This introductory study offers a critical overview of the major works of V.S. Naipaul from 1950 to the present day. Professor Mustafa's main concern is with literary issues, but historical, political, and cultural questions are also addressed, with comparative references to other postcolonial works. Paradoxically, a major segment of Naipaul's non-western, pro-decolonization readership seized on negative elements in his thinking, while western reaction to his ideas and themes led to set notions about Third-World society. Thus, his work has always been the object of radically divergent views, dependent on the perspective of the reader. In examining this issue, Mustafa introduces general debates about postcolonial literary production and its contemporary interrogation of narrative techniques, language, gender, race, and canon formation.

V.S. NAIPAUL

CAMBRIDGE STUDIES IN AFRICAN AND CARIBBEAN LITERATURE

Series editor: Professor Abiola Irele, Ohio State University

Each volume in this unique series of critical studies offers a comprehensive and in-depth account of the whole oeuvre of one individual writer from Africa or the Caribbean, in such a way that the book may be considered a complete coverage of the writer's expression up to the time the study is undertaken. Attention is devoted primarily to the works themselves – their significant themes, governing ideas, and formal procedures; biographical and other background information is thus employed secondarily, to illuminate these aspects of the writer's work where necessary.

The emergence in the twentieth century of black literature in the United States, the Caribbean, and Africa as a distinct corpus of imaginative work represents one of the most notable developments in world literature in modern times. This series has been established to meet the needs of this growing area of study. It is hoped that it will not only contribute to a wider understanding of the humanistic significance of modern literature from Africa and the Caribbean through the scholarly presentation of the work of major writers, but also offer a wider framework for the ongoing debates about the problems of interpretation within the disciplines concerned.

Already published

Chinua Achebe, by C. L. Innes
Nadine Gordimer, by Dominic Head
Edouard Glissant, by J. Michael Dash
V.S. Naipaul, by Fawzia Mustafa

V.S. NAIPAUL

FAWZIA MUSTAFA

Fordham University

CAMBRIDGE
UNIVERSITY PRESS

Published by the Press Syndicate of the University of Cambridge
The Pitt Building, Trumpington Street, Cambridge CB2 1RP
40 West 20th Street, New York, NY 10011-4211, USA
10 Stamford Road, Oakleigh, Melbourne 3166, Australia

First published 1995

Printed in Great Britain at the University Press, Cambridge

A catalogue record for this book is available from the British Library

Library of Congress cataloguing in publication data

Mustafa, Fawzia, 1952–
V.S. Naipaul / Fawzia Mustafa.
p.   cm. – (Cambridge studies in African and Caribbean literature)
Includes bibliographical references and index.
ISBN 0 521 40378 2 (hardback)   ISBN 0 521 48359 X (paperback)
1. Naipaul, V.S. (Vidiadhar Surajprasad), 1932 – Criticism and interpretation.
2. Developing countries – In literature.
3. Indies – In literature.
I. Title. II. Series.
PR927.9.N32Z78   1995
823'.914–dc20   94-37522 CIP

ISBN 0 521 40378 2 hardback
ISBN 0 521 48359 X paperback

For my dear parents, Sophia and Abdulla Mustafa

Contents

Acknowledgments   *page* x
Chronology   xi

1   Introduction   1

2   Bearings   30

3   Home   59

4   Abroad   88

5   The world   121

6   Right of abode   159

7   One way   196

8   Conclusion   219

Notes   227
Bibliography   243
Index   251

Acknowledgments

I am very grateful to Abiola Irele for his editorial skill, and the tact with which he exercises it. Working with him has been a pleasure as well as an invaluable experience. I am also grateful to Fordham University for granting me a Summer Faculty fellowship, and a single semester sabbatical to complete this study. Aitken, Stone and Wylie have also been kind enough to grant me permission to quote from the works of V.S. Naipaul, and I thank them.

Everyone I know has a well-articulated opinion about V.S. Naipaul, and no one I know has neglected to express his or hers to me, including my sister, Hana, and my brother, Mali. Among the many others to whom I am greatly indebted, Dale Lasden, Jamie Macguire, David Lelyveld, Nuzhat Ahmad, Carole Murray, Bonny Kwoh, Bonnie McDougall, Alison Bailey, Kate Mulvey, Terence McGuigan, and Mehreen Sadik all at one time or another have helped me think through my early engagement with Naipaul's work. I owe particular thanks to Susan Berger for reading portions of the manuscript and for continuing to speak her mind quite plainly. Finally, I would not have written this book but for Sara Suleri Goodyear, whose friendship over many undocumented years has always found unusual ways to force the issue. I thank her with the long-overdue salutation, "What next, Sach?"

Chronology

1932   Born, Chaguanas, Trinidad, August 17.
1948   Awarded Trinidad Government Scholarship.
1950   Travels to England to read English at Oxford
       University; starts occasional pieces for the BBC World
       Service *Caribbean Voices*.
1955   Marries Patricia Ann Hale.
1957   *The Mystic Masseur*.
1958   *The Suffrage of Elvira*; awarded John Llewellyn Rhys
       Memorial Prize for *The Mystic Masseur*; begins to write
       reviews for the *New Statesman*.
1959   *Miguel Street*.
1960   Commission by the government of Trinidad and
       Tobago to write on the Caribbean.
1961   *A House for Mr. Biswas*; awarded Somerset Maugham
       Award for *Miguel Street*.
1962   *The Middle Passage*; embarks on first trip to India.
1963   *Mr. Stone and the Knights Companion*.
1964   *An Area of Darkness*; awarded Hawthornden Prize for
       Mr. Stone and the Knights Companion.
1966   Travels to East and Central Africa.
1967   *The Mimic Men*; *A Flag on the Island*.
1968   Awarded W. H. Smith prize for *The Mimic Men*.
1969   *The Loss of El Dorado*.
1970   Settles in Wiltshire, England.
1971   *In a Free State*; awarded Booker Prize for *In a Free State*.
1972   *The Overcrowded Barracoon*.
1975   *Guerrillas*; D.Litt. University of the West Indies,
       St. Augustine Campus.

1977   *India: A Wounded Civilization.*
1978   Teaches at Wesleyan College, Connecticut, USA.
1979   *A Bend in the River*; travels through the non-Arab
       Islamic world.
1980   *The Return of Eva Peron with The Killings in Trinidad*;
       awarded the Bennet Award.
1981   *Among the Believers.*
1983   Awarded the Jerusalem Award.
1984   *Finding the Centre.*
1986   Awarded the T.S. Eliot Award.
1987   *The Enigma of Arrival.*
1988   Travels through the southeastern United States.
1989   *A Turn in the South.*
1990   Awarded Trinity Cross, Trinidad; knighted; *India: A
       Million Mutinies Now.*
1994   University of Tulsa, Oklahoma, MacFarlin Library
       opens its Naipaul archive; *A Way in the World.*

CHAPTER I

Introduction

> Look, boys, it ever strike you that the world not real at
> all? It ever strike you that we have the only mind in the
> world and you just thinking up everything else?
>
> (V.S. Naipaul, *Miguel Street*)

Few non-western twentieth-century writers of English have
gained a readership as extensive and various as V.S. Naipaul.
Few have been as prolific in both the genres of fiction and
non-fiction and managed to develop and sustain such a singular expressive and literary idiom. At the present time, perhaps
the most evident of the several features that distinguish this
idiom is its longevity. Readers continue to be surprised at
recognizing the same personae, voices, and narrative stances,
introduced nearly forty years ago, surfacing with the same
nervous energy, in each newly published work. This longevity,
however, does not reside in the persistence of Naipaul's narrative tactics alone; instead, it is their combination with the
consistency of what Naipaul writes about, primarily Third-
World subjects, that gives a particular resilience to his
expressions. For those readers unfamiliar with the places and
situations Naipaul's work has explored, his career takes on an
aura of a mission whose goal has been to find a way to make one
part of the world readable to another. Conversely, for those
readers who are familiar with the Third-World issues Naipaul
has continued to address, his habits of representation appear to
be increasingly made up of misperceptions and inappropriate
inquiries. For almost his entire career, therefore, Naipaul's
writings and their idiomatic inflections have been simultaneously celebrated and castigated with descriptions that range

between "objective" or "ahistorical," "unsentimental" or "culturally ignorant," "unafraid" or "hysterical."

More interesting and important than the extremes that Naipaul's reputations rest upon, however, is the function his works have been made to perform in debates about the accomplishments of, or the dangers that beset, Caribbean or post-colonial writing. That the body of his work has always been read as a primary gauge in this inquiry suggests that the importance of Naipaul's achievements does not really lie in the balance of views between champions and detractors, but more vitally in the exemplary space his writings have helped create in the understanding, and making, of late twentieth-century literary history. The steady emergence of Naipaul's novels, non-fiction, journalism, and travelogues, in other words, has allowed two generations of readers, scholars, and critics one of the most sustained, and possibly one of the most unique, opportunities to witness and participate in the formation of a literary practice born of the implosive capabilities of its post-colonial historical, cultural, and political divides.

The divides which Naipaul's work is seen to span emerge from the broad cultural and geopolitical shifts and demarcations created by Europe's colonial economic and administrative practice and the militarisms of its imperial spread. Naipaul's foci within this amalgam of vast historical eruptions appear to be examinations of the deracination and displacement of migratory peoples. Furthermore, his engagement with the social and cultural friction caused by ethnic traditions forced into proximity, and the disintegration or failure of old and new systems and rituals in the face of economic modernities, repetitively leads him to conclusions about the cultural and political poverty that seems to characterize an increasingly destitute greater Third World. The possibilities of thematic richness spawned by colonial history, however, should not be read as the imbrication or even consonance of events that history can be defined by, and of which Naipaul is deemed the witness. Rather, it is more productive and accurate to first assess the categories of literature, history, and culture within and between which Naipaul's stories and accounts attempt to negotiate or which, according to some critics, they override.

Naipaul's travels may have followed the routes of European colonial conquest, for example, but his 1974 essay, "Conrad's Darkness," undercuts the literalism of such exploration. When explaining the effect that reading *Heart of Darkness* had upon him, it is the episode where Marlow stumbles upon Towson's *Inquiry into some Points of Seamanship* that stands out in relief:

This scene ... answered something of the political panic I was beginning to feel.

To be a colonial was to know a kind of security; it was to inhabit a fixed world. And I suppose that in my fantasy I had seen myself coming to England as to some purely literary region, where, untrammeled by the accidents of history or background, I could make a romantic career for myself as a writer ... And I found that Conrad – sixty years before, in the time of a great peace – had been everywhere before me. Not as a man with a cause, but a man offering ... a vision of the world's half-made societies ... [it was] a kind of truth and half a consolation.

To understand Conrad, then, it was necessary to match his experience.[1]

Such an evocation strongly suggests that Naipaul's map is Conrad's writing rather than colonial history, and his quest canonical rather than historical. Happily, literature and history are not mutually exclusive; nevertheless, even while it remains important not to confuse them, especially in their sometimes competing narrative modes, it is precisely their possible junctures that Naipaul's writings appear to strive towards.

His pursuit of Conrad's agendas, therefore, begins to help identify the "kind of truth" that his explorations prefer to look for. If he believed that his own personal historical circumstance could be exploited if and when a transference between a participant and observer status were enacted, then the solace the panicked young colonial looked for was through an escape into an imaginary realm where his particular historical location would recede into a larger, more diffuse area of generalized categories. As Sara Suleri has suggested, the figure in Conrad's story who best embodies this desire is the manual's owner, the Harlequin: "the borderer on someone else's story."[2] That Naipaul's "imaginary" should have been "a purely literary region," then, ultimately proves to be the central dialectic of his ideological composition: the election to a universalist aspiration that posits abiding principles about human affairs. Thus, in claiming to have singled out Conrad and, astonishingly, Conrad's experience as an early beacon during his preparations to become a writer, Naipaul deliberately aligns his work with a specific literary tradition, and its singular preoccupation with its own canon.

Having already declared in 1962 that "Living in a borrowed culture, the West Indian, more than most, needs writers to tell him who he is and where he stands,"[3] Naipaul has long positioned himself closer to the heart of the "borrowed culture" than at the brink of any "new" identity-formations. This poses a series of queries about his relation both to English literature and to Caribbean history, since, according to him the latter is dependent on the former. The problem of subscribing to such an equation is made clear in an essay where Homi K. Bhabha explains some of the limits of the exercise of colonial authority through propagating the emblematic power of the "book." Bhabha reads the passage in "Conrad's Darkness" quoted above as well as the episode referred to in *Heart of Darkness* as moments in literature where an Idea of Order based solely upon itself and not the context into which it is inserted allows for the belief that a "universal" truth exists before a "particular" one. Thus, in Bhabha's estimation, Naipaul's debt to Conrad is:

a vision of literature and a lesson of history . . . These texts [Conrad's and Towson's] of the civilizing mission immediately suggest the triumph of the colonialist moment in early English Evangelism and modern English literature. The discovery of the book installs the sign of appropriate representation: the word of God, truth, art creates the conditions for a beginning, a practice of history and narrative . . . It is to preserve the peculiar sensibility of what he understands as a tradition of civility that Naipaul "translates" Conrad, from Africa to the Caribbean, in order to transform the despair of postcolonial history into an appeal for the autonomy of art.[4]

If a particular "civility" and the "autonomy of art" are indeed the grids whereby Naipaul constructs his narratives of the Caribbean and the greater Third World, then his relation to history is aesthetic rather than historiographical, and predetermined rather than explorative. To attempt to "transform the despair of postcolonial history," after all, is to memorialize rather than to historicize it, granting it a status as emblem rather than a participatory and lived experience.

What Rob Nixon dubs Naipaul's "slave society trilogy," *The Middle Passage* (1962), *The Loss of El Dorado* (1969), and *A Turn in the South* (1989),[5] for example, are each infused with pockets of nostalgia because the potential temporal and spatial blurring of history and myth-making keeps showing in the frustrations and seductions caused by their competing locational and, therefore, narrative possibilities. Populations of African descent in the regions traveled in *The Middle Passage*, for instance, are evaluated by the relative "distance" their communities exhibit from "Africa":

> For the Negro of the islands Africa is no more than a word, an emotion. For the Surinamer Africa is almost in his backyard. Beside the rivers the bush-Negroes have maintained their racial purity, their African arts of carving, singing and dancing, and, above all, their pride. Rediscovery was not hard. (*The Middle Passage*, p. 170)

If the eventuality of "coherence" or "confusion" rests with a community's maintenance or retrieval of former cultural practices, as though time, place, and event do not count as mediating factors, then Naipaul's evaluatory system suggests that the "forgetfulness" of some communities cuts them off from History. Surinam's collection of "whole" communities, in other words, prepares it for modernity, while the islands' fragmentary and misdirected yearnings do not.

Naipaul's early characterization of West Indian or Caribbean culture as "borrowed," therefore, merits further examination. Quite apart from implying a status of perpetual surrogacy, the charge also carries with it a monological view of culture as an abstraction, "Culture." Rather than viewing the Caribbean confluence of European, African, Asian, and American cultures through the transformative lens of colonialism, such

as Frantz Fanon's prior study, *Black Skin, White Masks*,[6] tried to
do, or George Lamming's *The Pleasures of Exile*[7] struggled with,
Naipaul's assessment relies almost completely upon a belief in a
system of preordained hierarchy and order. When he recollects
in a 1964 essay that, "It helps in the most practical way to have
a tradition ... the English language was mine; the tradition
was not,"[8] he characterizes his position as a young writer
starting out as paradoxical because of the absence in the
Caribbean of a tradition *equivalent* to the English. Homi K.
Bhabha, in another essay, explains that the kind of anxiety
Naipaul expresses

is resolved in the discourse of literary history through the inception of
an "origin" whereby history turns to a kind of myth, and the problem
of beginning is resolved as the progressive distinction between past
and present. The authority of the past is finally authored (and
authorized) in the present ... Produced in this way, both Literature
and History, as well as the history of literature, enable a perspective
of essential order, coherence, culmination and Culture.[9]

By trying to establish alternative but equally coherent "traditions" from local materials whose "unmediated reality" must
be revealed, Bhabha suggests that Naipaul's investment in the
"Novel" is deeply rooted in anxiety about "Cultural" rather
than "historical" authenticity, since Naipaul believes one leads
to the other. Indeed, aspects of this anxiety were shared by
many Caribbean and other "Commonwealth" writers of Naipaul's generation, who would only characterize their representations on levels of "equivalence." Hence the debates within
"Commonwealth Literature" about the particularity between
"Australian," "Canadian," "New Zealand," "West Indian,"
and anglophone African and Indian literatures as part of a
dialectical process in pursuit of a common culture. As the mark
of a common humanity, the argument continues, these
literatures are evidence of the establishment of distinct, alternative "Cultures" and "Traditions" and serve as the stamps
of national "independence." The other route to a statement of
"independence," and one followed by a greater number of
postcolonial writers, has been of course through the process
of "decolonizing the mind," where the alienation fostered

by colonization becomes the site from which writers posit a "liberation."[10]

To illustrate Naipaul's need to align rather than break away from his canonical investments, we can read his pursuit of "coherence," in the "story" of his career. It can be, and has been, seen to have developed with all the surprises and satisfactions associated with a nineteenth-century European novel poised at the point of a recognition that its boundaries may be limitless. Like any solid bildungsroman, his writing begins at home; his first published works (1957–1961) take the backwaters of Trinidad as their habitat; he then graduates to the wider parameters of the Caribbean basin and South America, India, and Africa, as he matures through fiction to the putatively greater realities of non-fictional prose and travelogues (1962–1971). Then, after having established the empirical fact of the world, he proceeds to dismantle the fiction of the "Third World," in the precise locutions of a sadder and a wiser man (1972–1984). Knighted in 1990, Naipaul continues to be short-listed as a candidate for the Nobel Prize for Literature, and his most recent enterprises, as the century closes (1986–1994), have been gestures of return and reconciliation.

It follows, then, that to "order" Naipaul's career into the narrative frame of a nineteenth-century novel is to read it as though its story is predetermined by an already established plot. Such a plot develops according to an Aristotelean paradigm, the resolution of which is a culmination of all that has preceded it, and which accords the hero initiation into an elect group after successfully participating in a particular cycle of maturation. The predetermined hierarchy of this cycle means that only certain events having to do with already codified achievements are privileged in such stories, to ensure that the equilibrium of a particular social order is either reestablished or maintained. The formalism of this exercise, however, tends to dehistoricize the events depicted despite the "facts" that are marshaled, which allows for an essentialist reading of his career – as though becoming a "Writer" presupposes inherent qualities – rather than an historical understanding in representations of it. The "story" of Naipaul's career, therefore, is in symmetrical conformity with his childhood desire for a "romantic career ... as a writer." It also helps to explain his early disclaimers about being classified as a Trinidadian, West Indian, or Third-World writer.

Tension still surrounds Naipaul's antipathy about being called a West Indian, Trinidadian, Caribbean, or Third-World writer. While never denying his Trinidadian beginnings – indeed, quite the contrary – he has long objected to being called anything but a Writer. Claiming that descriptive prefixes that are nationalistic or racially and ethnically bound are either "political" or, for him, meaningless, Naipaul has gone so far as to cancel a contract with a publisher for listing him as a "West Indian Writer." In a 1981 interview with *Newsweek*, where this anecdote is cited, he is quoted as saying, "I've been breaking away from that tag all my life ... It's all the things I reject. It's not *me*."[11] The "*me*," it seems, privileges only its professional function which, self-defined, is perfectly consistent with his "appeal for the autonomy of art." The appeal, which is hardly a minority stance, belongs to the ideology of a transcendent humanism which vociferously rejects a political cast to its character. Naipaul seems to be more comfortable with being called "rootless," an "exile," or "truly a man without a country or a cause," one who can declare that "Political gamesmanship" leaves him cold, and that honesty is his "only ideology."[12]

While it is anyone's prerogative to define his or her own place in this world, historical circumstances do exist that circumscribe some of our options. The fictions of uncompromised ethnic, racial, religious, cultural, or even national origins, no longer lend themselves so handily to any peoples of the former European empires. It is not surprising, then, that alternative categories based on functional criteria, among others, should have arisen. The professionalization of specialized labor, for example, has peopled an increasing portion of the western middle classes through the migration of former colonized populations. Naipaul's insistence, therefore, that he and his work not be limited to quasi-sociopolitical categories is understandable. When, however, he also states that "When I speak about being an exile or a refugee, I'm not just using a metaphor," it is important to remember that outside the metaphor lies a deeply self-absorbed existentialist state, not a political one.[13]

To include a study of Naipaul's work in a series on Caribbean and African writers may well appear to some to be provocative at best, or obstinate at the worst, but what must be kept in mind nonetheless are the historical and, in this case, discursive circumstances at play. The host of writers to have emerged from the Caribbean region, be their works in Spanish, French, Dutch, or English, and whose audiences may be local, Euro-American, or international, have all had to grapple with the hybridity and amalgam of their cultural compositions which have resulted from the archipelago's European colonization. It could hardly have been otherwise. Much has already been written about the "colonial legacy," or "heritage" embedded within the aspirations and efforts of the first generation of Caribbean writers; of the troubled relation between the lived experience of their communities, classes, and ethnic groupings and the false consciousness, or alienation, fostered by colonial education; about the voluntary exile of a whole generation to Britain and France to seek a metropolitan milieu for a craft or vocation that had yet to take root, as it were, at home. A critical mass exists of prescriptions handed out by local critics for what Caribbean literatures should be like, and of pronouncements from British and French overseers intent on being arbiters of any literature from the former colonies.[14] Whichever compass these writers have endorsed, including rejections such as Naipaul's, one fact remains: a proliferation of fiction, poetry, and plays resembling European forms, aesthetic concerns, and practices emerged from a part of the globe where they had not existed before. The nomenclature and subsequent territorial battles about these literary productions aside, stories began to be told in ways that they had not been told before, and about situations, places and events that tested and challenged in a new or unique manner those very means of telling that were employed.

A banal truism is helpful here: a writer's place of birth does not necessarily dictate what he or she chooses to write about;

similarly, a Caribbean setting for a story does not have to make its writer Caribbean. The historical circumstances and discursive fields in which and from which a writer learns, however, and in which he or she participates – and sometimes changes – do provide helpful referents with which to understand his or her work. The designation "Caribbean" is not nationally specific, nor is its geographic spread the arbitrary compass in which to circumscribe its writers, and neither is it solely an experiential junction. Instead, it represents a major historical and discursive area of the heteroglossia of postcolonial cultural practice or, in non-Bakhtinean terms, texts and writing possibilities spawned by specific transformations initiated by the processes of colonization. This places the work of writers socially and culturally initialed in the Caribbean in concert with work from other postcolonial regions, but in a series of dialogic relations rather than by a "common experience." The ceaseless potential of "dialogue" within this vast and changing discursive field necessarily includes the so-called First Worlds as scenes of reciprocity and contestation as well as participation.[15] Naipaul's well-known affinity with an English tradition, therefore, is not a betrayal of his origins, but a discovery of one possibility, or even one aspect, of the inevitability of Caribbean and postcolonial literatures.

Perhaps the most illustrative case history that can best explain Caribbean writers' originary and participatory role in both the creation of postcolonial literatures and their dialogic relation with other modes of intellection and activity is that of the literary movement known as negritude. A group of Caribbean and African students, principally Aimé Césaire, Léopold Sédar Senghor, and Léon Damas, studied in Paris prior to the Second World War, fought with the Allies during it, and eventually started a journal, *Présence Africaine*. The publication rapidly became a vehicle with which to explore the existential centre of black Being. Obviously steeped in the ascendancy of European existentialism of the time, the group also consciously looked to the Caribbean and African American figures of the so-called Harlem Renaissance – such as Langston Hughes, Countee Cullen, W.E.B. Du Bois, Marcus Garvey, and Claude

McKay – as key referents of their literary and metaphysical enterprise. Moreover, Garvey's efforts at organizing economic self-reliance and his "Back to Africa" movement, and Hughes' manifesto declaring, "We younger Negro artists who create now intend to express our individual dark-skinned selves without fear of shame," represented, for the younger writers, circuits in a network of conceptual possibilities. However, despite the studied heterogeneity of Claude McKay's novels such as *Banana Bottom* (1933) and *Banjo* (1929) (much of which is set in Marseilles), the cultural productivity of the Harlem Renaissance did not simply stand as an unmediated precedent for the younger francophone colonials. In part, obviously, this was because of the different linguistic, political, historical, and social issues at stake. Instead, through a series of gestures aimed at a profound break with the tutelage of colonial subordination, this first negritude generation recognized that they would not need antecedents since, they were beginning to discover, a belief in the absence of "precedence" could also be one originary mark of postcolonial expression.

The notion of starting anew, therefore, inspired this generation of negritude poets to initiate a program of self-invention. In order to do so, they undertook to reconstruct a sense of a common African "past" and "ethos" to function both as an alternative "traditional" referent and as a vision of the future. The forging of this new negritude consciousness, therefore, spawned a multitude of fascinating trajectories which, in their operations, reveal the magnitude and extent of colonialism's cultural influences. For example, Aimé Césaire, principal among this group, coined the term "negritude" in his major poem, *Cahier d'un retour au pays natal* (1939) and, in his *Discours sur le colonialisme* (1955) read the ascendancy of fascism in Europe as a colonial consequence. Nevertheless, Césaire subsequently became a political player in Martinique's status as a department of France. Léopold Sédar Senghor of Senegal, who also entered politics and became a head of state, used his poetry to pursue an aesthetic based increasingly on an essentialist race consciousness, the implications of which are a political embarrassment. Like Césaire, Senghor's political career is also responsible for the model of African and French assimilationist "self-determination." In France, the surrealists led by André Breton had "discovered" the new poetry and showered endorsements and approval, a circumstance unwittingly similar to the endorsements required of the African American slave narratives of the nineteenth century, and the "white" patronage necessary for so many artists of the Harlem years. Jean-Paul Sartre, in his introduction to Senghor's *Anthologie de la nouvelle poésie nègre et malgache* (1948), recast the significance of this literary devlopment into a quasi-marxist dialectic and read it as the process of disalienation for the colonial disenfranchised.

By 1952 Frantz Fanon, the young French-trained Martinican psychoanalyst, incorporated a critique of negritude and its reception into his analyses of the psychopathology of colonization, in his work *Black Skin, White Masks*. In marked contrast to the nationalism of Césaire and Senghor, Fanon's subsequent work and writings associated with the Algerian revolution – where the language of the populace is Arabic and the cultural matrix of the resistance to the French a secular Islam – became the primers for resistance movements throughout sub-Saharan Africa and elsewhere. Rather than a chain of events, or a series of "influences," then, it is more useful to read a quick description of the negritude movements as illustrative of the courses of dialogism – the proliferation of often "unlikely" exchanges – that constitutes the heteroglossia of the Caribbean or postcolonial circumstance.[16]

The generational proximity of Naipaul and the francophone Caribbeans engaged with the negritude movement is illustrative of another factor that helps explain Naipaul's early literary and ideological anxieties. Because of the places and times during which they all formulated their aesthetic or political allegiances, wittingly or unwittingly their works represent a hinge between representations of the colonial and postcolonial eras. Only these generations of Caribbean writers have had to face the immediacy of what Sara Suleri phrases as "the question of whether it is possible for a postcolonial writer to exist in the absence of the imperial theme."[17] Another examination of the course of the Trinidad-born writer's career, therefore, will help explain some of the initial struggles peculiar to Caribbean and postcolonial writing. After all, how does a writer resign membership from a version of history and then proceed to construct native histories out of precisely the same materials? What idiom can be developed to accommodate without fracture the ambivalence of its own authority? And what difficulties accompany the issue of "novelty" when the idea of the new is used to erase the idea of the past? It is Naipaul's use of details from his own life in his expository and fictional writing, and the almost transparent role that other biographical facts have played in the establishment of his public persona, that best help to characterize his work in postcolonial discursive practice. The emphasis is important because Naipaul's use of biographical information in his writing constructs an overdetermined relation between notions of the Author and the multiple usages of what is called the colonial subject. It is a deliberate and brilliant ploy that allows his anxiety about being a Writer to substitute for a more historically exacting engagement with his topics.

Born as Vidiadhar Surajprasad Naipaul in Chaguanas, Trinidad, on August 17, 1932, the writer can claim descent from a Hindu grandfather, who migrated, at the turn of the century, from Uttar Pradesh in India to Trinidad under the British colonial system of indentured labor. Both the island of Naipaul's birth and the subcontinent of his ancestry serve as two extremes in Britain's colonial enterprise; the one an afterthought of convenience and contingency in its Caribbean machinations, and the other the center-piece, as it were, after the British failure of empire in North America. The colonial setting of Naipaul's childhood in Trinidad, therefore, provides the scene wherein he is schooled in the minutiae of the struggles attending cultural displacement – "to be Indian in a non-Indian world"[18] – as well as the polyglot hybridity of a colonized and colonial population. At a count of just over a million, the population of Trinidad claims ancestry from the Caribbean region, Africa, India, China, the Middle East, and Europe.

Naipaul's formal schooling, furthermore, was in an educational system whose program was mapped out in nineteenth-century British India, under the guidelines of Macaulay's much-quoted "Minute on Indian Education," in which he declares the purpose of colonial education to be to "form a class who may be interpreters between [the British] and the millions whom we govern; a class of persons, Indian in blood and colour, but English in taste, in opinions, in morals, and in intellect."[19]

Despite its regional and historical modifications, such a curriculum in the Trinidad of the 1930s and 1940s had yet to make adjustments towards the newer demands of an impending era of decolonization.[20] Thus it seems reasonable to assume that the scholarship to Oxford that Naipaul was awarded in 1948, and which took him there in 1950 to read English, positioned him, almost strategically, to await and oversee, as it were, the then nascent alternatives of migration or return emerging for colonials in a postcolonial and post-independence era. Would he participate in a tertiary migration for parity and acceptance with a diminishing colonial power and, as did so many of his compatriots, new immigrants in Britain? Or would he declare solidarity with the novelty of decolonization and its nationalisms like the greater Third World? A third alternative, however, turned out to be the curiosity of pursuing his precolonial origins, which, coupled with the adolescent and romantic desire to be a Writer, allowed Naipaul to capitalize on two colonial "privileges": literacy and mobility.[21]

The next phase of Naipaul's tutelage can be considered as a period of apprenticeship during which he found the intellectual base from which he could chart the boundaries of his writer's world. Long cathected on the idea of being a "Writer," Naipaul claims to have spent the first few years out of Oxford hunting for experience. He freelances for the BBC Caribbean Service, becomes an occasional reviewer for publications like the *New Statesman*, marries, and, with a determination akin to a messianic quest, begins a process of self-generation of himself as Writer. With curious precision, Naipaul dates the start of his career with the typing of "Bogart" in 1955, the writing of which revealed one "tract of experience ... My very particularity" as the hitherto elusive "subject sitting on my shoulder."[22] Having found his "subject" – portraits and stories of life and communities in Trinidad – Naipaul's subsequent success with the publications of *The Mystic Masseur* (1957), *The Suffrage of Elvira* (1958), *Miguel Street* (1959), and the celebrated *A House for Mr. Biswas* (1961) secured him inclusion within the new literary-historical category of "Commonwealth Literature." This new coinage, created by a coalition of the British Academy and publishing enterprises, was conceived to accommodate, or, as some would argue, contain and exploit, the new writings in English by subjects of the dominion.[23]

Having already shown some impatience with constraints in the Trinidad of his youth, Naipaul seems to have eschewed the safe-houses of "Commonwealth," or "West Indian" literature. Marking the end of his apprenticeship, Naipaul wryly notes that, "To become a writer, that noble thing, I had thought it necessary to leave. Actually to write, it was necessary to go back. It was the beginning of self-knowledge" (*Finding the Centre*, p. 34). The "tract of experience" out of which Naipaul first began to write, and which "book by book" eased him "into knowledge," was dependent, he implies, on the trope of exile, framed by actual leave-taking and imagined return. This early imbrication of "experience" and "knowledge," figuratively composed of his ambitions to be a Writer, and encompassing the "heritage" of his birth – colonial subject, East Indian Trinidad, Hinduism, India, – emerges in the following decade to have been only the first site of an intellectual excavation of, or for, what he terms, "self-knowledge." The endeavor, it seems, required the alternative choices of digging into strata of "history" that were waiting to be unearthed or restructuring the same into new sedimentation. This equation between "experience" and "knowledge," discovered so early in his career, is the framework that allows him to anticipate disappointment and a quality of nostalgia that shows in so much of his work.

The varieties of knowledge that Naipaul cites as the work of writing, however, are also "incomplete" (*Finding the Centre*,

p. 20). As though to address these ellipses, he embarks on a series of travels that take on the character of an urgent inventory of places, experiences, and narrative exercises. In the early 1960s he returns to the Caribbean, by invitation and commission, and extends his purview of a region in which Trinidad is only a part. He goes to India for the first time in 1962, and spends a year there sorting through the dissonance of the familiarity bred of his upbringing and the disappointment of what he finds. In 1966 he visits East and Central Africa, experiencing first hand its political transitions, and acquainting himself with its old Arab slave trade routes; and, by the end of the decade, he returns once more to the western hemisphere. His literary and travelogue production during this period is prodigious. The first return to the Caribbean is documented in *The Middle Passage* (1962), his first English-set novel, *Mr. Stone and the Knights Companion*, appears in 1963, and his testament about India, *An Area of Darkness*, in 1964. In 1967 both *The Mimic Men* and *A Flag on the Island* are published, and *The Loss of El Dorado*, something of a history of early European governance of Trinidad, soon after in 1969.

Settling in England for a longer than usual period in 1970, Naipaul's first venture into an African theme, *In a Free State* (1971) is finished, the first collection of his essays spanning more than a decade, *The Overcrowded Barracoon* (1972) is compiled, and *Guerillas* (1975), another Trinidad-based novel, the first to gain widespread attention in the United States, appears. His second book on India, a commentary on the Emergency declared by Indira Gandhi entitled *India: A Wounded Civilization*, is published in 1977, and in 1978 he tries his hand at teaching, at Wesleyan College in the United States. He closes out the third decade of his career with his most sustained engagement with Africa, the novel *A Bend in the River* (1979), and, while traveling in the Muslim world gathering materials for the controversial *Among the Believers* (1981), the second volume of his essays, *The Return of Eva Peron with The Killings in Trinidad* (1980) is collected. In addition to the six works of fiction and the seven of non-fiction, the decades of the 1960s and 1970s are also marked by the more than half-dozen prestigious literary prizes and awards, and by a readership extending beyond the span of his travels. Now an internationally established writer, in conformity with his earliest visions, Naipaul's most productive period appears to have achieved a synthesis between his "knowledge" and "experience" in the evidence of his international reputation.

It could also be argued that by traveling to the literal areas of the world that thematically constitute his personal history, Naipaul discovers a textual agenda by developing an idiom with which to express the seemingly unprecedented observations he was able to exercise in the Americas, England, India, and Africa. The construction of this idiom develops through Naipaul's versions of the histories, current events, human interest encounters, and landscapes of diverse places, but always offered with the transience and finite passage of a traveler. This device serves as a temporal and linear limit for a piece, allowing Naipaul an episodic progression which, in his non-fiction, can be seen to rely on a personal rather than historical positioning of his narrative voice to the immediate matters at hand. Similarly, in the fiction of this period, Naipaul's protagonists tend to struggle with an historical circumstance which is often elusive until after their respective actions prove to have been either anachronistic or futile. This sense of miscalculation has a ring of inevitablity because, it would seem, the transience of characters such as Ralph Singh in *The Mimic Men*, Jimmy Ahmed in *Guerrillas*, and Salim in *A Bend in the River* is thrust upon them by the absence of tradition in the wake of historical and political change. Each protagonist, as a result, is forced to be mobile without necessarily having any place to go, which favors each of their plots with an apparent contradiction between their temporal and spatial determinations. Therefore, the fiction can adopt the trope of "incomplete" knowledge as the *faux pas* of a postcolonial mimicry. Meanwhile, the non-fiction repetitively draws on Naipaul's interviewees' opinions with the seeming accuracy of transcripts, only to find, by the end of a piece, that their cumulative effect is that of a compendium of, precisely, "incomplete" knowledge.

The transient passage of the traveler, then, becomes the metaphor for examining such alienations in both Naipaul's fiction and non-fiction, but only when the narrative structures themselves are offered as the final unifying principle of a story or an account does Naipaul's idiom take on its peculiar strength. By allowing a determinism premised on the tropes of alienation to shape the plots of his fiction, and by maintaining the stance of observer and reporter for the narrative voice of the non-fiction, Naipaul's power is seen to rest in the writerly distance he forges between himself and his work. Much of his reputation rests on this "objectivity," or, to phrase it another way, the distinction he establishes between the area of the past and the condition of the present. One belongs to a mythology and its images of journeying never to return, and the other to the lucidity which frees one from the need to return. By the 1980s, it seems, Naipaul had dealt with both these temptations by tracing and retracing their seductions until he had neutralized them within an idiom whose effectiveness is that it functions with an equal efficacy in disparate parts of the world.

Naipaul continues to travel, and the pattern of return in his work is increasingly evident. Since the publication in 1981 of *Among the Believers*, he has revisited Africa and India, and conducted an extended tour through the southern United States. His 1983 essay, "Prologue to an Autobiography," coupled with his reflections on the Ivory Coast, "The Crocodiles of Yamoussoukro," appears in 1984 as *Finding the Centre: Two Narratives*, and the 1987 publication of his novel, *The Enigma of Arrival*, continues the use of overt autobiographical borrowings. His first extended book about the United States, *A Turn in the South* (1989), is soon followed in 1990 with what rounds out his trilogy about India, *India: A Million Mutinies Now*, which is a voluminous reassessment of his notions about contemporary India. And, with *A Way in the World* (1994) called "a novel" in the United States and "a sequence" in Britain, Naipaul's comfortable re-settlement with the imaginary historical constructions of European and Caribbean figures first encountered in *The Loss of El Dorado* (1969) confirms his agenda of a personal circumnavigation of the topics and themes his career has pursued. Since 1981, all of Naipaul's work appears more reflective, increasingly autobiographical, and curiously buoyant. This would appear to endorse the view that an older but still peripatetic Naipaul has curtailed the edges of his anxieties as he has truly come to grips with the expanded world he discovered when first leaving the island of Trinidad forty-five years ago.

By examining Naipaul's career through the framing device of authorial intent and its subsequent realizations in the chronology of his publications, many readers choose to understand Naipaul as a writer in search of his subject whose voyages of discovery function within an empirical realm where "The world is what it is" and nothing else.[24] Therefore, almost in the spirit of the tale about the emperor's new clothes, these readings insist, it is the Writer's job to expose anything that pretends to exist but which is plainly not there. By not questioning this empirical view of his career, it also becomes possible to conclude that his contributions to the ways in which the "new" societies of the former colonial world can be understood are ground-breaking and original. With the discipline and persistence akin to an ethnographer's, Naipaul's continued engagement with the greater Third World carries the verity of an observer who has dedicated a life-time to his study and who has consequently earned, by all formal criteria, authority. The added fact that Naipaul is by origin a Third Worlder himself only enhances a notion of his strategic advantage towards the areas he writes about, for it suggests that the understanding he brings comes from within rather than without the societies under examination. In other words, because Naipaul appears to *be* his subject, the collapse he documents can also be read as an unfortunate rather than inevitable consequence of contemporary, ongoing history.

The mannered elegance and fluidity with which Naipaul writes, furthermore, closely echoes the tradition of English letters, from the travelogues and the novelistic forms he creates to the sensibilities of a specific English civility he draws upon. This provides Naipaul recourse to an idea of humanism in his vision that he can display as the conscience of the modern world. By taking it upon himself to travel along the routes of imperialism's spread, the argument continues, Naipaul's depictions of disarray and colonial consequence are sobering reminders of what the west is not. Consequently, Naipaul is cast as a spokesperson for a postcolonial world even as this world also sees him as its harshest critic. The uncompromising stance that he seems to take only increases the aura of integrity for which he has become known, and firmly places his efforts within the compass of an empirical but humanistic value system: Naipaul is not afraid to name the worlds he encounters and observes, and his eye is always focused on the human costs of ill-conceived and willful attempts at the management of human affairs. Indeed, the despair he has expressed often borders on a sense of nihilism which surfaces in his fiction as nothing short of apocalypse. That debt, mismanagement, corruption, failure, despotism, civil strife, and war continue to plague so many postcolonial nations only seems to confirm this kind of reading of Naipaul's career and work.

Two appraisals of Naipaul's work, one British and one North American, will serve to illustrate the vigor with which such canonical and empirical readings have embraced him and his work. By 1973, for example, the British critic William Walsh was confident that

Naipaul answers positively the question posed by Leavis, "Is there any great novelist whose preoccupation with 'form' is not a matter of his responsibility towards a rich human interest, a complexity of interests, profoundly realized? – a responsibility involving, of its nature, imaginative sympathy, moral discrimination and judgement of relative human value?"[25]

Within this set of criteria, Walsh continues, Naipaul meets the demands of a moral and humanist agenda in a way that implicitly allows for evaluation against a supposedly transcendental norm. It precludes arguments of a political or ideological nature in the very act of pulling Naipaul out of the stagnant "Commonwealth" pool and placing him in the rubric of Leavis' "Great Tradition." Such an appraisal is the logical culmination of the supposedly benign overview delivered towards the end of the 1972 revised edition of *The Concise Cambridge History of English Literature*. Concluding the subsection of "The Age of T.S. Eliot," entitled "Literature of the West Indies," R.C. Churchill states:

Naipaul, Harris, Clarke, Salkey and other West Indian novelists who may one day come to be regarded as among the mid-twentieth-century's classic writers, major or minor, will not find themselves considered by posterity as any less universal in their appeal because they are so closely associated with the colour and the speech (to say nothing of the colourful speech) of Trinidad, Guyana, Barbados and Jamaica. Such writers, novelists and poets alike, have brought a new idiom, in every sense, to literature in the English language, as their calypso-singing compatriots have brought a new rhythm to popular music and their cricketers a new vitality to sport.[26]

While the spirit of this entry is inclusive, and the distribution of its praise democratic, the argument's premise remains deeply colonialist. West Indian literature, pop music, and sports can only be understood as tributaries feeding the depleted water table of the former colonial source.

Similarly, in 1977, Alfred Kazin's endorsement of Naipaul and his work to the readers of *The New York Times Book Review* builds its thesis around the statement that Naipaul is a quintessential "stranger" before he is anything else. With a curious disingenuousness, Kazin writes that Naipaul "looks very Indian. For all I know, he looks *East* Indian," and his books about the old western empires remind him of "Dickens on American manners and Chekhov on Sakhalin Island's prison colony rather than Norman Mailer on the steps of the Pentagon." Furthermore, Kazin also feels that, "since Naipaul is just as confident a loner as Nabokov, is as historically pent-up as Solzhenitsyn, as funny/sad as Beckett, the fact that he is not better known, that he is always asked to tell his own story over again as some lesser writers are not," is cause for concern. While appearing to draw upon a world of literature without boundaries, what such a statement reveals is the almost nationalistic self-authenticating impulse to which Kazin's "natural" comparisons lead him. The transcendental norm of "greatness," and the pluralistic compilation of extraterritorial writers are given an empirical status into whose framework Naipaul's deracination blends nicely.

Kazin implicitly suggests that Naipaul's work, along with those of the other writers cited, houses an operative paradigm for "objectivity," because he uses his "migratoriness" as an historical rather than "psychological" trope in his work: "my deepest sense of him is that he recognizes himself as a historical effect and that he has used this in his writing with something like the British power that once awed poor Indians in Trinidad." Kazin's fiercely sympathetic view of Naipaul unwittingly, or wittingly, colludes with the opinion that Naipaul the writer is free of a narrow self-authenticating impulse because his deracination and its cultural composite allow him entry into a literary canon of extraterritorial works that already exists. Thus Kazin can categorize Naipaul as "totally without ideology," a view which neatly complements the British invitation into their Great Tradition.[27]

Such appraisals, obviously, are riddled with their own contradictions, and have been chastised accordingly. Selwyn R. Cudjoe starts his revisionist assessment of Naipaul's work by dismissing close to forty books, theses, and studies of Naipaul's work written over twenty-five years as "idealist." This would frame these works well within the parameters of the above readings, which are guilty of being, in Cudjoe's words, "non-historical misreading[s]" that fail "to locate Naipaul's work in its tradition and to identify or consider its ideological orientation."[28] To view Naipaul's work as fundamentally "humanist," after all, is to ultimately grant it a "universalist" value which immediately subsumes any number of historical particularities. One of the fallacies that allows for this inductive leap is equating the notion of "international" with that of "universal," a misreading which privileges the notion of Author over that of History, and, in the case of Naipaul, grants his purview a single, blanket authority.

To read Naipaul's work as Walsh and Kazin do, therefore, can be understood as engaging in what Anthony Appiah has called "the Naipaul fallacy," a coinage that deals with the act of manipulating non-western topics in order to make a reader complicit with the writer, and aims to caution against both moves. The fallacy, Appiah explains, is the habit of only being able to account for non-western situations, issues, and cultures by "embedding [them] in European culture."[29] The implication here is that the "universalism" or "trancendence" with which Naipaul is credited is, in fact, nothing other than an endorsement of so-called western values, whether in their liberal or conservative guise. Another term, "Naipaulicity," which Chris Searle defines immediately in his subtitle, "A Form of Cultural Imperialism," similarly analyzes Naipaul's affinities with a bourgeois ideology by measuring the residues and perpetuation of colonialist sympathies in his reporting on the Grenadan revolution.[30] Among the most sustained, thoughtful, and carefully documented critiques of Naipaul's colonialist sympathies and colonial referents is Rob Nixon's full-length study, *London Calling: V.S. Naipaul Postcolonial Mandarin* (1992). Nixon's concentration on Naipaul's travel books brings into dramatic relief just how deeply invested Naipaul's allegiance is to the designs and desires of Victorian travel writing. Naipaul's powerful and influential readership among the elites of Europe and North America is equally implicated in Nixon's reading. Similarly, Joan Dayan's review of Nixon's book, "Gothic Naipaul," is a vigorous indictment of Naipaul's indelible propensity to deal "in reactionary flotsam."[31]

Differences in political and ideological affiliations, however, cannot fully account for such divergent readings. The seductions that Naipaul's work still exercises for some originates from what Hayden White explains as "a technique of ostensive self-definition by negation ... [which] appears as a kind of reflex action in conflicts between nations, classes, and political parties ... If we do not know what we think 'civilization' *is*, we can always find an example of what it is not."[32] Thus one way of understanding the use of Naipaul's views about the non-western world by an empirically minded and positivistic audience (the "kinder, gentler" people both Nixon and Dayan cite) is for the purposes of "self-definition." This is a frequent reaction, not only because some of his readers are closet colonialists themselves, but because the weight of what has already been written about Naipaul's topics during the era of colonial codifications is still felt in subsequent accounts through the textual residues of colonialist reflexivity. Literary theory, particularly deconstructive practice, discourse theory and Lacanian readings, has taught us that colonialist reflexivity – the habit of colonial representations intended to objectify "others" – and postcolonial self-reflexivity – the habit of strategic self-positioning within an objectified space – are manifestations of the ambivalence generated by colonial discourses. The ability to break the cycle of colonialist inscriptions, therefore, has proved to be an involved textual exercise that requires, among other things, a rereading of historical facts. The complexities associated with literary theory and the study of colonial discourses are central to an understanding of Naipaul's textual universe and the difficulty faced by postcolonial writers.

Studies such as C.L.R. James' *The Black Jacobins* (1938), Aimé Césaire's *Discourse on Colonialism* (1955), Frantz Fanon's two seminal works, *Black Skin, White Masks* (1952) and *The Wretched of the Earth* (1962), as well as the more recent work of Edward Said, *Orientalism* (1978) and *Culture and Imperialism* (1993), Aijaz Ahmad's counter to Said, *In Theory: Classes, Nations, Literatures* (1992), and inquiries such as Homi K. Bhabha's and Gayatri Spivak's theoretical investigations into the constitution of the colonial subject, are among a huge body of work that has reread the history of colonialism. Along with a new generation of scholars, these studies show how the long tradition of European representations of non-European places and habits – either histories and travelogues or novels – emerged hand in hand with colonial consolidation and imperial reign. The complicity between the political agendas designed to allow for colonial domination and these representations, we now know, led to formulae which allowed those in power to act as though only their accounts were authoritative. This authority was further strengthened through the translation of colonialists' versions of the colonized into social and political policy that, even to this day, can be used to dictate what the

Second and Third Worlds are, how they are to be understood, and why any interest should be taken in them.[33]

The practice of eliminating any reciprocity between writing's subject and object – the colonizer dictating the terms of definition of the colonized – has been the dominant strategy of colonialist representations. European, or First World, or "western" writings about Africa, India, South-East Asia, the Pacific Islands, China, Japan, the Caribbean, and the precolonial Americas, consequently, have engaged in such monologic discourses for so long that contemporary works must necessarily labor under the burdens of overcoming these well-established imaginary constructions, if the process of self-representation or re-presentation of former subjected peoples is to take place. Writing about the non-"western" world, therefore, demands of contemporary scholars and writers a certain vigilance against the dangers of reinscribing in their texts received colonial assumptions. This brand of vigilance often requires re-education about the colonial past, since the educational systems that produced most of us were themselves formulated within a colonial framework. In the view of many critics such as Cudjoe, Appiah, Searle, Nixon, Suleri, and Dayan, Naipaul has often failed to exercise enough vigilance, or to acknowledge the need to rethink the colonial past.

A host of prescient critiques of colonial and domestic social control in the nineteenth century has long since been written, such as David Walker's *Appeal* (1829), and Frederick Douglass' *Narrative of the Life of Frederick Douglass* (1845). In the Caribbean, J.J. Thomas' response to James Anthony Froude's *The English in the West Indies: The Bow of Ulysses* (1887) remains exemplary as a direct challenge to a specific attempt to justify more direct colonial control in the Caribbean; Thomas' *Froudacity: West Indian Fables By James Anthony Froude Explained* (1889) was written towards the end of the Trinidadian lexicographer's life, and challenged the assessment and methods of a well-respected British historian. As C.L.R. James explains, however, abilities such as Thomas' to expose "a genuine sense of outraged superiority stimulating political ignorance and myopia and not averse to plain lying,"[34] were the exception

rather than the rule. Until recently, furthermore, many of
these nineteenth-century works contesting the rationalizations
of colonial rule or slavery were neglected, banned, or hyster-
ically challenged as to their "authenticity." Thus their current
reinstitution as historical documents that offer an alternative
source of historical knowledge is a result of the recent systematic rereading of post-sixteenth-century modes of colonial
representions. Analyses such as Thomas' are now complemented by the understanding in contemporary scholarship that
colonial representations were deliberately, and necessarily,
damaging political and ideological discursive practices.

Where the prior colonialist texts followed the course of
postulating a hierarchy within the human species in order to
categorize the different races of man,[35] for example, or used
non-European or non-white or non-Christian cultures as sites
upon which to project notions of the Other, colonial discourses
are now acknowledged to have established historiographical
and narrative structures with which the subordination of entire
peoples and civilizations have been justified and deemed
"natural." The formidable power of this discursive authority is
made vividly clear in examples such as the pseudo-scientific
literature used to justify the Atlantic slave trade and slavery
even while a polity based on human and civil rights was being
implemented in Europe and the United States, or in the
imperial convenience operative in works like Hegel's *The Philosophy of History* (1833–1836), which relegated the entire continent and peoples of Africa "outside of History," thus paving
the way for the massive European "scramble" for the continent
in the late nineteenth century. Since so many of our disci-
plinary practices are still predicated upon the instrinsic
formulations of such nineteenth-century texts, numerous contemporary accounts documenting the failure or disappointment
of so-called Third-World endeavors run the danger of still
harboring the residues of imperialist proscriptions.

One of the most effective documents in the vast production
of nineteenth-century "knowledge," for example, was James
Mill's pre-Macaulayan and enormously influential *The History
of British India* (1817). As Suleri explains in her study, *The*

Rhetoric of English India, Mill's text became the virtual bible for the Indian civil service, and his major premises can be said to have helped consolidate the British Raj by mid-century:

Whatever is worth seeing or hearing in India can be expressed in writing. As soon as everything of importance is expressed in writing, a man who is duly qualified may obtain more knowledge of India in one year, in his closet in England, than he could obtain during the course of the longest life, by the use of his eyes and ears in India.[36]

Mill's claim may well appear farcical, but the assurance of its utterance must not be underestimated. The statement represents the establishment of a cultural polemic of such extraordinary strength precisely because the unquestioned paradigm of its historiography is the triumph of a particular brand of scholarship and *literacy* over alternative methodologies and categories of knowledge. British power in India, in other words, did not lie solely with the East India Company's monopolies and militias, but more forbiddingly in British codifications of "Indian" knowledge or – quite starkly – in English books about India. Edward Said's study, *Orientalism* (1978), remains the seminal work to have charted the convolutions of such colonial discursive practices in its treatment of what we now call the Middle East, and has been instrumental in opening up the academy to a rereading of the colonial past.[37]

In the light of such scholarship, it becomes increasingly clear that Naipaul's obsessive privileging of the Word and Book and the "coherence" and "order" leading to "knowledge" they represent is partially responsible for his implication within colonialist discursive practice. Coupled with the intentionality of his manufacture of "lived experience" in his travels and sojourns, Naipaul's "bookishness" can with justification be read as Orientalist. His writings, therefore, lend themselves to an indictment, the charge of which is political and, by extension, one which not only explores the issue of a writer's "authority," but also that of the *ethics* of writing and reading about non-western worlds.

It is not coincidental, therefore, that Naipaul's writing should function as one of the illustrative sites of critics' efforts to theorize, and problematize, the discourse of colonialism and the construction of the colonial subject. Both the history that Naipaul purports to document and the history from which his writing stems allow for an examination of the discursive complications that exist in an *a priori* relation to postcolonial enunciation as a whole. Naipaul's work has been deployed to cover a broad range of concerns. Homi K. Bhabha's work on the colonial subject, for example, utilizes Naipaul's work as the exemplary texts upon which his theoretical investigations are realized. He reads Naipaul's representations by exercising the methods and analyses of deconstructive practice and psychoanalytic theory to trace Naipaul's replication of the constructions of "difference" that constitute focal points of repression in colonialist representations. Social scientists such as David Rosenthal and H. Hoetink, on the other hand, refer to Naipaul's observations for substantiation of their own examinations of linguistic and "racial" practices of the Caribbean region. The latter use of Naipaul's work presumes the "colonial subject" to be the combination of colonial factors that account for the social composition of present-day societies and polities. Their reading of the "colonial subject," therefore, is akin to tracing the etymology of a "topic," or looking for an amalgam of empirically locatable cultural and behavioral practices. The term, "colonial subject" (and Naipaul's implication within its discernment), therefore, is used in two quite different ways: on the one hand, one that sees it as embodying colonialism's ability to distort and sometimes deny, within its hegemonic discursive practice, a primary enunciatory position for any people within its compass; and on the other, one that empirically documents colonial patterns. Those critical of Naipaul tend to adopt the former usage, while those who endorse Naipaul's observations the latter.

All the same, rather than just aligning Naipaul's work in a continuum with texts such as James Mill's, and rather than casting him as irredeemable, it may be equally instructive to examine how his fiction and non-fiction have dealt with the other hazards of colonial discursive formations and their inscriptions of authority. What are the crucial strategies and tactics embedded in the textual and narratological exercises of

Naipaul's work? What negotiations need to be made, for example, between the shadow of colonialist stereotypes and Naipaul's characterizations of Caribbean and other peoples? How are his formulations of postcolonial "mimicry" and "borrowed cultures" to escape the charge of exclusionary monologism? Can they? Is there a theoretical difference between empathy and antipathy that transforms a text's grammar of *subject* and *object* in Naipaul's work? Under examination, his language supplies a more difficult and complex understanding both of the postcolonial condition and of the remarkably divergent readings he already has elicited and continues to elicit.

The following six chapters more or less divide Naipaul's work up into the four decades of their chronological elaboration. Thus, rather than reading a steady progress towards a maturation in his long career, I am more concerned with illustrating the reiterative quality of it. The readings that follow therefore are not developed around the thematic clusters to be found in his oeuvre, nor divided between his fiction and non-fiction. And, while the geographic grouping of his locations and settings have meant that many of his readers are divided between those who are only familiar with, say, his "Indian," or "Caribbean," or "African" books, my lateral organization is premised in part on the belief that regardless of place, the development of Naipaul's work is basically linear.

CHAPTER 2

Bearings

You ever hear that people tell the truth in Trinidad and
get away?

(V.S. Naipaul, *Miguel Street*)

The history of the Caribbean, which includes the history of the
northeastern rim of South America, is one of enactments and
events that span every political, social, and cultural development to have been played out in major areas of the world since
the end of the fifteenth century. The Spanish conquest and
subsequent imperial rule lasted without external interference
for over a century and minimal internal resistance resulted in
the dramatic depopulation of the Amerindian peoples within
just a few decades of European arrival. The agencies of disease,
enslavement, massacre, and eventually intermixture have
meant that only isolated communities such as the Caribs of
Dominica and scattered remnants of other Amerindians in
the Guianas have survived. The history of the region, therefore, carries the burden of a profound erasure, the traces of
which haunt the area with a memory but no recognition of an
autochthonous cultural base. What remains startling about
Caribbean history, then, is the stark transparency of its European manufacture: of its populations, social structures, political
organizations, and the outside orchestration of the region's
participation in the events of the larger world.[1]

The play of multiple colonialisms in the region began in
earnest in the seventeenth century. The piracy of the Spanish
Main by the British, French, and Dutch led to Northern
European colonization of most of the region except Cuba,
Puerto Rico, Santo Domingo, and Trinidad. The rapid trans-

formation of the area into the center of a booming sugar plantation economy was predicated on a massive influx of labor, dramatically escalating the Atlantic slave trade which, by various estimations, brought up to 10 million Africans to the western hemisphere over the course of four centuries.[2] By the time the Caribbean sugar monopoly was broken in the late eighteenth and early nineteenth centuries, and mercantilism had given way to Europe's industrial development, more labor, under indenture rather than slavery, was brought from India, the East Indies, and China to fill the gap created by emancipation. The tension that exists within the discursive realm that the Caribbean represents, therefore, is unprecedented in the multiplicity of its concerns. Ranging from competing European hegemonic discourses that have entrenched themselves as "official" histories, to the until recently denigrated creolized and populist-generated "unofficial" alternatives, the polyglot composition of the region has given rise to an extraordinary series of taxonomic problems.[3] What offsets Naipaul's Caribbean writings, therefore, are the *kinds* of referential choices he has made in representing the region.

Primarily, the group that Naipaul's early work draws upon is the East Indian Trinidadian community into which he was born.[4] As a group, its historical experience since the nineteenth century typifies the insularity of a largely endogamous community who were employed almost exclusively in agricultural labor under indenture. As relative newcomers, carrying with them a mainly rural village experience of British India, and their internal frictions and demarcations between Hinduism and Islam, their cultural contexts through the migratory process remained more intact than for many of their Trinidadian–African predecessors. Many arrived as transients only to discover on their return to India that they had more opportunities and advantages in Trinidad. The communities that settled and multiplied had become by the mid-twentieth century a significant portion of the population. As is always the case with overseas communities over time, Trinidad's East Indian communities, both rural and urban, developed idiosyncrasies and cultural changes in their efforts to maintain their customs and traditions so that the Hinduism and Islam, the Hindi, and Urdu, the adherence to categories of caste, and their kinship patterns all transmuted to adapt to the colonial setting of Trinidad's already stratified society. Even the isolated rural communities suffered a sea change for, eventually, their insularity only deepened their rigidity to custom as it had been practiced in India at the time of their initial emigration. The East Indians of the urban areas, however, became the most deracinated of the group, and their integration into the society at large has been understood as a polarized rather than strictly segregated development of the urban setting. Thus, the intricacies and nuances that inform the social and cultural make-up of Hindu East Indians in Trinidad provide the referent material from which Naipaul's early fiction draws. The localized moment of *Miguel Street* (1959) and the early stories of *A Flag on the Island* (1967) depict scenes of the transitory and static tension of urban migrations, *The Mystic Masseur* (1957) follows the commodification and entrepreneurial use of Hindu cultural capital, and *The Suffrage of Elvira* (1958) charts the literalism of communal polarities in the face of enforced democratization. These early literary navigations cohere into a steadier course with the books dealt with in the following chapter. *A House for Mr. Biswas* (1961) explores the matrilineal and patrilineal tensions within a kinship system on the cusp of change, while Naipaul's first travel book, *The Middle Passage* (1962), serves primarily to contextualize the regionalism of the area, of which the Trinidad of his stories has been the starting point.

It would appear, then, that Naipaul's choice of material is a natural one. At the same time the local and situated matrix from which it evolves is aestheticized to the degree that Naipaul's use of satire to contextualize the creolized nature of the community ultimately measures it against the norms of a social order propagated by British imperialism's "civilizing" mission.[5] This general impulsion is brought into sharp relief by the time of *The Middle Passage*, where Naipaul's referents are almost entirely made up of nineteenth-century British accounts of the region. Nevertheless, the stylistic experimentation of this first period of his career is instructive and illuminating about the narrative and genre options that seemed to offer themselves to him. In contrast to the manifestly autobiographical explorations of George Lamming, or the recuperative stand of Wilson Harris, both of whom offer overtly polemical cases for the generation of a postcolonial Caribbean literary aesthetic,[6] Naipaul's Caribbean fictions are more concerned with an insular narrative universe where the internal "coherence" emerges from an aesthetic of "universal" values.

Read together, then, Naipaul's early work serves as a site of experimentation that the writer's apprenticeship requires as he learns from working and reworking the same materials into gradually more self-sustaining narratives. The culmination that *A House for Mr. Biswas* represents, in other words, has been rehearsed, recast, and severally rewritten through the exercises of *The Mystic Masseur*, *The Suffrage of Elvira*, and *Miguel Street*. Thus, the first decade of his career represents both his most sustained "Caribbean" signature while it also translates into the paradox of his need to distance himself from it. In hindsight, this paradox that Naipaul represents has helped complicate an understanding of the literary endeavors of the region during the transition between the colonial and post-independence eras. Many of the observations and arguments that follow, therefore, are intended to serve as introductory cartography of the techniques, topics, ideological groundings, and the almost vocational deliberations that characterize Naipaul's literary production about the region during the 1950s and early 1960s. The "new" foray into non-fiction represented by *The Middle Passage*, with which the next chapter ends, consequently focuses upon the "experience" of a Naipaul who has narrativized a topic rather than having "studied" it.

THE MYSTIC MASSEUR (1957), THE SUFFRAGE OF ELVIRA (1958), MIGUEL STREET (1959)

While *The Mystic Masseur* (1957) is Naipaul's first book-length publication and his first novel, and *The Suffrage of Elvira* (1958) his second, the manuscript of *Miguel Street* was the first he

completed. Its seventeen episodic sketches of characters and
events associated with a composite fictional Trinidadian street
community are loosely held together by Naipaul's boy-
narrator who, by the end of the volume, leaves for study
abroad. Not only does his departure herald a transience that
Naipaul will continue to develop in most of his later work, but
it is also a device that allows the narrative to fluctuate between
a mature voice recollecting the impressions of childhood and a
child's limited vision. Closely parallel to the levels of the
narrator's maturity as either observer of or participant in the
events of the sketches is the volume's play with "code-switching."[7] Rather than demonstrating the multiple switching
between languages and usages of any given character,
however, the code-switching happens at the level of the
framing narrative itself. The standard English of the narrative
interludes or transitions is constantly challenged by the dialect
and distinct syntax of a more local Trinidadian English so that
eventually, as the narrator grows older, and his English
becomes more standard, the level of his "education" becomes
the measure of both his distance from the world of the street
and the *means* whereby the street community is given its
"coherence."

The boy-narrator of *Miguel Street*, therefore, is the first of
Naipaul's narrative frames with which his fiction achieves
"coherence" in the face of its otherwise loose composition and
uneven development. The narrative voices of *The Mystic
Masseur*, *The Suffrage of Elvira*, and *A House for Mr. Biswas* all
variously play with the same steady interpellation so that their
singular demonstrations of a particular, *standard*, literacy
gathers an ideological force, which, furthermore, is the basis
for the satirical maneuvers that each of the books engage
in; namely, that the multiple examples of *misreadings* and
misapprehensions in all four fictions reveal the slippage between
literacy and illiteracy within the communities represented,
allowing Naipaul to lampoon the affectations of what he later
calls "half-made societies," and "borrowed cultures."

The troping of literacy consequently emerges as the central
figure of the early fiction. Sign-writing in particular is a talent

that all the narrators or protagonists share. In *Miguel Street* it becomes the narrative's ironic means of codifying the characters' claims to artisanship, such as Popo's carpentry and Hat's tailoring, which the narrator has already cast doubts upon. Similarly, the efficacy of sign-writing is explored in *The Suffrage of Elvira*, where one of the principal characters, Baksh, advertises his enterprise as: "M. BAKSH/London Tailoring Est./Tailoring and Cutting/Suits Made and Repair at City Prices" (*Elvira*, p. 15). Later, in *The Suffrage of Elvira*, during the political campaign to gain election to the Legislative Council, one of the candidates, Harbans Singh, watches helplessly the sabotage as his slogans exhorting the community to "VOTE HARBANS OR DIE!" become "DIE! DIE! DIE (*Elvira*, p. 40), thus allowing the narrative to hint broadly at the permutations of its dramatic irony. Finally, Mohun Biswas, in *A House for Mr. Biswas*, begins his young adulthood as a sign-writer, a circumstance that leads to his courtship of Shama, which, at that point in the novel, represents a false start in his upward mobility. Collectively, then, the unselfconscious "errors" in the shop signs, placards, and hoardings of all Naipaul's fictions set in the Caribbean and the greater Third World become the indicators of pretensions towards literacy that Naipaul transposes to many of his later fictions and travelogues.

The ability to read and write *standard* English in an anglophone Caribbean setting, the satirical edge of Naipaul's early fiction insists, is the only claim to legitimacy. This is because this same literacy allows one a place in the larger discursive field of an articulated History. Since Naipaul later attributes this capability to writing's "work" and the "knowledge" it achieves, the litanies of characters' misapprehensions in all the early fiction doggedly parallels the demonstrations of their misreadings as well. Subsequently, Naipaul will habitually attribute the many failures of the postcolonial worlds he encounters to this "confusion." The overwhelming occurrence of *Miguel Street*'s enactments of misapprehended and misread situations, as a result, not only becomes the occasion for Naipaul to enact his narrator's gradual disengagement from the world of the street and Trinidad but to also cast it as an achievement. The characters' many false starts, in other words, be they professional, vocational, familial, or "artistic," provide the measurement whereby the narrator's act of recollection salvages them from "incompletion." As his first completed manuscript, and first sustained engagement with a narrative voice that must employ the idea of escape in order to unify its subject, *Miguel Street* serves as a fascinating introduction to both the ambivalences and certitudes of Naipaul's fictive base.

Miguel Street's first sketch, "Bogart," for example, is often cited in the context of Naipaul's 1983 essay, "Prologue to an Autobiography," in which he traces the advent of his life in fiction. After quoting the first two sentences of the story:

Every morning when he got up Hat would sit on the bannister of his back verandah and shout across, "What happening there, Bogart?"

Bogart would turn in his bed and mumble softly, so that no one heard, "What happening there, Hat?" (*Miguel Street*, p. 9)

Naipaul writes, "That was a Port of Spain memory. It seemed to come from far back, but it was only eleven or twelve years old" (*Finding the Centre*, p. 4). The immediate significance of this observation is its acknowledgment of the fusion of time and space in the act of recollection. The "Port of Spain memory" localizes the occasion but does not limit its applicability – "Every morning when ... " – while the passage of its trans- mission carries the double awareness of imagined and finite time. Curiously, however, a few pages later in "Prologue," after Naipaul has given a condensed description of his family's migratory history and encapsulated the intracommunal social stratifications which characterized the nascent urban develop- ment of that time, he goes on to claim that "Luck was with me, because that first sentence was so direct, so uncluttered, so without complications, that it provoked the sentence that was to follow ... The first sentence was true. The second was pure invention" (*Finding the Centre*, pp. 8–9). The category of "Luck," it seems, belongs to a rhetoric of accident, suggesting as it does the serendipitous nature of discovery. Nevertheless, such fortune notwithstanding, what is more important is that the narrator is so positioned that he can situate Hat's "call" so that it is "heard," whereas Bogart's "response" is not. The narrator's control, in other words, only takes hold at the point where "invention" intervenes. Thus, in the same way that the juxtaposition of the first two sentences of "Bogart" engendered the rest of the book, Naipaul's explanation implicitly suggests that the relationship between fact and fiction is a productive and *reliable* symbiosis, and that the difficulty of writing fiction rests in calibrating the relationship of the two. What does not seem to be at issue here is the possibility that the "fact" or "reality" in question is as constructed as any "fiction."

An alternative reading which Naipaul's explanation also suggests is one that complicates the relationship between language and representation. The strength of the opening of "Bogart," Naipaul states, lies in its ability to leave "out everything – the setting, the historical time, the racial and social complexities of the people concerned – [the opening] had suggested it all ... And together, as sentences, words, they had set up a rhythm, a speed, which dictated all that was to follow" (*Finding the Centre*, p. 9). By granting language a superordinate status over its referents, Naipaul consciously and unconsciously suggests a constructionist rather than essentialist relationship between the two. This deference to the self-perpetuating capability of "sentences, words," therefore, is also a comment on the process of invention and its constructions of meaning rather than a valorization of writing's transparency. At the same time, however, the comment also seems premised on an unquestioned assumption that what writing enunciates is in consonance with what is being written about.

The dialectical process that Naipaul credits to "fiction" merits a further observation because of the self-acknowledgment of its subterfuge. Recollection and invention together, by his own account, not only activate the self-perpetuation of "sentences, words," but also license the repression of history, "race" and class in order to create space for the creation of a Dickensian category of "character." It is precisely this substitution of individualistic and idiosyncratic "types" that allows Naipaul's fiction to resist the less romantic but no less poignant

challenges of a materialist verisimilitude. Thus the foundation
of his fictive base lies in his attempts to recreate, adapt and
transpose a specific narrative tradition on to his locale, rather
than look for alternative narrative categories that may stem
from the more local and alternative habits of expression.[8] The
latter-day subtextual information that the essay "Prelude to
an Autobiography" appears to provide for *Miguel Street*, therefore, is not a gesture towards the earlier volume's materialist
ellipses, but rather a further sublimation of them. By contextualizing the writing of *Miguel Street* through the same ploy of
pitting what information was "real" against what was not,
Naipaul reifies the license of fiction's artifice to dehistoricize its
subjects. The alternative subtext of *Miguel Street*, consequently,
must also be seen as Naipaul's obsession with a monological
view of aesthetics.

Accordingly, the more heavy-handed examinations of
literacy and aesthetic issues in *Miguel Street* occur in the
sketches about the poet and calypsonian, "B. Wordsworth,"
the resident mad man, "Man-Man," and the self-appointed
teacher, "Titus Hoyt I.A." B. Wordsworth, for example, by
his own admission is, "Black Wordsworth. White Wordsworth
was my brother. We share one heart. I can watch a small
flower like the morning glory and cry" (*Miguel Street*, p. 46).
Where "B. Wordsworth" enacts a literal transposition of a
Wordsworthian pastorale, enchanting only to the narrator,
Man-Man manages to affect the entire community. His tale
initially deconstructs literacy's privilege by literalizing the
notion of inscription when he chalks the pavements with
extended vowels. Furthermore, his eerie sermon, "He show me
husband eating wife and wife eating husband ... He show me
brother eating sister and sister eating brother. That is what
these politicians and them mean by saying that the island
going to become self sufficient" (*Miguel Street*, p. 42), is only a
prelude to his attempt at figural embodiment. The crucifixion
scene he stages suggests that the testimonial he represents is
well aware of the determinist plot of its scriptural origins.
When he is actually stoned and forced to give up his calling, in
other words, the metaphor of cannibalism is reinstated to its

symbolic function, and, consequently, the Word to its status as codification as the Book.

Titus Hoyt is equally literal-minded. His school and social clubs are earnest but hollow gestures at community organization, and his tutelage of Elias, one of the narrator's contemporaries, is illustrative of how empty Naipaul sees such "mimicry" to be. Elias' third division in the Cambridge School Certificate examination, and his subsequent multiple failures to improve that score give both the truth and lie to Titus' enterprise. Education, or its semblance, as the narrator's own success suggests, remains of value despite or because of Naipaul's pleasure in pointing to its elusiveness. Titus' real ambition, for instance, finally proves to be his desire for congratulatory recognition in the newspapers, regardless of how self-manufactured it may be. But this shift from a parody of formal education – which is also encapsulated in *The Mystic Masseur* when the protagonist Ganesh is told during his first day as a teacher to "Form not Inform" (*Mystic Masseur*, p. 24) – into one of the more vibrant world of newsprint provides both *Miguel Street* and all the novels set in the Caribbean with an alternative, almost competing realm of (il)literacy.

The newspapers and their local and international coverage constitute a constant and recurring presence within the three books, and represent consequently a notion of stability, but more importantly, in Benedict Anderson's terms, participation within an "imagined community."[9] In *Miguel Street* this notion is toyed with because mention in the papers is usually for a crime but is still presented as the universal mark of honor. Hat "always read the papers. He read them from about ten in the morning until about six in the evening" (*Miguel Street*, p. 20), granting him authority within the narrator's purview. At the same time, however, Bolo the Barber, in "Caution," intones with feeling, "You mustn't believe anything you read in the papers" (*Miguel Street*, p. 129). Thus the extremes of the newspapers' effect, despite Naipaul's satiric cast, bear further examination. Helpful here are two astute observations by Anderson: "if we ... turn to the newspaper as a cultural product, we will be struck by its profound fictiveness," because the arbitrariness and juxtaposition of the events depicted and reported "show that the linkage between them is imagined" (Anderson, p. 33). He also stresses that the activity of reading the papers presupposes that "each communicant is well aware that the ceremony he performs is being replicated simultaneously by thousands (or millions) of others of whose existence he is confident, yet of whose identity he has not the slightest notion" (Anderson, p. 35). By understanding that the newspaper performs a novelistic function of creating the means whereby a community can conceive of itself, Naipaul's habit of obsessively quoting, or creating, headlines, articles, reports, and newspaper competitions in his first four books helps locate an important conceptual pulse that his fiction depends upon.

Bolo, for example, stops believing anything in the papers only after a series of disappointments with the various competitions newspapers use to bolster their circulations. The Missing Ball Competition is the cause of his loss of faith with the *Trinidad Guardian*, while the endorsement via advertising and reporting of the Co-operative Housing Society scheme in the *Gazette* sees Bolo as victim to a scam and he stops reading it. That Bolo has been obsessed with the games rather than the "news" is less ironic when we realize that their promise of material gain represents the commodification of desire as a substitute for economic opportunity. Thus, while Bolo controls his frustration, his restraint is chillingly measured by whose hair he allows himself to cut, signaling a curious moment of self-knowledge. His self-discipline, nevertheless, is not enough to protect him from the way information comes, until the end, when the sweepstakes he eventually wins no longer represent the promise of gain, and he isolates himself entirely. Newspapers as agencies of desire allow for the ploy and curse of gambling to enact its own morality play throughout the volume, but its dialectic of temptation is less a symbol for the vagaries of Fate or Chance than for the unreliability or fictiveness of information, or the lies that maintain colonial dependency.[10]

Thus, Hat's propensity to make impossible bets, and his dedicated reading of newpapers, firmly plant him within a world where information is severally moot, unreliable, elusive, and capricious. This is in keeping with his own conduct in "Hat," where he allows spectators to believe that the twelve children he has brought to a cricket match may all be his. Similarly, his relationship to his nephews, Boyee and Errol, is couched in innuendo, strengthening the surrogacy of his paternity precisely because it belongs to a fictional realm. His practice of watering milk, furthermore, resists entirely an admission of guilt despite the general knowledge of it. His rationalization that, "You ever hear that people tell the truth in Trinidad and get away?" at first appears to be one of the many self-deprecating statements made about Trinidad in relation to the world, or England in particular, but his punishment within the judicial and penal system – British colonialism's most powerful institutions –nevertheless is blind to such nuance. Thus, the rift between Sergeant Charles and Hat over this same situation allows Hat one of his most passionate declarations about information: "*Which* water in *which* milk?" (*Miguel Street*, p. 159). Also challenged in this instance is the narrator's gesture of interpretation when he plays the role of go-between between Sergeant Charles and Hat. Thus the fictiveness of the way information comes via the newspaper serves as a narrative rather than thematic device throughout the volume. In the absence of a unifying plot, Naipaul's loose collection of characters appears within a narrative space that is constructed upon the same principle of arbitrary inclusion and juxtaposition outlined by Anderson.

Two other juxtaposed themes rather than narrative devices that help explain Naipaul's early attempts to craft fiction out of "experience" are also introduced in a somewhat haphazard way in *Miguel Street*. They are a nascent consciousness about the status of women within the setting and, by extension, about how depictions of familial domestic situations lend themselves to an examination of the power relations and exercises of authority within a colonized community. Curiously, issues of gender play a far more significant role in Naipaul's early fictions, even while questions about authority appear to be resolved within a male-centered frame. What could be politely

termed as Naipaul's ambivalence about women in his later
novels such as *Guerrillas* and *A Bend in the River*, to name only
two, appears instead as a curiosity bred of concern in the early
stories. *Miguel Street*'s *machista* ethos, for example, is constantly
parodied in Hat's refrain about the induction of characters into
the street's company of "we men." Hence, the gendering of
the community's social spaces is more blurred than a forth-
right phallocentricism usually suggests. Mrs. Bhakcu and
Mrs. Morgan, the wives of two protagonists, do indeed define
themselves solely according to their husbands' status, but only
as much as the Trinidad of the sketches is defined by evocations
of England, typified by examples such as the examinations
corrected by "Mr. Cambridge." Women are objectified by the
male gaze of the street's gatherings, but so are the cricketers
within the same kind of gaze of the street.

Similarly, Naipaul exercises some sensitivity towards the
issues of adultery and bigamy, which happen with great frequency throughout *Miguel Street*. Mrs. Morgan's discovery of
her husband's infidelity in "The Pyrotechnicist," and her
immediate public outcry – "It was a cry of great pain" – lends
the volume its most concentrated theatrical spectacle, complete with lights fluttering on and off, and its tableau of "the
thin man held up so easily by the fat woman" (*Miguel Street*,
p. 72). While George's wife's lot in "George and the Pink
House" is cause for regret on the street, it is not afforded the
"respect" that the runaway adulterer Mrs. Hereira in "Love,
Love, Love, Alone" receives. Here, class is the factor that
moves the men of the street to accost Toni, Mrs. Hereira's
lover, after he has beaten her. What this sketch brings into
relief is the double standard of Miguel Street's internal civil
register. Relations between men and women serve as the baro-
meter with which the community measures the maintenance of
its codes, but its fluctuations also reflect the intervention of
class, and to a degree, race, in their modulations, which ultimately remain consistent with the colonial paradigm of social
relations.

Hat, one of the narrator's surrogate father figures in *Miguel
Street*, is finally convicted for wife beating, Bogart indicted for

bigamy, Popo jogged into productive action only after his wife runs off with the gardener; these and other characters caught by marital and filial indiscretions, attest to the moral scrutiny Naipaul attempts. It is the character of Laura in "The Maternal Instinct," whose eight children are fathered by seven men, however, who provides the clearest line of early feminist consciousness on the part of Naipaul. Nathaniel, the father of Laura's last two children, and her companion of note, is cited as an unacceptable transgressor of the fluid street code towards women. Laura's ability finally to expel him from her life appears a triumphant gesture of independence; nevertheless, when her eldest daughter announces her own pregnancy, Laura breaks down, and at the news of her suicide simply states, "It good. It good. It better that way" (*Miguel Street*, p. 91). Laura's failure is Naipaul's most detailed portrait of the internalized subjugation of women within this setting.

In *Miguel Street*'s third sketch, "George and the Pink House," Naipaul leads his narrator through a pristine characterization of a male-centered vision. The narrator first acknowledges that, "I found it hard to believe that George had a wife and a son and a daughter" only to follow with the further admission that "George's wife was never a proper person. I always thought of her as George's wife, and that was all. And I always thought, too, that George's wife was nearly always in the cow-pen" (*Miguel Street*, pp. 22–23). The narrator's incredulity about this domestic equation is due less to his disbelief that anyone could possibly choose to be with George, than to a skepticism about the fictions an imposed norm of "the nuclear family" generates within the setting. When Elias, George's son, defends his father's violence to Hat and the narrator, for example, his rationalization draws upon a Christian ethic that blithely flies in the face of manifest injustice by propagating martyrdom as a general panacea to exploitation and tyrannical behavior. Because it poses itself in the Name of the Father, Elias cannot comprehend or acknowledge the brutality of his father's exercise of authority. That the son should take such an attitude while his mother and sister ultimately bear the brunt of the blows, points to the profound repression that underscores both patriarchal and colonial domination: only the wholesale subordination of woman in the former, and subordination of colonial subjects in the latter, can maintain these structures of power and authority.

George beats his family, but privileges his son, possibly beats his wife to death, then opens a brothel, and finally barters off his daughter in marriage during a hideous display of sexist ribbing from the predominantly American military guests. Though the agent of brutality for his family, George too is depicted as brutalized, thus cementing the old equation of master/slave, colonizer/colonized. The descriptions of domestic violence that dominate Naipaul's Caribbean fictions are grim to say the least, but they are also part of a portrait of the blindness willed into situations where the appearance of familial and marital loyalty must be maintained at, literally, all costs. The states of mind that Naipaul's depictions of domestic violence suggest are chillingly reminiscent of the demands of colonial filiation. For all the rough edges of its execution, therefore, *Miguel Street* nevertheless lays the foundations for Naipaul's increasingly more concentrated examinations of the colonized condition. In both *The Mystic Masseur* and *The Suffrage of Elvira*, *Miguel Street*'s communal space is reworked into a more overt "national" framework, and the domesticity of its Dickensian "characters" into a sophisticated allegory of colonialism in *A House for Mr. Biswas*.

Naipaul's first novel utilizes a narrator faintly reminiscent of *Miguel Street*'s boy-narrator, but one who adopts the posture of a biographer, or mock-biographer, as Kenneth Ramchand describes him.[11] Both the tone and the fact that the narrator's source material is primarily made up of the protagonist's autobiography and self-promotional publications immediately establishes the satirical cast of *The Mystic Masseur*. The novel is ostensibly Ganesh's story. Starting his career as a school teacher after successfully completing secondary school and the rudiments of training as a teacher, Ganesh capitalizes on his education by combining it with his pretensions to being a pundit after he inherits his uncle's Sanskrit texts. Entering a marriage that benefits him financially, and gaining a father-in-law, Ramlogan, with whose commercial enterprises he continues to compete throughout the novel, Ganesh's upward mobility through financial success to political office is offered as emblematic of the rise of the first generation of colonial entrepreneurs who unethically capitalized on the political opportunities the era offered.

However, as a character who becomes a public figure within the cultural, political, and social landscape of the Trinidadian setting, he is also immediately emblematic of part of the island's hybridity. His status as emblem, however, is not limited to a crude version of a Naipaulian colonial, to be developed later into the more troubled "mimic man." Instead, Ganesh also serves as an important social and cultural marker for Hinduism, not as a system of belief, but as the resident Hindu institution which offers recourse to an *idea* of amelioration in the heart of Trinidad's Hindu Indian community. The recurring references to him in *Miguel Street*, *The Suffrage of Elvira*, *A House for Mr. Biswas*, and stories in *A Flag on the Island* such as "My Aunt Gold Teeth," furthermore, provide an early example of Naipaul's intertextual enfolding whereby he is able to create an internal narrative authority premised upon recognition and familiarity. The election campaigns of both Ganesh in *The Mystic Masseur* and Harbans Singh in *The Suffrage of Elvira* are uncomplicated satires of actual historical events: Trinidad's first election under universal adult suffrage in 1946, and its second in 1950 to achieve self-government. The settings of both novels thus allow for a quasi-historical familiarity of events that fashion their fictions' guise within a "national" rather than "nationalist" framework.

When the narrator of *The Mystic Masseur* suggests in his introductory remarks that, "I myself believe that the history of Ganesh is, in a way, the history of our times" (*Mystic Masseur*, p. 18), he announces the mock-heroic dimension of the novel's political fable. Furthermore, by taking as his authority Ganesh's own publications, the narrator also establishes a game of textual authority that anticipates the intertextual role that Ganesh will play throughout the early fictions. The

inflation of the significance of Ganesh's writings, therefore, is
the first gesture of the novel's pleasure in playing with the idea
of "literacy," and the conflations and subterfuges that characterize the multilingual aspect of Trinidadian cultural poly-
genesis. To start with, Ganesh, the elephant-headed Hindu
god, is, among other things, the god of writing whose invocation is talismanic at the start of any number of Sanskrit and
Hindu texts. To make the protagonist of his first novel the god's
namesake, then, is not only Naipaul's small gesture to his
Hindu heritage, but it is also the first layering of an elaborate
intertextual elbowing that the novel houses between the competing cultural literacies – of Hinduism, colonial education,
English, commerce – that converge, conflate, and displace one
another during the course of Ganesh's political creolization.

The coalescent literacies are set against the orality of all
Trinidad's rural and urban communities. The textual layering,
however, does not only take the form of allusion and cross-
referencing, such as Ganesh's glosses of Hindu texts, or in the
linguistic games between notions of standard English and the
local versions of it. It is also played out in a series of demeta-
phorizing tactics where Naipaul allows characters, including
the narrator as a young man, to misread the significance of
"books" by confusing quantity – the number and size of books
– with content. When introduced to Ganesh, for example, the
narrator and all the characters present are awed by the
number of books he has. To capitalize on their awe, Leela,
Ganesh's wife, supplements the news of the purchase of the last
three volumes with the following incontrovertible fact: "But
they was big books, big books. Six to seven inches altogether"
(*The Mystic Masseur*, p. 15). Another aspect of Naipaul's satire
is the novel's plot, which is so firmly rooted in a notion of a
progressive development into modernity that the novel refuses to
recognize that *alternative* readings may occur when a translation or application of a cultural referent is shifted from one
context to another. Thus the novel's effect is the chronicle of
Ganesh's success as a flawed and misguided achievement
within a political and social milieu that cannot as yet read itself
as the tangled amalgam of badly translated texts.

Since Ganesh's initial success is premised on his reputation as a masseur whose healing capabilities are attributed to a mystical power that includes the skewed emblem of "books," his clients' gullibility and superstition become yet another occasion for Naipaul to play with the idea of misreadings. At the same time, however, the novel also suggests that Ganesh's manipulation of his clients' superstition shows that he "reads" with considerable sophistication. For example, Ganesh is able to capitalize on the ownership of his uncle's Sanskrit texts, and then respond to occasions such as the boy who thinks he is pursued by a black cloud with a clever application of popular pyschology and theatrical gestures of exorcism that pay lip-service to the practice of *obeah*. He further compounds the appearance of his authority over the unknown by switching between speaking Hindi or English when appropriate, and by writing a stream of books and pamphlets that also alternate between self-assertion, glosses on Hinduism, and "mysticism." Then his negotiations with Ramlogan over Leela's dowry suggest more than just a shrewd ability to out-haggle an opponent. They suggest a keen reading of the proprietorial conventions of kinship transactions where caste, class, and pure cash are elaborately woven into the perpetuation of a specific, predetermined, and endogamous communal pattern.

One of the early indices of how widespread and prevalent the trope of misreading and subsequent cultural devaluation is within *The Mystic Masseur* is the figure of the wandering Englishman, Mr. Stewart. Ganesh's encounter with him, on a simple symbolic level, is an encounter with an "Other," the complementary image of himself and his career of cultural appropriations. Mr. Stewart appears as a transplanted, ahistorical, and apolitical self-annointed Hindu whose seduction at the altar of a skewed essentialism is as absurd as it is emblematic. He helps trigger Ganesh's will to write, provides him with the proscribed formulae of *The Science of Thought Review*, and endorses a pretentious practice of meditation and non-participation. As inspiration, therefore, it is Mr. Stewart and the license of his colonial misreadings rather than recourse to a textual Hindu authority that sets the stage for Ganesh's soon to be brilliant career.

At the end of the novel, furthermore, the award of an MBE
by the absent authorities in Britain is a gesture premised
entirely upon the British authorities' misconstrual of Ganesh's
participation in a labor dispute. Naipaul's fictional story of one
of Trinidad's candidates in its first elections under universal
adult suffrage, is, therefore, in many ways a relentless parody of
the "adult" in a colonial setting. The adolescence and willful
petulance that characterize the events and behavior within the
story are the ills held up for ridicule and correction. Consequently, the implication of the novel's judgment is that the
island was not yet ready for such "responsibility," and that the
"irresponsibility" of granting such privilege too soon is also
complicit in the general failure. The satire's moral and social
fulcrum is one that is reminiscent of a late-imperial paternalism, best examined, and ultimately endorsed, in Forster's *A
Passage to India* rather than in Kipling's more simplistic formulation of the white man's burden.[12]

At the same time, though, Ganesh's use of the press during
his career of self-promotion, and especially his exchange via the
gossip columns such as "A Little Bird Tells Us," with his
father-in-law, Ramlogan, during the years of their estrange-
ment, place newspapers within the heart of the island's
orality. While it is Biswas' career as a journalist during the
latter chapters of *A House for Mr. Biswas* that is Naipaul's most
comprehensive account of the press's reach into the multiple
imaginings of the communities' desires, *The Mystic Masseur*
nevertheless lays the groundwork for a conception of the island
as an imagined community. So, despite the satirical cast of
both *The Mystic Masseur* and *The Suffrage of Elvira*, the two
novels can also be read as an anticipation of Fredric Jameson's
assertion that "All third-world texts are necessarily ... allegorical ... they are to be read as what I will call *national
allegories*, even when, or perhaps I should say, particularly
when their forms develop out of predominantly western
machineries of representation, such as the novel."[13] Naipaul's
use of satire to dismiss the viability of Trinidadian nationhood
on the one hand, and his narrative evocation of its early years
on the other, is a central tension which helps explain his

continued ambivalence about postcolonial political possibilities. It places him with a large group of other postcolonial
writers because, even while Jameson has been brought to task
for the sweeping compass of his pronouncement,[14] there often is
in early postcolonial fictions perceived or imagined imperatives
to provide for the historical and cultural context in which the
story, or novel, is set, and the political urgencies out of which it
has emerged.

Because of the constraints of colonial history, the construct of
the "nation" often figures predominantly as the conceptual
frame within which postcolonial stories can be told.[15] These
"national" imperatives rest on three broad demands: the audience unfamiliar with the place and culture asks to be informed
or corrected, and, secondly, the audiences who are informed
read for accuracy, insight, and, to use Jameson's term, futurity,
whatever form the representation may take. The third demand
is more diffuse because it entails a less prosaic and literal
criterion. Because the writer is engaged in narrativizing a
subject hitherto "untold," his or her version carries the possibility of setting in motion, for better or for worse, a codification
of the subject within an "official" textual and discursive realm
– a process that is predisposed to closure and determinism. In
other words, the narrative claims an "authenticity" as to its
status as history.

The coalition, therefore, of an internally self-authenticating
narrative and the concept of "nation," produces an enormously powerful text because, as Homi Bhabha explains at the
start of his anthology, *Nation and Narration*, "it is from those
traditions of political thought and literary language that the
nation emerges as a powerful historical idea in the west. An
idea whose cultural compulsion lies in the impossible unity of
the nation as a symbolic force."[16] Naipaul's first two novels
and their satiric treatment of the emergence of the Trinidadian
"nation," therefore, can be read, in the light of Jameson's
dictum and Bhabha's initial premise about nation and narration, as two demonstrations of how Naipaul's Trinidadian
example illustrates the *absence* of symbol from the idea of
"nation." By appearing to expose this "absence" Naipaul

implies that it is the novelist's role to create a local narrative whose tropology will serve as the ground for a new symbolic order.

If Naipaul's means of achieving this objective are satiric and ironic, then his deliberately distorted satirist's focus needs to be dealt with before the narrative can assume its symbolic authority. In response to George Lamming's charge that Naipaul's early novels are "castrated satire," for example, Gordon Rohlehr chooses to point out that:

The position of the ironist in colonial society is indeed a delicate one. Lamming can see little that is risible in a society whose history is one of underprivilege. One appreciates his point. The early Naipaul is at times the irresponsible ironist, subtle, but lacking in a sensitive participation in the life he anatomizes ... Satire is the sensitive measure of a society's departure from the norm inherent in itself. Since Naipaul starts with the conviction that such a norm is absent from his society, his task as satirist becomes doubly difficult ... This explains the mixture of farce and social consciousness which occurs in the two early novels.[17]

The double jeopardy through which Naipaul's early novels negotiate, Rohlehr continues, is between sympathy and antipathy. The absent norm with which he credits Naipaul's satires, accordingly, is implied by the "Chaucerian" grin of the narrative stance whereby the "reader is invited simultaneously to recognize the degree of distortion and to share in the author's grin" (Rohlehr, p. 123). Ultimately, Rohlehr maintains, the sum total of Naipaul's satire by the time of *The Middle Passage*, is a nightmare vision of Trinidad because it seems unable to participate in either a "national" or moral purpose, thus undermining the island's recourse to any sense of "authentic" viability.

Jameson's reading of "national allegories," however, evokes another function of satire and its collusions with a "utopian impulse," where the latter is "driven secretly by the satirist's rage at a fallen reality" (Jameson, p. 80). Read this way, Naipaul's satire takes on the dimensions of a nostalgia for the colonial order and its propagation of a supposed "civility." This formulation does indeed fit into a reading of Naipaul's works as ultimately colonialist in their sympathies. Jameson's essay, despite the vast global sweep of its application, however, does not include the Caribbean region in its purview. His concerns are more with regions and cultural histories which, between their contemporary Third- and Second-World status, represent postcolonial situations that have entered the late capitalist global order from autochthonous pasts, be they feudal–dynastic or "so-called primitive, or tribal." Latin America, in Jameson's argument, offers a third model which he predicts Africa and Asia will eventually follow. But the Caribbean is not on his map, despite its overdetermined constitution of colonial and "third world" features.

With this realization, it becomes necessary to reread an easy indictment of Naipaul's colonialist leanings in his Caribbean work because the secret sharer of his satire's revelations needs to be identified. If Naipaul's anticipation of a political allegory is not of a nationalistic kind, for example, it nevertheless does carry a distinct ideological inflection that appears blind to its own complicity with a larger hegemonic practice that takes as its goal a society's progressive ascension to a secular but moral, indeed civil, modernity. The target of Naipaul's satire in *The Mystic Masseur*, after all, is the *misuse* of the Hindu tradition's longevity and religious practice, which in turn is also a comment on the factionalism that its deployment within Trinidad's transition to decolonization causes, precluding the possibility of a "nationalist" rubric. The novel's thrust is that the bastardization of cultural capital is the means whereby Ganesh gains success, and the subsequent political dividends he is able to enjoy have far less to do with any kind of grand idea or vision than with opportunism and chicanery. Nevertheless, double dealing and knavery are the features that do indeed lead to an economic boom and self-sufficiency in Ganesh's district of Fuente Grove. Embedded here, therefore, is the assumption that economic development within a capitalist setting overrides the need for cultural struggle and its often concomitant nationalist rhetoric. Paradoxically, the exposure of corruption through farce does suggest again that some ideal exists if its corruption can be manifest, and that political integrity, like "civility," is an ahistorical but "cultural" requirement. Thus, the novel establishes the groundwork for Naipaul's subsequent theses on the philistinism of Trinidad's political matrix in *The Middle Passage*, which will also become the basis for most of his subsequent analyses of postcolonial political situations.

Naipaul's allegory, therefore, does not focus only on the local Trinidadian example. The allusions to Indian independence movements, as Selwyn Cudjoe has pointed out, serve as an analogous projection, within the allegorical site, of modeling Ganesh's career, albeit satirically, on a famous Indian nationalist: Mahatma Gandhi. While the text is replete with such references, especially during the campaigns of Indarsingh – recently returned from a British university – and of Ganesh for the Legislative Council seat, the satiric mode's effect lies less in just denigrating the success of Trinidad's first election by universal adult suffrage[18] than in its suspicion of reactive and imitative rather than "rational," well-thought-through nationalist movements in general. The importance of India's independence movements to the rest of the British empire notwithstanding, Naipaul's recourse to them as icons for the East Indian communities within that empire is not only a comment on the process of becoming "Trinidadian," as Cudjoe suggests, but more chillingly on the *fictions* allowed to proliferate in the name of many mid-twentieth-century nationalisms. Cudjoe also attributes *The Mystic Masseur*'s "mysticism" to Naipaul's attempt to reconcile Trinidad's Hindu Indians to their "social environment" where the figure of Ganesh represents, eventually, the "transformation to Trinidadianism" (Cudjoe, p. 41). The national allegory, for Cudjoe, therefore, is precisely along the lines of Jameson's dictum because, he argues, "What begins as a purely particular and parochial matter becomes a general and national matter, and in the process that which is purely Hindu merges with the general and sociopolitical history of the country" (Cudjoe, p. 41). From this angle, Ganesh's story does indeed suggest that one individual's or community's story is the nation's story too.

The Hinduism of Naipaul's novels, however, is hardly "pure." The very crossing of the ocean of the laborers from

India precluded the religion's transportation in any orthodox sense, and its subsequent practice by migrants is, theoretically, necessarily compromised. Thus the profound contradictions inherent in the religion's fearful hierarchy of exclusion and prohibitions belies its political deployment in an egalitarian polity.[19] Naipaul's depictions of the rituals practiced, therefore, are almost always reductive; for example, Aunt Gold Teeth's fetishism, or Ganesh's brahminical initiation, which has a minor character named Dookhie running after him saying, "Cut out this nonsense, man. Stop behaving stupid ... You think you really going to Benares? That is in India, you know, and this is Trinidad" (*The Mystic Masseur*, p. 21). Examples such as this are repeated throughout the novel, indeed in all Naipaul's works where Hinduism – and other religions – are encountered in their evolution from one form of practice to another. *The Mystic Masseur*, in particular, stresses disjunctions which cannot be repaired when a cultural translation takes place from one political arena to another.

The political allegory of *The Mystic Masseur*, therefore, is a complex compendium of self-invented propositions that create a pastiche of political, and cultural rationalizations. The local materials from which cultural, political, and economic capital can be generated, in other words, are the exploitable resources of a marketable item – a talismanic Hinduism – that, during the course of the novel, momentarily *reinstates* cultural practice as a social function. In this reading, then, the depiction of the Hindu East Indian community empties the "national" out of the allegory and substitutes instead a story of colonial hybridity rather than a detail of the larger Trinidadian political canvas. In this way *The Mystic Masseur* is the first of a long series of works in which Naipaul charts his version of the paradigms of postcolonial nationalisms, whose rhetoric manages to resist the novelty of their constructions by either inventing or parroting the *cultural* referents of irretrievable or withheld traditions. Thus the novel also houses the first outline of a colonial "mimic man," a parody of the prototype of a "flawed colonial mimesis," where to be anglicized is not only not to be English, but, in Naipaul's depiction, to fail the Macaulayan recommendation too.[20]

The figure of Ganesh, consequently, foreshadows that of
Ralph Singh of *The Mimic Men*, as it does of many other
characters in most of Naipaul's work, including his non-fiction.
What must also be remembered, as Rohlehr, Lamming, and
countless other critics from the Caribbean have noted, is that
the process of Naipaul's own anglicization, principally through
his writing, is in a fascinating dialogic relation to the figures he
creates. This is not to insert a biographical intervention, so
much as to establish that the allegorical sites of Naipaul's
fictions are more complex than a blanket view such as Jameson's would allow: the issue of cultural belonging as an existentialist quest rather than the issue of national rootedness or
"identity" dictates, indeed often distorts, Naipaul's
engagement with political realities. Ganesh Ramsumair's
transmutation into G. Ramsay Muir MBE, for example, does
suggest that his career marks the character's voyage to
"whiteness," a conceit that persistently recurs in all of Naipaul's work as the sign of colonialism's power to posit the fact of
"whiteness" as the predetermined end of all its cultural
identity-formations.

The Suffrage of Elvira continues *The Mystic Masseur*'s political
themes by staging the campaigns waged, in a remote part of
the island, by the candidates of the next election, after Trinidad and Tobago has achieved self-government. The elevation of familial, kinship, ethnic, and petty rivalries to the
power of a force in national elections provides the gist of the
satire, and follows *The Mystic Massuer* with a chronological
faithfulness: by the 1950s the island is still not ready for
self-determination. Where *The Mystic Masseur* focused on
Ganesh's story, *The Suffrage of Elvira* substitutes the story of a
campaign in one district. While Surujput Harbans is the
candidate, it is his wooing of his constituents in Elvira rather
than his career that provides the story's action. The rivalries
between Baksh the Muslim, Chittaranjan the Hindu jeweler,
Ramlogan the Hindu rum-shop owner, and Dhaniram the
local pundit, as well as the candidacy of Preacher who
appears to have the black vote, are all combined to create a

series of intricate but chaotic situations that Harbans must muddle through.

Surujput Harbans' attempts at forming dubious alliances is always consumed by the present tense of his encounters with accidents – such as his near collision with Jehovah's Witnesses, or the convoluted fate of a stray dog – so that his habit of reading them as "signs" of impending misfortune appears to divorce him from the possibility of control. The passivity he displays and the aura of victimization he nurtures, however, is ultimately revealed to be comfortably reactive since his financial arrangements for a predetermined outcome to the election do eventually see him through. Thus, while superstition is a convenient vehicle with which to introduce the illusion of competition into his campaign, thereby allowing Naipaul to frame the entire exercise as a display of deep political dubiety, it is also the agency whereby, like Ganesh in the prior novel, Harbans wields his power.

Both *The Mystic Masseur* and *The Suffrage of Elvira* are novels that satirize a national political process, but not before they have established an awareness that the participants are already schooled in a long tradition of political brokering. Harbans' first meeting with Baksh at the beginning of the novel, for example, culminates in Baksh and his son, Foam, acquiring a van with a loudspeaker with which to "manage" the campaign. Baksh's subsequent candidacy, just before polling day, nets him $2,000, and is understood as a strategic maneuver that is quite unnecessary to the outcome of the election. Similarly, Harbans' negotiations with Chittaranjan over the marriage prospects of their children take place within an elaborately choreographed minuet where Harbans' apparent compliance is finally revealed to have been cleverly deceptive. While he has no intention of going through with the arrangement, he nevertheless plays the role of prospective father-in-law to Chittaranjan's daughter to perfection. In the end it is the younger generation, Baksh's son Foam, Lorkhoor the Hindu manager of Preacher's "Christian" campaign, Nelly, Chittaranjan's daughter, and the pundit Dhaniram's abandoned daughter-in-law, the *doolahin*, who are offered as examples of members of the community who eventually outmaneuver the entrenched corruption of their elders.

Their relation with the community turns out to be a productive alienation that begins to emerge in the community through the agency of "education." Nelly's move to London is offered as an escape from an anachronistic system of arranged marriages, and happens only after her "honor" becomes the occasion of the reconciliation between her father and his nemesis, Ramlogan. Harbans' use of the "scandal" to renege on the almost-arranged marriage of Nelly to his son is another moment the narrative offers as a release for the girl. In the case of Dhaniram's daughter-in-law, who runs away with Lorkhoor the renegade campaigner, Naipaul offers an even greater escape, having characterized her life with her in-laws as nothing short of slave labor. The text's pleasure in the independence and maturation of the younger characters, in other words, underscores the triumph of the satiric because it suggests that after the election the possibility of change exists.

The careful documentation of the personal gain that the principal characters of both novels enjoy is, of course, a measure of the corrupt practices they engage in while participating in a public, or civic, service. Nevertheless, neither *The Mystic Masseur* nor *The Suffrage of Elvira* even attempts to explore the possibilities of a rubric beyond the communal within which a polity based on either coalitions between groups or consolidation around an idea could emerge. The tussles within the communities represented, therefore, are emblematic of the polarization characteristic of Trinidad's ethnic and class divisions, and are offered as such. Naipaul's use of satire to arrive at this bleak prognosis, even while the process of "decolonization" was underway in Trinidad, prompts a last look at the considerable criticism of his "irresponsible" irony when adopting farce or satire as the generic modes with which to cast Trinidadian life.

George Lamming's much-quoted accusation that Naipaul's early "books can't move beyond a castrated satire," for example, rests on the claim that, "When such a writer is a colonial, ashamed of his cultural background and striving like mad to prove himself through promotion to the peaks of a 'superior' culture whose values are gravely in doubt, then satire, like the charge of philistinism, is for me nothing more than a refuge."[21] Lamming's charge is that Naipaul's overview is basically Eurocentric and therefore the values, be they cultural or moral, that appear to be in such confusion within the stories, and which provide the grist for satire, irony, or farce, are judged so by an external, and hostile moral and civil code. Rohlehr argues against Lamming only in the instance of *Miguel Street*, pointing out that, "in a society which is seen as having no true standards, irony is bound to operate in reverse, the ironist starting with an abnormal situation and hinting at a sanity which is absent from his world ... The farce has become a nightmare ... If satire is a means of running away, it is equally a means of fighting ... the confrontation of a nightmare, not the seeking of a refuge" (Rohlehr, pp. 125–126). Both Lamming's and Rohlehr's views on the function of satire and irony in Naipaul's early work acknowledge, rather than articulate, the ambivalence inherent in the choice of referents Naipaul adopts at the narrative level of his sketches. The slippage from farce to nightmare shadows the overt and deliberate disjunction Naipaul writes between the "Dickensian" cast of his island characters and their Caribbean setting.

Perhaps the most effective device with which the satires appear to engage in the political ramifications of decolonization and self-determination is Naipaul's trick of investing his characters with a built-in skepticism and self-denigration. Hat's protestations in *Miguel Street* about the health services or judicial system set the tone, and the much-cited banquet at Government House at the end of *The Mystic Masseur* provides a grotesque tableau of similar self-deprecation. These gestures of self-denigration are in keeping with the colonial portraits of colonized peoples, as they are with analyses of the psychic toll of colonial domination. It is in the allegorical consequences of such manifestations of "self-hatred" that Naipaul's early work is most effective. For, while the satiric allows Naipaul to side-step an historical engagement with Trinidad, it offers no protection against the social issues that "tradition" and the domesticities of the world he grew up in create. Scenes of wife and child abuse abound in *Miguel Street*, and the subordination of women, particularly daughters, underscores the action in both *The Suffrage of Elvira*, and to a lesser degree *The Mystic Masseur*.

After all, the materiality of colonial social institutions such as the educational system, the civil service, and the judiciary on the one hand, and the alternative economic bases of commerce, agriculture, and animal husbandry on the other is geared, it must be remembered, towards the administration and mainte- nance of a *dependent* social system. The conditions of existence within such a society, therefore, necessarily operate within the confines of predetermined and limited opportunities, where a pyramidal structure oversees the perpetuation of a severely articulated system of social stratification. *Miguel Street* is a fictional rendering of one of these less privileged strata in Trinidad, and it is, therefore, in the brutal domestic situation of the characters' lives, rather than in a social polemic, that the issue of colonial dependency is addressed. Rather than simply a sign of moral decay or anarchy, then, the scenes of domestic violence and sexist double standards also serve as an allegorical device for examining the vicissitudes of a colonial dependency's material and psychosocial aggressions. Thus, it is only when Naipaul enters the domestic spaces of his fictions that any exploration of a state that resembles colonial dependency takes place. For this reason, *A House for Mr. Biswas* is Naipaul's most politically astute novel.

CHAPTER 3

Home

Elvira, you is a bitch.

(V.S. Naipaul, *The Suffrage of Elvira*)

A HOUSE FOR MR. BISWAS (1961)

Despite the novel's opening statement of Mohun Biswas' death, the first few paragraphs record the narrative's only sustained moments of satisfaction. They are Biswas' appreciation of his wife's loyalty to himself and their children, and her independence from her mother and sisters, as well as his articulated wonderment at "being in his own house, the audacity of it" (*A House for Mr. Biswas*, p. 8). Indeed, the coda the Prologue offers is made up of an inventory of Biswas' possessions, and the proprietal victories he appears to have achieved with his family, and his "claim to one's portion of the earth" (*A House for Mr. Biswas*, p. 14). The third-person narrative with its omniscient narrative voice, however, also contextualizes Biswas' success by portraying the general paucity that underlies all his claims. The mortgage on the house, the solicitor's clerk's scam, the neglect of Biswas' mother, Shama's struggles, and Biswas' illness all announce the limitations to Biswas' sense of achievement. To begin the novel with a coda, futhermore, underscores the determinist tendency of the plot, which will indeed proceed to develop as though Biswas' life is already curtailed.

Biswas' birth is at once problematic, causing as it does prophecies of doom for his parents, Bipti and Raghu. The family is depicted as mired in poverty and driven by superstition, so that Biswas starts life as a marked infant, differentiated from his siblings, the carrier of an unlucky sneeze, and pursued by prohibitions. Naipaul's deliberate allusion to the Oedipus story is played out when, as a child, Biswas inadvertently becomes the cause of his father's death. The details with which his father's funeral and mourning rituals are described inaugurate the novel's singular obsession with accumulating minutiae, so that a strain of the macabre grows as a central impulse of the narrative's development. Immediately after the funeral, the family undergoes a siege by Dhari, a neighbor and owner of the calf that drowned under Biswas' care, who, with other neighbors, relentlessly digs around the house for Raghu's reputed savings. Their nightly visitations reach proportions of terror, sealing the complete hostility that faces the bereaved family until they are forced to dispossess themselves of the house and land. Without the father's protection, the family can no longer stay together and a series of dispersals gets underway. Dehuti, the only daughter, is sent as a poor relation servant to Tara, Biswas' maternal aunt, while the brothers Pratap and Prasad are sent to distant relatives to graduate into the cane labor system to which they have already been apprenticed. The family portrait that emerges has a sociological significance in its demonstration that the only recourse the family has is in a system of extended kinship, and not in any of the island's social institutions.

The long novel documents in detail the course of Biswas' life: the evolution of his marriage and immediate family, and the evolution of his "self-reliance" as a professional and "individual" within a newly forming social order. The resilience and resistance of East Indian familial custom emerges as the social web that both protects and inhibits the social mobility of its adherents. Biswas' early experience of being shunted between various familial units is posited as the cause of his need to disengage from the dependencies it creates, but the story of his youth and maturation is incrementally the story of how far-reaching the web's cast is. The irony that the land his mother is forced to sell is later discovered to be rich in oil is the novel's early indicator that capital and its acquisition through inheritance or enterprise may be the only way to free oneself from reliance on a feudally structured kinship system. However, rather than a simple desire to be rid of family, Biswas' obsession lies more with his need to declare his individuality, so that his eccentricities, though no more unusual than those of others in the novel, take on the dimensions of a rebellion. That the bulk of the novel takes place within the gradually unwinding meshes of the Tulsi family allows a large enough canvas for a thorough exploration of the profound consequences attendant upon a community's transition from a quasi-feudal to a capitalist mode of operation.

Selwyn Cudjoe's interpretation of the novel places this shift from a feudal structure to a capitalist one as the central tension informing Biswas' role. Reading Biswas as an emblem of "the newly emerging social order,"[1] he casts Biswas' assertions of individuality as synonymous with his professions of "manhood," thus implying that "independence" is a passage from one patriarchal order into another. Within the articulation of the same argument, however, Cudjoe also equates the democratizing rhetoric of Biswas' "rebellious" espousal, while still a member of the Tulsi household, of a reformist Hindu "Aryan" cult's platforms with "some of the central doctrines of capitalism: the equality of men and women and the freedom of choice" (Cudjoe, p. 55). The conflation Cudjoe creates here, of course, is between capitalism and democracy, an economic system and a political ideology that have deployed each other's rhetoric but not necessarily wedded them. Cudjoe's argument, therefore, ignores the fact that the capitalism to which he attributes the island's emerging social and economic order is a neo-colonial late capitalism where the island's infrastructure is designed almost purely as an appendage of the metropolitan order.

While the transitions that the novel's communal organizations undergo are aptly analogous to the analytic paradigms of the move from the country to the city, from feudal to capitalist operations, or from pre-industrial to industrial modes, they are even more accurately illustrative of the shift that occurs when the appropriations of the colonial state mutate into the dependencies of the neo-colonial situation. Biswas' role, then, carries the double burden of being illustrative of a general historical process, as well as embodying the consequences of a specific and local moment. The story of Biswas' early life lived at the edges of his mother's extended family, therefore, serves to both prepare and educate the reader about how the elastic bonds that operate within the East Indian communities are analogous to the ties that develop within the early stages of colonial administration. Biswas' married life within the confines of the Tulsi system, by extension, represents the profound ambivalence bred by the debilitating circumstances of an entropic co-dependency that resembles the aggressive rootedness of the authoritarian colonial state. And finally, Biswas' career as a journalist and his acquisition of the house on Sikkim Street signify with a mixture of poignancy and dramatic irony the depleted potentialities of a postcolonial "independence," complete with its self-delusions.

The political histories that the domestic dramas of *A House for Mr. Biswas* enact are also occasions for Naipaul to stage another series of explorations into more literal aspects of filiation: namely, the transfer of authority between father and son, and modernity's consequent re-evaluation of the status of women. Gestures towards analyzing a woman's role and status within Trinidadian Indian communities, where, we are told repeatedly, "wife beating" is the norm, serve as a thematic frame within which Naipaul can further draw upon the virtues of modernity and the obstacles it must face within a specific colonial context. Addressing the problems of victimization of women and the commensurate objectification of children makes Biswas and his immediate family the vanguard of social change within the extended Tulsi household. All the familial units within the Tulsi system, however, are similarly engaged, and the internal friction is a major feature of the novel's examination of the palpable disruptions caused by social change. For example, even though all the children of Hanuman House – the central Tulsi residence for major portions of the novel – enjoy a privileged minority status that is ultimately democratic in its conferral of resources, their participation in the continuation of the status quo is never taken for granted. Mrs. Tulsi's special grooming of her sons, the two "gods," and the subsequent non-Hindu schooling of the other children (Biswas' own failure in his schooling as a pundit already having been rehearsed within the novel), are all undertaken with an awareness of the changes in social patterns the island and the family experience during the course of the story. The burden of the future, in other words, lies as much with the younger generation as it does with figures such as Seth, the family's senior male, and Biswas, both of whom exhibit as keen a sense of the future as any others of the Tulsi household. The combination, therefore, of gender and generation, manifested in the spousal as well as filial compass of the novel's theme, emerges as a more embedded and more complex center of the novel than its more celebrated metaphorical rendering of Biswas' search for a house of his own. It is also this aspect of the novel that draws deeply upon autobiographical resources, pitching Naipaul into a most difficult fictional terrain.

Most commentaries on *A House for Mr. Biswas*, including Naipaul's own, acknowledge that the novel is a fictional version of the life of the author's father, Seepersad Naipaul.[2] The novel's emotional gauge, as a consequence, extends beyond a merely fictional and allegorical register, to also include the intensely personal. Rob Nixon opens his study with the acknowledgment that *A House for Mr. Biswas* "remains [Naipaul's] most remarkable work. Nothing since has equalled the inventiveness and emotional generosity of that homage to his father's misfortunes in the strained circumstances of colonial Trinidad."[3] In addition to this, it is also well documented that much of the novel is closely based upon events and circumstances of Naipaul's childhood. Naipaul's 1983 Foreword to the Vintage paperback edition of *A House for Mr. Biswas* (1984) reports that since passing the proofs in 1961, he had not reread the one novel closest to him, "the most personal, created out of what [he] saw and felt as a child" (*A House for Mr. Biswas*, p. 1).

Listening to the BBC World Service while in Cyprus one evening in 1981, however, Naipaul was surprised to hear an installment of the novel read during the program, *A Book at Bedtime*. He describes his response as follows:

I listened. And in no time, though the installment was comic, though the book had inevitably been much abridged, and the linking words were not always mine, I was in tears, swamped by the emotions I had tried to shield myself from for twenty years. *Lacrimae rerum*, "the tears of things," the tears in things: to the feeling for the things written about – the passions and nerves of my early life – there was added a feeling for the time of the writing – the ambition, the tenacity, the innocence. My literary ambition had grown out of my early life; the two were intertwined; the tears were for a double innocence. (*A House for Mr. Biswas*, p. 1)

Quite apart from the emotional weight that Naipaul ascribes to the novel, readers familiar with his work before *A House for Mr. Biswas*, will notice that this passage and the subsequent account of the nurture of his ambition to be a writer, are startlingly reminiscent of one of *Miguel Street*'s oddest and most formulaic sketches, "B. Wordsworth." *Lacrimae rerum*, it seems, is the central lesson B. Wordworth imparts to the young narrator:

I said, "Why you does cry?"
"Why, boy? Why? You will know when you grow up. You're a poet, too, you know. And when you're a poet you can cry for everything." (*Miguel Street*, p. 46)

And, when the narrator leaves a dying B. Wordsworth at the end of the sketch, he leaves with a new self-consciousness that, despite its bathos, is nevertheless precise: "I left the house, and ran home crying, like a poet, for everything I saw" (*Miguel Street*, p. 52).

The essentialism of "B. Wordsworth" is not only a parable about aesthetic function within a cultural vacuum, but more interestingly about a boy's search for the law of a father, or an authority other than his mother's. Similarly, Naipaul's account of his reaction when hearing a portion of his novel read on the radio so many years later still finds his neediness associated with that era of his life inescapable. The compensatory and elegiac gesture to the memory of his father that the novel is designed to perform reveals the origin of its urgency not only in Naipaul's recollections, but most particularly in the earlier stories, written at a time when Naipaul's "double innocence" intruded upon his vocation to be a Writer.

A collection of stories published as *A Flag on the Island* in 1967 contains several stories written before and at the time of those of *Miguel Street*, as well as one meant for that volume entitled "The Enemy."[4] The episode that "The Enemy" depicts is the prototype of a central moment in *A House for Mr. Biswas*, an episode concerning Biswas' son, Anand's, relation with his father. "The Enemy" explores the boy-narrator's relationship with his parents, before and after their separation, during a period which eventually includes his father's death, and the narrator's move from the country to the city. In keeping with the allegory of the colonized, this story is a less guarded first-person account than any in *Miguel Street*, primarily because the story involved is a more personal one, allowing Naipaul to explore the flexibilities of a voice that overtly and directly takes itself as its subject after having established its location in relation to others. Furthermore, the story's rural setting introduces a sinister register that is muted in the urban setting of *Miguel Street*. Because "The Enemy" provides a context for the narrator's familial and social location within the sketches, the sinister cast of the siege that the family experiences due to the father's treatment of the cane workers is an almost confessional acknowledgment of the mentality bred by the plantation system's mode of operation. Even the narrator's skepticism about his father's reputation as a dictatorial overseer is an illustration of the ambivalence that riddles this rural milieu. In this way, "The Enemy" sets out to try and delineate the oppositional contours of a rural and an urban existence at that time in Trinidad.

Thus the narrator's central dilemma in "The Enemy" is whether to stay on the plantation with his father, or return to the city with his mother, who can no longer endure the terror of hostile plantation workers. It is resolved when he chooses to remain with the father: "I chose the crayons and my father," thus initiating the boy's alignment with an adult social order. Where the mother's "abandonment" eventually provides the absence during which the father dies, prior to his death the father teaches his son three things: namely, that a divine father supersedes a corporeal one, a statement that ironically, even cynically, underscores the trope of paternal surrogacy in the *Miguel Street* sketches; the law of gravity, the demonstration of which – dropping a box of matches and swinging a bucket half-filled with water – serves as an awkward lesson in empiricism; and, finally, the transformative effect of mixing primary colors. When the father's death occurs during a storm that conveniently provides a theatrical excuse for its cause: "I would have to bear the cross of a father who died from fright" (*A Flag on the Island*, p. 68), the narrator deftly deals with an incipient oedipal anxiety. Thus it is a gesture of self-naturalization when the narrator forgets his father and begins "to look upon myself as the boy who had no father." He continues, "In fact, when we moved to Port-of-Spain and I saw what the normal relationship between father and son was – it was nothing more than the relationship between the beater and the beaten – when I saw this I was grateful" (*A Flag on the Island*, p. 68). The Law of the father, here, is strangely and cleverly reduced to the register of a colonial social order where the "natural" process of socialization into a symbolic order appears distorted and robbed of its functional value.

The mother's substitution into the father's role as the beater, therefore, goes beyond a simple parody of this social order. Despite the mother's status as "The Enemy," graphically rendered in the shoelace-tying episode, where the narrator's ineptness at tying his laces creates an anxiety that makes it impossible for him to do so, her substitution as the authoritarian figure does eventually engage the challenge of the Oedipus metaphor. After the narrator's accident while helping to demolish Hat's latrine wall injures his arm, his dreamwork begins in earnest. Gaining consciousness amidst a parodic nightmare scene of a bus surrounded by squawking chickens and women, the narrator sees clearly for the first time the depth of his mother's concern for him. The recognition scene reaches a crescendo when, in the last paragraph, the narrator is able to retrieve, albeit belatedly, the imaginary for a moment: "I wished I were a Hindu god at that moment, with two hundred arms, so that all two hundred could be broken, just to enjoy that moment, and to see again my mother's tears" (*A Flag on the Island*, p. 73). The resolution here of both a castration anxiety and the restitution of the mother as object of desire is of course a dig at the story's allegory of the constitution of a colonial subject.

The refiguring of these episodes from "The Enemy" in *A House for Mr. Biswas*, however, carries more complex implications about filiation, and serves a narrative rather than emblematic function regarding the issue of familial authority. The episodes of "The Enemy" are redistributed in *A House for Mr. Biswas* among more characters, and are the indicators of a central shift in the narrative's understanding of Biswas' frustrated efforts to gain independence from his in-laws for himself and his family. The episodes are framed by two events. First, his quest by the time he has two children has seen him take up a reluctant residency in one of the Tulsi family estates, the Chase, and about to embark on the second, the plantation at Green Vale. Biswas' shopkeeping duties at the Chase represent his forced acquiescence to the Tulsi system of governance wherein his duties as son-in-law require him to conform to their needs. His little acts of defiance while still resident at Hanuman House, the main Tulsi residence, culminate in his humiliation at the hands of another son-in-law, Govind. Govind's status as son-in-law, furthermore, has served as an example of the territorial stakes the Tulsi system is premised upon. Second, after Biswas has served as an unsuccessful driver at Green Vale, and after the destruction of his "first" house there, his bout with insanity leads to yet another return into Hanuman House, this time carried in the arms of Govind. Thus Biswas' re-entries into the bosom of the Tulsi establishment towards the mid-point of the narrative are accompanied by a series of new realizations about his own status, and the conditions of possibility of his own existence.

The shoelace-tying episode involves Savi, Biswas' five-year-old daughter and Anand's sister, and Shama, Biswas' wife. The child's inability to tie her laces becomes the occasion for Shama to strike her with some ferocity, not because she is a callous mother, but because after having returned to Hanuman House, her maternal home, Shama is thrust back into the pitiless world where "the sisters still talked with pride of the floggings they had received from Mrs. Tulsi" (*A House for Mr. Biswas*, p. 199). Rather than illustrating a time-honored tradition, however, the episode is more concerned with the profound seductions that provide the security which accompanies the familiar when posed as an alternative to the "new." Biswas' quest for a house of his own, with its accompanying material and economic independence, has begun to teach him that desire and its fulfillment require very different efforts. Witnessing the reinitiation of his children into the rituals of Hanuman House, therefore, allows Biswas to acknowledge both the urgency of his need to be free of the extended family system as well as the extent of his dependency upon it.

Furthermore, by complying with the plan to *insuranburn* the Chase enterprise, Biswas has become complicit with the titular partriarchal figure of the family, Mrs. Tulsi's brother-in-law, Seth. At this point in the narrative, the poles of authority represented by the matriarchal figure of Mrs. Tulsi and the soon to break away Seth come into sharp relief. Seth's plan represents his manipulation of the public sphere in the interests of the family business, in this instance couched as carried out on behalf of Biswas, the errant son-in-law. Mrs. Tulsi's authority, on the other hand, functions almost exclusively within the family's internal narrative of loyalty to the memory of the dead patriarch, Pundit Tulsi. Her hypochondria is a not very subtle ploy, for it is a form of emotional blackmail to command the allegiance of her clan by exploiting their filial status. Thus Savi's shoelace-tying episode, where she resisted tying the laces even as she was forced to go through the motions of doing so, foreshadows the moment of acquiescence and rebellion that arises during this period of Biswas' transition. By witnessing the transformation that his wife and daughter undergo upon their return to Hanuman House, Biswas makes two efforts: a failed one at reclaiming his immediate family, and a successful one at leaving them, at least temporarily.

With Shama returning to Hanuman House with some frequency during this period, principally to have two more babies, Biswas' eldest daughter Savi is required to fulfill several figurative roles. In her mother's absence, Savi becomes the recipient of Biswas' sudden generosity at Christmas time. His present of a doll's house, extravagant and overdetermined in its symbolism, becomes the occasion for an even more dramatic gesture of rejection by Shama when she destroys it in the interests of harmony amidst the vicious but petty rivalries within Hanuman House. Biswas' response is to take Savi with him to Green Vale, where the child spends an unhappy week fervently adhering to prohibitions she associates with the Tulsis. Her parents' subsequent pride in her behavior leads to the moment of their reconciliation. However, almost immediately after this episode, Biswas' descent into a nervous breakdown begins. Alone at Green Vale, and under orders from Seth to start dispossessing the laborers of land upon which they have depended, Biswas' task becomes blurred with his fears of extreme bodily vulnerability: "He was rocking hard on the creaking board one night when he thought of the power of the rockers to grind and crush and inflict pain, on his hands and toes and the tenderer parts of his body" (*A House for Mr. Biswas*, p. 229).

Biswas' breakdown cannot complete itself, however, until the full implications of his dependencies and his vulnerability, accrued over his whole life, are reintroduced and made clear. Biswas' unintentioned implication in his own father's death at the beginning of the novel has already allowed Naipaul to school his protagonist through a series of surrogate father figures and male role models. With regard to his own children, then, Biswas' gestures as a father take on the added significance of having to model themselves on his own dimly understood experiences as a child. Having witnessed Savi's difficulties, therefore, Biswas must also experience his son's. Anand's humiliation at the mission school, where he was unable to reconcile his need to relieve himself with his distaste for the facilities provided, is immediately reminiscent of his father's humiliation at about the same age while undergoing apprenticeship as a pundit when he too chose to let his bowels move without availing himself of the facilities. The twinned experience is the trigger which moves Biswas to start preparations to build a house of his own.

Using his children as the excuse, Biswas orchestrates a coalition between his own and his wife's family by borrowing money from one, and land from the other. He hires a builder, Mr. McClean, and proceeds to watch the construction of a structure that becomes increasingly depleted even as it is being built. The drain on Biswas' resources that the house demands, and the entropic form it begins to embody – including the surreal asphalt snakes, seeping through the ceiling, that begin to populate Biswas' nightmares – fast become emblematic of Biswas' dilemmas concerning the issue of both independence and fatherhood. Naipaul's use of the building metaphor and the asphalt snakes as a frame within which to explore questions of authority between individual and community concerns has the double duty of representing the struggles of an individual trying to break away from one system into another, as well as those of one generation embarking upon the construction of a new and ascendant history. The marked signature of failure that accompanies Biswas' efforts throughout the novel strongly reiterates the suggestion that familial and colonial dependency breeds circumstances in which it is far more difficult to sever relations between the old and the new, or the past and the present, than a simple desire to do so may imply.

That Biswas' breakdown should take the form of extreme bodily vulnerability underscores the metaphoric aspect of his self-appointed role. Before the doomed house is habitable Biswas visits his own relatives, his maternal aunt Tara and her husband Ajodha, figures who provided him shelter when Bipti his mother was unable to. He is joined by a cousin by marriage, Rabidat, whose father, Bhandat, Biswas had once worked for in one of Ajodha's rum shops. The visit recalls his life before marriage, and its shadowy duplication by mid-point in the narrative begins to coalesce and reveal the aetiology of Biswas' breakdown. His activities during those earlier times included visiting his uncle every Sunday, where they develop the habit of Biswas reading aloud the week's accumulation of "a syndicated American column called *That Body of Yours* which dealt every day with a different danger to the human body. Ajodha listened with gravity, concern, alarm" (*A House for Mr. Biswas*, p. 49).[5] (When he reaches the appropriate age, Anand occasionally fulfills this function too.) After satisfying Ajodha's quirky hankering, Biswas would then settle down with Tara's volume of *The Book of Comprehensive Knowledge*. Biswas' propensity for reading at once sets him apart from Ajodha's other nephews, Bhandat's sons Rabidat and Jagdat. These boys, nevertheless, have been the agents for Biswas' initiation into the adult world of sex and sexual knowledge, thus vying with his reputation for learning. Therefore, his uncle's fixation with information about bodily harm, coupled with the surreptitious tutelage of Rabidat and Jagdat create in Biswas a fearful entry into adulthood. The era comes to an end when Bhandat brutally beats Biswas with a belt when he suspects him of informing Ajodha of his practice of skimming profits as proprietor of Ajodha's rum shop.

This early experience is further complicated by the rumors surrounding Bhandat's kept mistress and Biswas' own knowledge of his wife-beating habits. By going to his mother for recourse, and finding none, Biswas is able to declare, "You see, Ma. I have no father to look after me and people can treat me how they want" (*A House for Mr. Biswas*, p. 67). While the loose confederation that this side of Biswas' family represents is posited as the communal alternative to the Tusli establishment, housing as it does the seeds of Biswas' fears and rebellion, it is also an arena in which Biswas' first attempt at independence is tested. That it leads to his sign-writing career and marriage into the Tulsi family, the place of his greatest incarceration, is less ironic than illustrative of the overwhelming hold that familial structures exercise in this particular setting. Biswas' first overt attempts to claim his children's loyalty are gestures that are at once imitative as well as proprietary. Anand's encounter with his father, unlike the narrator's in "The Enemy," must negotiate a complex series of obstacles before it can overcome the record of Biswas' failures. Only when a transfer of a male authority between father and son occurs does Biswas' mental breakdown complete itself, and offer a kind of cathartic release.

The pace at which the events leading up to Biswas' breakdown are depicted is dogged and obsessive. In his attention to minutiae, Naipaul is able to convey the oppressive weight of Biswas' unraveling. The devolution of Biswas' fears is precise: threatening laborers, fear of being alone, of bodily harm, of fire, of reading, and of people; his obsessions with the newspapers on the wall, the house and its asphalt snakes, his dreams, his children, and his wife. On the eve of his wife's and children's visit, he imagines killing his eldest children and himself; finding his pregnant wife's presence unbearable, he kicks her in the stomach. At this juncture, Anand is faced with the choice of whether to leave with his mother or stay with his father.

The bond created between father and son is simple. When asked why he had chosen to stay, we are told: "'Because' – The word came out thin, explosive, charged with anger, at himself and his father. 'Because they was going to leave you alone'" (*A House for Mr. Biswas*, p. 279). The child's time with his father closely resembles the episode in "The Enemy," but the time they spend together in the unfinished house is also plagued with even more terror until the storm that destroys the structure also brings about Biswas' complete collapse. With the storm raging, and his father comatose, Anand voices the final release when he begins to scream. Biswas' protection has materialized, and a transaction of responsibility has occurred between father and son. Once back in Hanuman House, Biswas' equilibrium is re-established in the knowledge that the Tulsi protection remains, *despite* himself; he neglects to record the birth of his newest daughter.

In "The Enemy" the father simply dies during the storm, but his death eventually leads to his son's reconciliation with the mother. In *A House for Mr. Biswas*, the reworking of the father's and son's sojourn in the country allows the novel to embark on its detailed examination of Biswas' subsequent career of difficult familial negotiations and professional aspirations. That Biswas becomes a journalist is by no means only a detail faithful to Naipaul's father's life. The role of the press within the larger story of the island's struggle for self-determination is examined with relentless attention even though the characterizations and descriptions of Biswas' various assignments resemble the satire and humor of Naipaul's earlier fictions. What is brought to maturity in Biswas' story, therefore, is the gradually discernible independence and authority provided by a faithful adherence to a belief in literacy and writing. After all his failed attempts to both resist and accommodate his status as son-in-law of the Tulsis, it is only through his career as a journalist that he is able to establish the economic and functional basis upon which he can negotiate a reciprocal relationship with them. From this point in the narrative until he buys the house on Sikkim Street, Biswas' position is one of an equal to those of the same station within the Tulsi hierarchy even as the family establishment moves, during the period of its dismantling, from Hanuman House to Port of Spain, up to Shorthills, and finally back to Port of Spain.

Naipaul's privileging of the Word and the Book as Biswas' life-line is amply illustrated throughout the novel. Its introduction, moreover, closely resembles the passage in Conrad's *Heart of Darkness* where Marlow stumbles upon Towson's manual. Biswas acquires and reads diverse volumes such as Marcus Aurelius' *Meditations*, Epictetus' *Discourses*, *Bell's Standard Elocutionist*, *Hawkins' Electrical Guide*, *Collins' Clear-Type Shakespeare*, *Reform the Only Way*, *The Super Sensual Life*, *Arise and Walk*, *Newspaper Management*, and *How to Write a Book*, as well as the works of one Samuel Smiles. All the books are as "alien" to the novel's setting as Towson's *An Inquiry into Some Points of Seamanship* is to Marlow's. The comfort and security that the manual provides Marlow, who, after all, is a seaman, is magnified over a life-time in Biswas' case. Indeed, the *reference* that the books give Biswas during his initial interview at the *Sentinel* allows the narrative a moment outside the humor that the books' apparent arbitrariness has provided. When asked by the editor, Mr. Burnett, "You read those people just for pleasure, eh?" Biswas' response, "Just for the encouragement" (*A House for Mr. Biswas*, p. 321), provides the context that allows him to achieve a practice of literacy that becomes his redemption.

Biswas' short story writing phase provides the novel with one of its several self-reflexive moments. The reflexivity is several because the registers upon which it plays include the biographical, the autobiographical, the intertextual, and the metaphorical. Ensconced as a journalist, and his tutelage of Anand and Savi in hand, Biswas enrolls in a correspondence course with the Ideal School of Journalism, based in London. In a series of bejeweled platitudes, the Ideal School recommends strategies with which aspiring journalists can locate subjects about which to write: seasons, windows, the village green. Phrased in the style of a bad manual's recommendations, Naipaul places Biswas' perplexity at the same edge to which he places himself, more than twenty years later, in "Prologue to an Autobiography." The Ideal School's statement that, "Even people with outstanding writing ability say they cannot find subjects" (*A House for Mr. Biswas*, p. 342), is refracted in Naipaul's admission that, "Half a writer's work, though, is the discovery of his subject ... I had without knowing it fallen into the error of thinking of writing as a kind of display. My very particularity – which was the subject sitting on my shoulder – had been encumbering me" (*Finding the Centre*, p. 18). Biswas' subject, however, remains elusive. All his stories stumble at the fearful blockage of their beginnings, the repeatedly insistent first sentence, "At the age of thirty-three, when he was already the father of four children ... " (*A House for Mr. Biswas*, p. 344).

The subsequent unfinished quasi-erotic fantasies that Biswas writes and rewrites are illustrative of precisely the problems confronting postcolonial writing when faced with the grafted literary values and habits of an alien culture, coupled with the willed repression of colonial tutelage. Similarly, when Biswas discovers Dickens and starts reading him with his son, Naipaul ascribes to his protagonist his own childhood habit of transposing the action and characters into a Trinidadian setting. This internalization of received literary paradigms in turn becomes the occasion for Biswas and Anand's further bonding, where the narrative starts in earnest to privilege the son, allowing him gradually a reciprocity with his father that Biswas was unable to enjoy:

He said, "I don't want you to be like me."
Anand understood. Father and son, each saw the other as weak and vulnerable, and each felt a responsibility for the other, a responsibility which, in times of particular pain, was disguised by exaggerated authority on the one side, exaggerated respect on the other. (*A House for Mr. Biswas*, p. 374)

Seth's breakaway from the family heralds the end of the Tulsi hegemony. The gradual unraveling of the centralized authority is played out in Shorthills, where, in concert with the disintegration of the family structure, the estate is cannibalized, and the family wealth embezzled. Similarly, Biswas' career as a journalist parallels the changes occurring in the island's political consciousness; indeed, the press serves as the conduit for the novel's monitoring of both the social and political climate of its times. From the seeker of curiosities for sensationalist features and reports, Biswas becomes an "investigative" reporter when the *Sentinel*, under a new editor, decides to take on a more "responsible" role in the face of the war in Europe. Biswas' coverage of the various institutions, organizations, and figures on the island now has to echo the "official" line of the government. The use of an editorial policy serving as a form of censorship is suggested, and the initiation of the Deserving Destitute's Fund, a circulation ploy of the same kind as Missing Ball competitions, has Biswas thrust into the difficult world of advocacy and poverty. Resisting bribery as best he can, the deputation to Biswas from Shama's widowed sisters for coverage of their plight results in one of the novel's most overt observations about the inequities of the economic situation on the island. Against the background of household noises – "A Child was being flogged downstairs" – Biswas reflects:

How could one speak of a woman as destitute when she lived on her mother's estate, in one of her mother's three houses; when her brother was studying medicine in the United Kingdom; and when another brother was a figure of growing importance in the South, his name all over the paper, in the gossip columns, in the news columns for his business deals and political statements, in his own stylish advertisements ("Tulsi Theatres Trinidad proudly presents ... ")? (*A House for Mr. Biswas*, p. 447)

What Biswas fails to see, but what the narrative nevertheless makes evident, is that the widows' predicament stems from their status as women within a deteriorating structure that no longer can accommodate their new needs. Their casualty is not dissimilar to Biswas'.

Nevertheless, Biswas' sojourn as a community welfare officer is a studied portrait of the earnest but ill-informed development projects associated with "nation building" and government-sponsored social improvement. Thus, when Owad, one of the "gods," returns from his training in Europe full of socialist rhetoric, the family's response is emblematic of what Naipaul will later refer to as the responses of borrowed, half-made cultures and societies, where the applications of received ideas remain impractical and often absurd. The economic health of the setting is also mapped in detail, principally through Shama's book-keeping adventures and in her role as collector of her mother's rents. The income derived by the brothers-in-law Govind and W.C. Tuttle from the presence of American troops during the war, brings into relief the changing contours of the whole economy where multinational capitalism begins to replace the older colonial order. Biswas' exclusion from this source of new opportunities while he is a civil servant places him firmly at the diminishing center of an entropic circuit of late colonialism's reach. The debt that buying the house at Sikkim Street plunges Biswas into is the final, determined gesture that the narrative provides to underscore fully the tolls of colonial dependency.

With Anand and Savi abroad on scholarships, it remains for Shama to deal with Biswas' disappointment, sealing the achievement of their marriage with both loyalty and protection. That Savi returns to help support the family while Anand remains away growing increasingly distant is both an acknowledgment of Naipaul's willed distance from his own family and a statement about the seductions of migrancy that so characterize the options opened for the last generation of colonial subjects. Without exception, the children are each portrayed as exempt from the trials that Biswas endured because of the single agency of education. The narrative voice itself engages in a moment of imbrication with them when it reflects upon memory and repression, recognizing that the house on Sikkim Street represents the coherence and order that their father's life lacked: "From now on their lives would be ordered, their memories coherent. The mind, while it is sound, is merciful . . . So later, and very slowly, in securer times of different stresses, when the memories had lost the power to hurt, with pain or joy, they would fall into place and give back the past" (*A House for Mr. Biswas*, p. 581). The nuclear unit of a bourgeois ideology is materialized as a house that is remembered as a home; the reach of empire rests in the adoption of its colony into its post-imperial fold.

THE MIDDLE PASSAGE (1962)

Naipaul's first travel book was commissioned by the government of Trinidad and Tobago at the suggestion of its prime minister, Eric Williams. Naipaul has acknowledged that the traveling for and the writing of *The Middle Passage* were undertaken with a combination of uncertainty and nervous exhaustion after the completion of *A House for Mr. Biswas*. As *The Middle Passage* unfolds, these preconditions rapidly make themselves evident as Naipaul's narrative voice almost immediately takes refuge in a nervous energy that fluctuates between petulance and disdain. The first chapter, "Middle Passage," also establishes a formula that will henceforth serve as a central tactic in all his subsequent travel writing as well as surface as a persistent habit in his major fiction of a later period: the detailed description of his travel to the target destination. Indeed, the sketches of fellow travelers, of the daily routines,

the vessels, living quarters and facilities, food, drink, rec-
reations, chance and deliberate encounters, conversations
engaged in or, just as often, overheard, are offered in exacting
detail so that their accumulation establishes an aura of verisimilitude associated with a *roman verité*.

The Middle Passage, however, announces its uncertainty even
before its first chapter in the volume's two epigraphs from J.A.
Froude's *The English in the West Indies* (1887) that Rob Nixon
has succinctly characterized as "the most shrilly racist of
Caribbean travel books" (Nixon, p. 45). As Nixon goes on to
argue, Naipaul's textual authority is made up of stalwarts of
Victorian "authority," quotations from whom are liberally
cited throughout the volume. For Nixon, Naipaul's recourse is
a tactic he uses for confirmation of his own observations which
reveals, for the first time, the *obsessive* nature of his investment
in Victorian assurance. His uncertainty, then, stems from his
illusion that in order to offer any informed opinion about the
places he is commissioned to "explain," he must first school
himself in the historiography of the region. What is startling, of
course, is that he should choose the very authorities whose
interest in the Caribbean is purely imperial. He does, in effect,
borrow references in order to argue against the "borrowed"
cultures he believes he encounters.

The ideological base that Naipaul borrows from his Victorians is, then, a belief that "order" is the prime directive that
allows a society to "cohere" at its centre. Put somewhat
crudely, this "order" stems from the practice of a shared
enterprise of survival *as* a people. The unifying idea that
evolves over time manifests itself in a peoples' accomplishments
– civil, political, economic, and cultural – that form a "tradition" from which subsequent "progress" can continue to
happen, further enriching the group and the idea. Leadership,
creativity, innovation, and "knowledge" are the necessary
ingredients. Hence, the methodology that Naipaul's Victorians
– Froude, Trollope, Kingsley – employed in assessing West
Indian societies of their time was to observe and then measure
to what extent those societies had maintained the principles
and values of the parent culture in an alien setting. The
empiricism of their exercises served well to elevate and estab-

lish the *record* of travel's "experience," observation, and anecdote to the power of knowledge and authority.

Armed with these references, Naipaul's travels are depicted
with a novelist's eye for detail and symmetry. The title
chapter, with its reference to the slave voyage of Africans to
the Americas, immediately establishes travel, or the journey,
both as a metaphor and as a narrative framing for the explorations underway. That the ship about to take Naipaul back to
Trinidad has just arrived with a cargo of new immigrants
from the Caribbean neatly underscores the cyclical nature of
both arrival and departure, providing Naipaul with his first
opportunity to craft an elaborate trope for postcolonial
migrancy. It surfaces again in *An Area of Darkness* (1964), and
with increasing sophistication, in the stories of *In a Free State*
(1971) and the novels *A Bend in the River* (1979) and *The
Enigma of Arrival* (1987). The distaste that Naipaul expresses
about the ship, *Francisco Bobadilla*, furthermore, marks the
advent of Naipaul's use of physical discomfort – his own as
well as others' – as a gauge for his reading of the functioning,
or completeness, or societal health of the place in which he
finds himself. Finally, the opening chapter's scripts of conversations among Naipaul and the other passengers, as well as the
liberal quotation from Caribbean newspapers, initials the
means whereby Naipaul sketches the level of education,
values, and "ignorance" that seem to announce themselves in
the various settings. By appearing to let his examples speak for
themselves, Naipaul finds a way to create a sense of distance
between himself as observer and the people and places he
observes.

Naipaul's first major stop is the Trinidad of his birth, a place
over which he has already exercised a narrative control. The
outpouring of rapid opinions more than tinged with a personal
antipathy at once places the island within a psychosocial
landscape of the narrative voice's fear of confinement. The
implicit Hegelian frame which Naipaul uses to dismiss the
island's "accomplishments" is evoked in the quasi-apostrophe
to "Ambition." That Trinidad's apparent disrespect for this
trait is also the fulcrum of Biswas' thwarted life underscores the
way in which this chapter serves as an explication of Naipaul's

crafting of his fictional analyses of its Trinidadian setting.
Without heroes, the island is dismissed as a non-nation since it
breeds no sense of self-importance, ambition, or value. Hence,
Naipaul is able to implicitly justify his own antipathy by
claiming that, "The threat of failure, the need to escape: this
was the prompting of the society I knew" (*The Middle Passage*,
p. 43). Furthermore, when editorializing on the island's relation to and understanding of modernity, Naipaul embarks on
his studied deferral to his Victorian referents and their procla-
mations about the habit of Trinidadians to denigrate local
products, from food to ideas. By equating the readings of his
authorities with his own, Naipaul unconsciously engages in a
profound historical represssion. The composition and material
conditions of the society of Trollope's, Froude's, and Kingsley's
scrutiny, after all, can hardly be made to resemble the Trinidad of Naipaul's mid-twentieth-century return until an
acknowledgment of the intervening years of colonial subordination has been made.

Similarly, rather than recognizing the seeds of a growing
North American hegemony – through technological access,
primarily – Naipaul attributes Trinidad's reliance upon
outside expertise as yet another sign of Trinidadian lethargy
and self-doubt. Where the story of "Bogart," in *Miguel Street*,
was able to enact a subtle transference of influence between
England and the United States by staging the mime between
Hat as Rex Harrison and Bogart as Humphrey Bogart, "Trinidad" in *The Middle Passage* is, oddly, less analytical. By attributing Trinidadian preferences for American B-grade movies
over more studied British film fare as a sign of both bad taste
and "fraudulent" cosmopolitanism, Naipaul chooses to fault
his compatriots for allegedly ignoring their folk-culture, calyp-
sos, and repressing their past in favor of Europe's. Without
acknowledging the class differentiation of the groups he
chooses to compare, or the *agency* of colonialism's programmatic subordination and denigration of subject peoples, he
engages in the practice of blaming slavery's victims rather than
its perpetrators. This slippage contains an uncanny danger, for
it is not blind to the psychosocial effects of the history of slavery

or colonization; indeed, Naipaul focuses on the "self-contempt" of black Trinidadians in ways similar to Fanon's observations about black Martinicans, but only to the point of identifying the habit, rather than as a part of an analysis of a dialectical historical process. Only reference to a group's autochthonous past, he suggests, can salvage its aspirations towards cultural authenticity and national health.

The "West Indian fantasy" of willed repression, Naipaul continues, is the reason for its need for writers to tell them who they are and where they stand. The extraordinarily self-authenticating impulse of this declaration first appears to be a participatory gesture whereby Naipaul declares his allegiance to the common Trinidadian enterprise of national and cultural self-definition. His subsequent critique of contemporaneous literary production from the region and "American Negro writing," however, quickly establishes his disaffection with "race" and "protest" writing which he claims is limited by its divisive single interest. The other kind of writing produced in the region according to Naipaul, is about the middle class, but it too has proved to be troubled by a "color" barrier, but this time of a "mid-Atlantic whiteness." By moving from an indictment of "black" ideology to an indictment of a "white" one too, Naipaul cleverly elides the pigmentation of his own contributions to the literature of the region. He settles instead into an examination of his own work's genre, satire. Making a sudden leap into a discussion of comedy, he quotes Graham Greene's definition, which states that comedy "needs a strong framework of social convention with which the author sympathizes but does not share." Naipaul's following observation, "By this definition the West Indian writer is incapable of comedy; and, as we have seen, he is not interested in it," would appear to be a self-negating statement, canceling out his own work: however, the momentary contradiction is quickly resolved when Naipaul concludes that only a strong framework of social convention can guarantee a literature a universal appeal. Rather than citing the strong social conventions that dictate *A House for Mr. Biswas*, Naipaul instead settles for "the tribal world of an African writer like Camara Laye" (*The

Middle Passage, p. 70). Nationality does not matter, universality does.

What is resolved here, of course, is that the "strong framework of social convention" represented by the maintenance of the customs, traditions, and the kinship structure of Trinidad's Hindu Indian community salvages it and *A House for Mr. Biswas* from the indictments Naipaul issues, and further lifts his status out of the existing "West Indian" pool. This section of "Trinidad," then, marks the advent of Naipaul's release from the fear of intellectual, cultural, and "racial" incarceration he experienced on returning to the island, and provides him with the main aesthetic framework within which to shape the rest of his career. Before continuing to explore the composition of Naipaul's developing aesthetic framework, however, it is instructive to make note of what his economy of dismissal either ignores or is ignorant of; namely the other, more thoughtful "alternative" literary, historiographical and analytical works produced from within the region. Within the anglophone tradition itself, Naipaul neglects to acknowledge C.L.R. James' history, *The Black Jacobins* (1938),[6] which provides a brilliant analytical paradigm for understanding the political constitution of "color" during the formative years of the Caribbean's modern history. Similarly, within the francophone tradition, Fanon's critique of Mayotte Capecia's 1948 novel, *Je suis Martiniquaise* in his study, *Black Skin, White Masks*, offers a far more productive understanding of the internalization of received colonial prejudices than Naipaul's hasty overview. Naipaul's commentary upon the francophone treatment of "race," in the chapter entitled "Martinique," furthermore, confirms his neglect when he elides Aimé Césaire's poetic corpus and its remarkable negotiations with "color" by choosing to reduce them in a clause: "the subject of Aimé Césaire's *Cahier d'un retour au pays natal* is blackness" (*Middle Passage* p. 198). And finally, from the hispanic tradition, Naipaul seems unaware of Alejo Carpentier's "discovery" of the *real maravilloso* in his 1949 novel, *El reino de este mundo*, which helped create a genre of narrative innovation – magic realism – that allowed for representation of the colonial experience that needed no recourse to either satire or irony.[7]

Thus, Naipaul's belief that "Culture" meets the requirements of "authenticity" only when a continuum with its original source is maintained through practice and its accompanying "tradition" not only underscores the rest of Naipaul's assessments of the communities of the Caribbean, but also reveals the framework of his aesthetic investment: a monological view of Culture that will not recognize the engendering capabilities of hybridity. Hence the privileging of the "Bush Negroes" of Surinam over nationalist Afro-Caribbeans and the Ras Tafarians of Jamaica whose allegiance to Ethiopia he sees as both absurd and dangerous. Even Naipaul's recognition of the discontinuities of tradition created by the middle passage and colonialism is accommodated in his new-found monological assurance, for his observations do offer alternative examples of cultural production which earns "authenticity" from a Caribbean folk-base. The calypso, accordingly, is Trinidad's real contribution to culture, but its commercialization, and the accompanying cultural commodification of steel drums within a nationalist agenda, cancel the possibility of building upon its promise.

For Naipaul, then, questions of cultural authenticity are absolutely integral to questions of nationalist possibilities. With a growing confidence accrued during the course of the second chapter, Naipaul concludes that, "Nationalism was impossible in Trinidad" (*The Middle Passage*, p. 72). He attributes this to the absence of a collective base from which the populace could coalesce behind an articulated purpose. To illustrate his contention, Naipaul adopts the metaphor of the picaroon to exemplify the individualistic and self-serving trickster-like characters who fought the first election in 1946. What follows as a consequence is a blueprint for the already published novels, *The Mystic Masseur* and *The Suffrage of Elvira*, so that what is offered as analysis has the effect of confirmation rather than discovery. The paradigm Naipaul proposes in order to address the apparent political vagaries of a "picaroon society," furthermore, is premised, not surprisingly, upon an ideology of

"civility." The inherited administrative structure and its hierarchy is sound, he implies, as long as the necessary accultur-
ation of the locals can be achieved. Naipaul concludes the
chapter with a survey of the manufactured racial divisions that
beset the island's constituencies, mainly between Indians and
those of African descent, which provides him with another of
the frequent occasions in which to offer a spate of harsh
generalizations about the region's complex etiquette of race,
color, and class.

Having contained his familiarity and discomfort with Trinidad within the discursive parameters of an argument whose
thesis rests upon identifying the island's refracted relation to
"borrowed cultures," Naipaul's subsequent readings of places
and societies are provided with a thematic context. British
Guiana proves to be more contradictory but ultimately more
promising than Trinidad. By devoting considerable space to
national political figures, whose hospitality Naipaul enjoys, he
is able to pursue his thesis about the possibilities for effective
nationalism because, as he maintains, the Guyanese example of
a short-lived coalition between organized political parties indicates a level of maturity.[8] Paradoxically, the harshness of
slavery under the neighboring Dutch, and the subsequent
domestic colonization of labor demanded by sugar, has created
in Naipaul's estimation a taste for independence among the
black populations, despite their lack of entrepreneurial
ambitions. Georgetown, the capital, elicits Naipaul's praise for
its antiquated Dutch architecture but also what will become a
characteristic Naipaulian petulance at the "inefficency" of its
services. Confident of his powers of discernment, Naipaul's
tendency to immediately generalize from an observation or a
comment or an experience, reaches an Orwellian conclusion
when he comments: "In British Guiana it is almost impossible
to find out the truth about any major thing. Investigation and
cross-checking lead only to fearful confusion" (*The Middle
Passage*, p. 132). Like the narrator of "Shooting an Elephant,"
Naipaul's frustrations exacerbate his already ambivalent feelings about the setting.

Surinam, a former Dutch colony, allows Naipaul a further base for comparing the varieties of colonial practice in the Caribbean. Thought of as a virtual extension of the Netherlands, Naipaul sees its relatively tension-free racial mix as a testament to "Dutch realism," which openly acknowledges racial difference. Therefore, the existence of a separatist nationalism is to Naipaul a "sad," because unnecessary, development, and one which, in its rejections, throws away a legitimate affiliation with a worthy European cultural tradition. This regret allows Naipaul to engage in one the volume's most extraordinary moments of editorializing. In order to demonstrate that the local creolized languages are simply not capable of replacing European ones and their rich expressive traditions, Naipaul applies the Arnoldian test of "touchstones." After asking a Mr. Eersel to "translate" lines from a Wyatt poem, his assessment acknowledges a "sweetness," but dismisses any real possibilities. Continuing to play these games of "translation," Naipaul concludes that the creolizing process is akin to engaging in "gibberish."

Naipaul also dwells with some passion upon the brutal and inhuman dimensions of the history of slavery in Surinam, principally through a late eighteenth-century account by an Englishman, John Stedman. Mary Louise Pratt has recently provided a critique of the ideological struggle about slavery between the British and the Dutch that informs Stedman's narrative. In the light of this broader comparative basis, where the compass of the struggle also included competing British and Dutch interests in South Africa, Stedman's harsh criticism of Dutch slave practices becomes disingenuous without his specific descriptions losing any of their power.[9] Thus Naipaul's indignation and compassion, however sincere, are offset by the partiality of his historical perspective. This becomes increasingly clear in his almost fatalistic charge of stasis that he sees as the inescapable consequence of slavery. He closes the chapter with a portrait he offers as emblematic of this condition: an isolated subcontinental Indian whose dereliction is a reflection of the country's. The image, which is coupled with that of the "Lazy Negroes," is not only locked into a colonial stereotype, but it is also anticipatory of what, in the years to come, and in a greater Third World, will settle into an angry Naipaulian despair. The depression into which Suriman plunges him more or less stays for the rest of Naipaul's travels in the Caribbean, and colors the responses he is able to muster. It perhaps accounts for the querulous and somber mood he takes to Martinique, where with an increasing impatience he suggests that Martinque's relation to France refuses to acknowledge its metaphoricity; Trinidad's aspirations towards England were at least structured like a simile.

Thus his reading of Martinican assimilation carries with it a scathing critique of what Naipaul suggests is a massive delusion the whole island suffers from. The basis of his antipathy is his estimation of the rigid stratification of race and color that operates within the island's insularity. Unlike Fanon, who offers a critique of the same phenomenon, Naipaul is content to leave his observations in an accusatory mode. The other critique Naipaul uses Martinique to introduce into his reading of the contemporary Caribbean condition is of the neo-colonial aspects of the region's abandonment to the tourist industry. The resulting reification of the social stratification, coupled with the wholesale importation of French habits of social valuation, or devaluation, allows Naipaul to reflect upon a curiosity of Caribbean-wide practice: the development of what can be called a racial eye. Rather than dispute or fault the existence of a special habit of perception, it must be kept in mind that this same "talent" is at the root of Naipaul's own special wisdom about the region, and is one of the first licenses, along with his upbringing within a pristine colonial diasporic moment, of his "authority."

Naipaul's fatigue overwhelms the rest of the volume. With the abbreviated haste of a weary and fraught traveler, the accounts of Antigua and Jamaica serve as a last compendium of confirmation of his original thesis about the Caribbean's "borrowed cultures" and "half-made societies." That Martinique should make him nostalgic for Trinidad, that the Victorians are replaced by quotations from the *1959 Yearbook of Jehovah's*

Witnesses, and that the local Antiguan radio station stocks tapes of Naipaul's own BBC broadcasts, limpidly suggests that his tour has revealed the region's imperfect graduation to a postcolonial status. The book ends with an appropriate juxta-position. After having read Jamaican nationalisms, from the apologist to the militant, through the category of "race" rather than history, in a formula that will resurface more than twenty years later in the novel *Guerrillas* (1975), Naipaul ends his journey in an exclusive retreat designed to anticipate all its guests' needs in a paradisical island seclusion. As his writing of the next two decades will confirm, Naipaul's last stop in *The Middle Passage* takes on the dimensions of a scene of meta-morphosis where he ceases to be a local and becomes instead a visitor.

CHAPTER 4

Abroad

> I left them all and walked briskly towards the aeroplane,
> not looking back, looking only at my shadow before me, a
> dancing dwarf on the tarmac.
>
> (V.S. Naipaul, *Miguel Street*)

In a 1964 piece published in *The Times Literary Supplement* entitled "Jasmine,"[1] Naipaul succinctly charts the transformations in perceptions of literature that he underwent from his schooling in Trinidad through his university years at Oxford. Offered as an insight into the ways in which a reader is affected by his or her cultural environment, the essay also provides a critique of the formal practices of studying literature, and the alienating effects he believes they achieve. Rather than attribute a Brechtian result, Naipaul faults the "scientific" study of "texts" because it divorces a reader from "wandering among large tracts of writing," and from relating "literature to life" (*The Overcrowded Barracoon*, pp. 26–27). Since part of the essay's objective is to try and explain the built-in alienation that a writer from a colony must overcome in order to bridge the experiential separation bred by colonial marginality, his antipathy towards literary scholarship offers itself as an interesting analogy. In his insistence that literary criticism is only an alienating activity, he refuses to acknowledge that the textual universe established by codifying "reading," or hermeneutics, contains in its exercises the bridges and trajectories that contribute to dialogical exchange.

Instead, he suggests that the dialectic created by a literature's tradition and the language in which it is written establishes an ideological milieu that he discovers to be insularly local. As a consequence, Naipaul claims to have had to learn "to separate the literature from the language," supplementing his already developed "love of language, the word in isolation." As a young colonial in Trinidad reading novels of the English literary tradition, he continues, he developed the habit of imaginatively transposing the stories into a Trinidadian setting, thereby engaging in the literature without the interference of knowing about England or its parochial concerns. The familiarity of the local subsequently gained by residence in England, however, has taken the fantasy out of his readings in the English tradition and substituted "knowledge" instead. Now, the density of the local coupled with the intertextuality of the tradition increasingly isolates English writing until, Naipaul fears, "Writing will become Arthur Miller's definition of a newspaper: a nation talking to itself," and, "Perhaps in the end literature will write itself out, and all its pleasures will be those of the word" (*The Overcrowded Barracoon*, pp. 28–29).

Naipaul then locates himself within his argument when he declares, "The English language was mine; the tradition was not" (*The Overcrowded Barracoon*, p. 26), and subtly clears a discursive space for a writer who needs to defy national or literary-territorial restrictions. This is further substantiated by arguing that literature's combined appeal rests with the fantasy it provides for an imagination that only has the word as reference, while "writing" provides the slippery foci that allow for the familiar and known to take an ordered shape. In Trinidad literature was fantasy; in England it is local knowledge. In Trinidad writing bestowed order upon the familiar; in England it is increasingly nationally private. By aligning himself with the pleasures of the word, therefore, Naipaul's implicit self-location as a writer transcends the local and its ideologies, freeing him to pursue the aesthetic course of universals. By referring to Britain as well as Trinidad in this formulation, Naipaul also manages to rationalize a separation between himself and his representations of home, thus complementing his separation from the English literary tradition. The essay's final coda, where he recounts an incident in British Guiana, describes the moment when he learned the name of a flower which had remained nameless during his childhood. After his initial exhilaration he concludes: "But the word and the flower had been separate in my mind for too long. They did not come together" (*The Overcrowded Barracoon*, p. 29).

His publications in the decade after *A House for Mr. Biswas* and *The Middle Passage*, not surprisingly, then, demonstrate this agenda of *writing-as-separation* he seems to have set for himself. His first "English" novel, *Mr. Stone and the Knights Companion* (1963), his second travel book, *An Area of Darkness* (1964), and the stories and novella, *In a Free State* (1971), each take him to different settings, while *The Mimic Men* (1967) and *The Loss of El Dorado* (1969), return to familiar territory but only in genres quite different from those previously employed. The realism of *The Mimic Men* and the textual history of *The Loss of El Dorado* are as removed from the satire and travel-journalism of the earlier decade as the name "Jasmine" is from the flower of Naipaul's childhood.

MR. STONE AND THE KNIGHTS COMPANION (1963)

Given Naipaul's antipathy towards the New Criticism of his undergraduate studies, and his dissaffection with its concentration on poetry, it is both curious and appropriate that he should open his English novel with a subtle evocation of T.S. Eliot's "The Love Song of J. Alfred Prufrock." Not only is the poem's cat imagery of the fog embodied in an actual cat, but the novel's protagonist, Mr. Stone, preternaturally resembles a prose embodiment of Prufrock. The ordered regularity of his adult life, upon which he reflects with some frequency, is a source of satisfaction, but intimations of mortality begin to intrude on his sense of well-being. Thus, as he approaches retirement, Mr. Stone develops a concern about ageing, and a mild anxiety about the status of his accomplishments to date. His subsequent marriage to the widowed Margaret Springer and the acceptance and success of his proposal at his place of work for a program to support retired employees, combine as events that allow him to feel he has accomplished something to be remembered by. The mild ups and downs of the novel's action are in consonance with the unexceptional cast of characters.

In writing such a novel, Naipaul appears to be testing his contention that all literatures are regional, and imbued with their own private languages, in this case an essentialist "Englishness." Since he identifies the English "vice" of the era as the habit of looking for "social comment" in their novelists, he centers his plot around his protagonist's embrace of just such a cause. Furthermore, the uniform regularity that obeisance to the social conventions of an English middle-class morality produces, dictates all the characters' actions. This conformity is well in keeping with Naipaul's other observation about the habits of an English readership: "an ordered society of the self-aware who read not so much for adventure as to compare, to find what they know or think they know" (*The Overcrowded Barracoon*, p. 28). Almost as an antidote to the lively chaos and rambling events of *A House for Mr. Biswas*, *Mr. Stone and the Knights Companion* presents the English middle class as reticent and dull – possibly the price of order in a well-regulated society. The only curiosities of the novel lie in the punctuation of Mr. Stone's fantasies and ruminations, which carry the same edge of eccentricity as those of the characters of the Caribbean fictions. Mr. Stone's attempts to trap a cat with cheese as bait, his habit of imagining out-of-body experiences, and his practice of writing and rewriting resumes of his professional life are all familiar character traits to Naipaul's readers.

The novel has been productively read as another of Naipaul's explorations into states of alienation. Mr Stone's Prufrockian disaffection does suggest that life in the metropole, so fantasized about by distant colonials, houses its own varieties of rootlessness and inner frustrations. Comparisons with both Mr. Biswas and Ralph Singh of *The Mimic Men*, furthermore, also suggest that Naipaul's preoccupation with existentialist questions breaks down the center/periphery dichotomy so prevalent in colonial and postcolonial representations. Nevertheless, the most engaging responses that *Mr. Stone and the Knights Companion* has garnered have been those that have

weighed it for its capture or achievement of "Englishness."
From the characterization of Mr. Stone, to the evocations of
time and place, critics have used the novel to "test" Naipaul's
ability to do so. While opinions have varied, the volume has
weathered as an exercise overshadowed by both *A House for
Mr. Biswas* and *An Area of Darkness*.[2]

AN AREA OF DARKNESS (1964)

An Area of Darkness is Naipaul's account of his first sojourn in
India, which lasted close to a year. Less chronological and
documentary than *The Middle Passage*, *An Area of Darkness* is far
more concerned with locating metaphors for Naipaul's personal odyssey as a writer than in explicating the subcontinent's
"mysteries." As the title suggests, the terrain over which the
narrative searches is the realm of the imagination, the metaphorical figures of which are in the interstices of cultural
memory created by migration. The sixty years that separate
Naipaul's "return" to India from his grandfather's departure
from it are close enough, temporally and spatially, to the sixty
years that separate Conrad's travels from Naipaul's.[3] The
textual echoing of *Heart of Darkness* within Naipaul's first
Indian narrative, then, resonates beyond the title's allusion, for
it also serves as Naipaul's guide into the textual unconscious of
writing's uncharted postcolonial potentialities. It is Naipaul
himself, then, who is the figure that the narrative explores as it
delves into the psychological composition of a voice that is
searching for signs and histories of its origins.

Early in the narrative, however, the habit of perception of
his racial eye introduces a sorry wrinkle into his explorations
when Naipaul provides a startling cartography of the racial
categories he believes he has encountered during the journey
out:

From Athens to Bombay another idea of man had defined itself by
degrees, a new type of authority and subservience. The physique of
Europe had melted away first into that of Africa and then, through
Semitic Arabia, into Aryan Asia. Men had been diminished and
deformed; they begged and whined. Hysteria had been my reaction,

and a brutality dictated by a new awareness of myself as a whole human being and a determination, touched with fear, to remain what I was. It mattered little through whose eyes I was seeing the East; there had as yet been no time for this type of self-assessment. (*An Area of Darkness*, pp. 15–16)

The extraordinary juxtaposition of racially personified continents and Naipaul-the-individual sets the perspectival focus of his persona, the obsession of which will indeed be "this type of self-assessment." Thus, as an illustration of his "wholeness," Naipaul offers an extensive description of the hysteria he felt when confronted with the labyrinthian maze of India's bureaucracy. In trying to reclaim the liquor requisitioned by customs on his arrival, he delves headlong into a stereotypical situation of being shunted from one department to another in a scene of escalating absurdity. Initially, the tone set appears to recast the satirical edge of his earlier fictions and the growing despondency of his Caribbean travels into a more exposed self-parody of the traveler thwarted by an intractable system. His self-portrayal, therefore, offers itself as self-aware, as though an admission of overreaction is also an admission of self-knowledge. However, since he has already introduced the slippery and subversive notion of "another idea of man," it becomes clear that the self-description developing, as persona, is actually offering itself as a category of analysis against a backdrop of fixed racial and cultural stereotypes.

Accordingly, as in *The Middle Passage*, and as will become a practice in all his subsequent travel writing, Naipaul provides a personal history of himself as a Trinidadian East Indian. In doing so, his introduction reiterates known information and reminds the reader about the curious posture that his colonial status forces upon him through the fact of the hybridity of his cultural referents. In the face of a trip to India, the Indian (read as brahmin, Aryan) takes precedence over the Trinidadian and Caribbean (read as displaced, isolated) that prevailed in *The Middle Passage*. Thus, his reflections about the imaginary India of his childhood, shaped by the experience of sporadic participation in Hindu ceremonies and memories of the artefacts and objects of his grandfather's migration provide part of the dialectic from which will emerge a new figure of cosmopolitanism rooted in the cultural amalgam of a post-imperial metropole. Naipaul's reconstruction of his imaginary India, however, cannot be pitted against the observations of his 1962 sojourn there until the narrative has negotiated yet another category that could potentially intrude upon his mission of self-definition as a writer and the constitution of his persona.

The status of immigrant in Britain, therefore, is dealt with singularly in the anecdote about Ramon, a Caribbean immigrant whose death and subsequent funeral in London become a scene from which Naipaul is deliberately excluded. Naipaul's reading of his rejection is also his justification for his own disassociation from the group:

I missed Ramon's funeral. He was not cremated but buried, and a student from Trinidad conducted the rites which his caste entitled him to perform. *He had read my books and did not want me to be there.* Denied a presence I so much wished, I had to imagine the scene: a man in a white dhoti speaking gibberish over the corpse of Ramon, making up rites among the tombstones and crosses of a more recent religion, the mean buildings of a London suburb low in the distance, against an industrial sky. (*An Area of Darkness*, pp. 43–44, emphasis added)

By attributing his exclusion from a group into which he could demographically be cast to the fact of his writing, his publications, Naipaul *writes* his separation from Trinidadian Indian immigrants in Britain by imaging the body of the dead Ramon. The next brief paragraph, which closes out this early section of the first chapter, quickly resurrects Ramon in a deft move of ironic memorialization: "Ramon died fittingly and was buried fittingly. In addition to everything else, he was buried free, by a funeral agency whose stalled hearse, encountered by chance on the road only a few days before his death, he had set going again" (*An Area of Darkness*, p. 44).

Released now to encounter India proper, Naipaul is rudely awakened when he suddenly finds himself in an amorphous area of invisibility: "And for the first time in my life I was one of the crowd. There was nothing in my appearance or dress to distinguish me from the crowd . . . It was like being denied part of my reality . . . recognition of my difference was necessary to me" (*An Area of Darkness*, pp. 45–46). As Sara Suleri has argued, this need for difference is triggered by "a moment of postcolonial panic," for it robs him of the romantic fiction of an essentialist cultural and historical location which he had naively sought. The narrator's project of "self-assessment," therefore, takes on an unexpected urgency which leads him to obsess upon the "idea of the foreign." "*An Area of Darkness* thus becomes a fascinating record of delusion," Suleri continues, because "Naipaul's obsessive need to apprehend his own hybridity . . . addresses the psychic terror implicit in . . . a sense of cultural malformation: its lack of alignment to the worlds that surround it forces the narrative to locate itself in representations of a wasted postcolonial body" (Suleri, p. 159).

Alternatively, for Rob Nixon, Naipaul's recognition of his difference at this point of the narrative "is one of those redeeming moments in *An Area of Darkness* where Naipaul allows us access to the fundamental contradiction in his identity as a travel writer, as he recognizes that the projected pleasure of identifying with a group is diminished by the accompanying threat of anonymity" (Nixon, p. 84). Comfortable with Naipaul's acknowledgment of this contradiction, Nixon attributes its dialectical affect to his need to nurture a "jealous" individualism and "his image of himself as homeless," which frees his persona to adopt both the mobility of a "natural traveler," and the posture of "imposing himself." Furthermore, he reads Naipaul's "psychological dependence on his difference," as evolving into a "vocational principle." Thus, whether from a sense of cultural malformation or difference as vocation, there issues a consensus among Naipaul's readers who agree that the crisis that visiting India engendered in him ultimately allowed him to fully rather than partially posit *himself* before positing the subjects and topics of his travel. The internal contradiction of his identity, in other words, gives Naipaul a lease on his career that his despondency in the Caribbean and isolation in England were unable to. Whatever relation to "truth" Naipaul's persona allows him, therefore, its historical facets need to function in the discursive space he constructs for himself with such care and calculation from within the seams of the colonial and postcolonial, and their juncture at the metropole.

Rather than aligning himself with new group formations, consequently, Naipaul chooses instead to adopt the role of overseer of just such formations through the agency of the Word. The idiosyncrasies that his persona gathers take on the weight of familiarity, granting his readers the illusion that their access to Naipaul's vision is through his sacrifice or exposure of the private in the interests of his public concern. The vocational thrust that this stand lends his work also diverts attention away from the not-so-secret fear he expresses about the malformation of a colonial's desire. Thus *An Area of Darkness* is the narrative in which he explores the "foreign" dimensions of this developing discursive possibility, for his first encounter with the subcontinent provides him with the only remaining separation to be written between himself and what he knows of his historical composition. Therein lies the fiction of Naipaul's persona, a fiction in which his investment as a writer is so profound that all his subsequent travel writing is rooted in the unchanging principle of his separation, or independence from *vested* historical affinities with his topics. By 1984, for example, while visiting the Ivory Coast, Naipaul claims with equanimity that he travels to satisfy a writer's curiosity that places him "in a novel of my own making, moving from not knowing to knowing ... The intellectual adventure is also a human one: I can move only according to my sympathy ... The kind of understanding I am looking for comes best through people I get to like" (*Finding the Centre*, p. 90). In the India of his first visit there appear to have been very few people that he got to like.

The sketches and descriptions of the several people the narrator encounters are interlaced with charged and sometimes furious editorials about India's poverty and the habit of its peoples of defecating in public. Poverty confounds and must therefore be relegated to the inadequate but overdetermined category of the "obvious," to which, he incessantly insists,

Indians are inured. Defecation, however, falls between Naipaul's horror and an attempt at satire when he accords the activity a Churchillian rhetoric. Despite their agency in the activity, Naipaul believes Indians to be blind to what he presents as a national habit. Thus the eye he casts around him is both mean-spirited as well as confused by the apparant lack of accord and the passivity it keeps encountering. Nevertheless, its restlessness gives the narrative an open range so that the episodic and almost random observations stagger along with the same kind of dissonance that the narrator accuses his setting of engaging in. The absence of "order" and analytic engagement that he constantly sees in the people and groups he meets is therefore matched by the narrative's own patchy progression. The literacy of an eye reading what it sees as a text and the emerging coherence that should appear is constantly resisted by the Indian setting so that finally the narrator's recourse to received assumptions stands out in raw relief.

His at first unacknowledged evocation of Gandhi's observations of India, for example, dwell with some satisfaction on the congruence of opinion they share with his own. Gandhi's status is colonial, hailing as he did from South Africa, and therefore like Naipaul, the narrator suggests, "He looked at India as no Indian was able to; his vision was direct, and this directness was, *and is*, revolutionary" (*An Area of Darkness*, p. 77, emphasis added). Or the apparant elusiveness of a shared civil context, when staying as a paying guest with one Mrs. Mahindra in Delhi, evokes feelings of affectionate indulgence since, the implication is, her actions were sincere but woefully misguided and capricious. Even recourse to local or ancient Indian texts fails to provide the center that would ground his observations in a sense of a locally ordered ethos. While in Kashmir, therefore, the restless narrative's respite arrives only when Naipaul falls back upon his own textually familiar and comfortable habit of citing the local hotel signs, hoardings, advertisements, and notices. Naipaul's function at the Liward (its spelling corrected to "Leeward" is noted almost thirty years later in *India: A Million Mutinies Now*) as the unofficial letter writer and hotel publicist, finally, provides him with the narrative base from which he can salvage some sense of control over his journey.

Other moments of comfort occur when he is able to find a direct connection between what he encounters and what he remembers as central to his Trinidadian Indian experience. The pause of recognition while traveling with a family party on a bus happens when a meal is served which, true to the prohibitions and etiquette of Hindu custom internalized by him as a child, triggers what Naipaul calls "a superseded consciousness" (*An Area of Darkness*, p. 149). Such connections seem to offer both the security of a traceable communal continuity as well as the now required evidence of his separation from it. He attributes the consonance of that moment of recognition to its having provided him with a perspective that turns out to be the hitherto unavailable cypher into the unreadability of an historical Indian landscape. What he now reads in the ruins of a structure misidentified as a fort, and in the pages of the *Kama Sutra* and reference to the *Mahabharata*, consequently, is a trait of what can only be called an Indianness – a quality or cluster of qualities that the narrative has been urgently trying to identify, believing as it does that such characteristics exist. Watching the sightseeing family in the bus apparently reveals to the narrator an Indian ability to so conflate the temporal with the spatial that the resulting blindness has become no obstacle because it is constantly steadied by an intuitive and equally blind trust in a sense of "the way things had always been done" (*An Area of Darkness*, p. 150).

While Naipaul is anxious to identify moments of readability in India – encounters, experiences, and observations to which his narrative can provide a frame – *An Area of Darkness* is less forthcoming about its own context. For example, no mention is made of the writing of *Mr. Stone and the Knights Companion* during his stay in India, nor is the companion briefly alluded to identified as his wife.[4] While such selectivity gives a semi-autobiographical cast to much of his non-fiction, and is realized with greater artistry in the novel, *The Enigma of Arrival*, almost twenty years later, the device of deliberate ellipses in *An Area of Darkness* allows the narrator's perceptual range to appear unencumbered. The effect generated is the sharpened precision of the narrative voice's *singularity* in relation to all that it encounters and perceives. Thus, while on the pilgrimage in the mountains the narrator's recurring preoccupation, other than the unsanitary conditions and the fluctuating dynamic of the procession up to the signs of the god, is his relationship with Aziz, the guide and hotel factotum. That characterizations of this relationship take on the guise of a lover's discourse is curious, to say the least, but also appropriate since it evokes the nascent sexuality and familial grafting reminiscent of colonial relations. That Naipaul is positioned as the employer who questions the affection and loyalty of Aziz is indication that the paradigm of order implicit in the narrative's internal register, and what it seeks in its investigations, is hierarchical. The coincidence of names cannot help but recall Forster's Fielding and Aziz and the occasion of their parting.

Thus the special status that India enjoys in Naipaul's imagination coupled with the amorphous sameness that he felt when he first encountered Indians in India supply him with another piece of the narrative equation that allows the supposed authority of the autobiographical to mollify the potential dangers of racializing cultural description. Another factor is added when the relative calm that Naipaul records about his stay in Kashmir is rudely interrupted in the book's final section. In an extraordinary but soon to be characteristic swerve of pace and preoccupation, Naipaul launches into a hasty but sweeping assessment of English India and its texts. His sudden refuge is provided, at this stage of the narrative, by the stock he feels he is able to take between his now "experienced" view of India and the quality of authority to be found in British representations of India and the empire in general, as well as in its nineteenth- and twentieth-century canon. The tightly textual quality of this section intrudes as a reminder that Naipaul's own authorization is underway, for in evaluating British texts he begins his fully participatory role in a literary-historical enterprise to which these commentaries elect him. As a writer he expresses a professional view; as a colonial he offers verification. The actual process Naipaul is using his writing to engage in, of course, is the practice of identity formation, and his digression into the textual space of English India allows him to address the most recent development of his personal constitution: namely, his status as a recognized Writer. The self-consciousness of this enterprise does suggest that by the time of *An Area of Darkness* Naipaul anticipates many of his critics in the realization that "his world" is a textual construct which predetermines the "reality" of everything, even that of its writer.

THE MIMIC MEN (1967)

The first-person narrative of Ralph Singh tells the story of a middle-class Indian West Indian of Naipaul's generation who, after a colonial education which includes a British university, returns with an English wife to the fictional island of Isabella. While there, he helps orchestrate a successful election, but only after his wife has left him. The party of which he is a co-founder is a nationalist, multi-ethnic, populist, and quasi-socialist organization which soon ousts him as its base becomes increasingly factionalized. His subsequent exile back in England at the age of forty sees him writing the memoirs of his active life from his room in a suburban residential hotel, and avoiding contact with any of his former friends, lovers, and acquaintances. The frame of the memoir allows the protagonist's voice to take on a ruminative but analytical tenor that probes both the political exigencies of his rise and fall as well as the social, historical, existential, and cultural composition of his life.

The tone of confidence of Ralph Singh's reconstruction of the circumstances and events of his life lends the novel a studied mood of dispassionate inquiry, where, despite taking himself as the subject, he appears to document the emergence of an historical phenomenon. The bulk of the novel, however, is not only a detailed review of historical or political situations, but also a meticulous piecing together of a childhood. Where the national allegories of *The Mystic Masseur*, *The Suffrage of Elvira*, and *A House for Mr. Biswas* each took their coincidence from aspects of the idea of the postcolonial nation, *The Mimic*

Men more completely embodies the metaphor in the person, life, and times of Ralph Singh. The detailed construction of the protagonist's subjectivity is more than just the establishment of a voice's consciousness, for its parameters are so carefully drawn from the nodes of each of his historical trajectories and then refracted back through the filter of colonial socialization that the result is a carefully constructed paradigm of an empirically determined state of mind.

Naipaul's postcolonial, therefore, is offered as a realist self-portrait that gazes back at its viewers with the look of one who knows that hidden in his flaws and blemishes lies the sickness of his soul. The realism of the novel functions severally. Ralph Singh's self-consciousness, which is also presented as a form of self-knowledge, to start with, is achieved by his ability to cast himself in the third person as he recollects his habits and their origins. The many references to the actual writing of the memoir, furthermore, play on a self-reflexivity to the extent that they achieve the formal status of a trope. The Wordsworthian allusion to the political history that was to be written, and which the memoir gradually becomes, settles the fiction within its own private textuality. And, by choosing to open the novel at the point in his life when as a student in England he faced the uncertainties of where and how he could fit into the unfamiliar milieu, Naipaul foregrounds the central ambivalence of his protagonist. A larger context is also provided when Mr. Shylock, his first landlord, not only serves as a model for the young student to emulate, to imitate, but more importantly as an historical correlative. An early allusion to the Jewish experience of the Holocaust in Europe subtly evokes both the tenor of a colonial experience and the vagaries of the diasporic condition. The second indicator of ambivalence occurs with the troping of snow, the image of which is synecdochal of the colonial desire for the metropole. When Ralph Singh calls it his "element," he alludes to the displacement of referents that occurs as a consequence of colonial education.

The rites of passage that his first stay in England represents, therefore, are encumbered by their filter through a colonial's experience, so the sexual knowledge, the class affiliations, and the attitude of fatalism that characterize Ralph Singh's young adulthood are each scrambled responses of ambivalence. The "shipwreck" metaphor that he offers at the outset of his story, as though all has ended before anything can begin, not only announces a determinist logic, but also encapsulates the post-colonial panic that the novel suggests is a condition of hailing from the Caribbean. The origin of the "shipwreck" image is explained later in the narrative, during the middle section which describes his childhood, when Ralph Singh recounts the humiliation he felt for his part-Chinese school friend, Hok, when they unexpectedly encounter Hok's black mother whilst on a school excursion.[5] The emotions stem from the struggle the boys undergo between the ambition to achieve nurtured by their education and their similar adolescent escape into imaginations fed by secret readings into their racial "origins." These are, of course, "Aryan" for Ralph Singh and "Chinese" for Hok. Pitched against their fantasies is the self-denigration each has developed towards their island hybridity represented by their variously mixed families. The resulting alienation manifests itself in a shame and humiliation that is far more than just a child's embarrassment about parents at a certain age, for it seems to take on the dimensions of a profound disability. The protagonist's change of name at school, and his "real" name, Kripalsingh, and the subsequent naming of his real-estate venture as "Crippleville," each emblematizes this disability complex. The betrayal of imagination, or the early onset of delusion, in other words, is one part of the problem, and the other rests with the interference that a growing class awareness brings.

Thus informed, the novel continues to attribute an almost unspeakable consequence to the category of "race,"[6] and an insurmountable division to the category of class. Naipaul's single formula about the consequences of colonial dependency, which carry an extraordinary determination in all his subsequent work, is solidified in this fictional proscription of the postcolonial condition. Presented in a realist mode, Ralph Singh's embodiment of what can be termed a postcolonial dyslexia, is played out as though an historical determinism forecloses any possibility of its cure, despite the fact that his voice is the one to articulate it. The nihilism that has been read into the novel is attributed to this determinism, and has been widely praised for the tone of self-indictment it is seen to reveal.[7] Thus the thin line that stretches between reading a first-person narrative such as *The Mimic Men* as fiction and attributing the protagonist's views to the author lends a deliberate transparency that adds to the novel's verisimilitude. For example, when the "self-deception" that Naipaul's traveling persona alludes to in *An Area of Darkness* is revealed to be the picture of an imaginary India that survived because of its *domestication* within the "alien" setting of Trinidad (*An Area of Darkness*, p. 197), it could become the link that Ralph Singh's assessment of his "shipwrecked" life fails to grasp, or it can be read as the kind of realization that finally empowers him to write his memoirs.

The clever device of conceiving of his "active" life as though in parentheses, bracketed by matching moods of pessimism between his first sojourn in London and his later exile there, not only informs the novel's self-consciousness, but effectively aligns the narrator's priorities by casting his "public" life as ultimately subordinate to his "private" one. He appears to privilege the psychological aspects of his social formation and location, which is precisely what allows the novel to steer so effectively its determinist path. What Naipaul uses this device to consolidate, consequently, is an agenda that his readers are by now familiar with:

It was during this time [of parenthesis], I have said, that I thought of writing. It was my hope to give expression to the restlessness, the deep disorder, which the great explorations, the overthrow in three continents of established social organizations, the unnatural bringing together of peoples who could achieve fulfilment only within the security of their own societies and the landscapes hymned by their ancestors, it was my hope to give partial expression to the restlessness which this great upheaval has brought about ... But this work will not now be written by me; I am too much a victim of that restlessness which was to have been my subject ... I was attracted less by the act and the labour than by the calm and the order which the act would have implied. (*The Mimic Men*, p. 32)

What is also privileged in the dialectic of the private and the public is writing and the way it oversees the protagonist's participation in the world.

Not all writing performs this function adequately, however. Since the wealth of Ralph Singh's maternal family and the poverty of his paternal side is presented as one reason for the class division within his sense of his familial location, his fluctuating affiliations are exacerbated by his father's literacy and his mother's lack of it. His ambivalence is further complicated by the political advantage he is able to gain as an adult in his father's reputation as a popular, grassroots, spiritual political figure. What this double ambivalence results in during the political campaign with Browne, his part-black old school friend, is the article about his father written for their journal, *The Socialist*. Not only does it give their coalition the veneer of legitimacy of a textually articulated base, but its political capital is such that the phantasmagoric rise of his father's cult status falls ripely into a fictional cast that is quite in keeping with the actual recurrence of charismatic leadership within the modern history of the region. Ralph Singh's article consequently builds on the lie, or metaphoricity, of the phenomenon rather than its sociological bearings, thus leading to his recollected assessment that in the article's deep dishonesty lay its expediency. The subsequent correspondence between Ralph Singh and Browne is also designed to legitimize their political alliance but, again it seems, their reluctance to write about their political task relegates the letters to the timid realm of received ideas. Naipaul is suggesting that only in the profit of an articulated literacy – one that addresses "truth" through "self-knowledge" and "knowledge," that the framing narrative itself is illustrative of – lies the salvation of colonialism's disruptions, a suggestion that by this stage in his career is beginning to carry the weight of a post-Enlightenment certitude.[8]

The novel's plot proceeds along the path of an almost rehearsed display of typical postcolonial themes. As a student in London, Ralph Singh's gradual deracination into cosmopolitanism is played out in the sexual territory of his encounters with neighbors, prostitutes, and Sandra, his English wife. The fetishistic and anxious nature of his sexual liaisons, and their interracial composition fall into relief when later it is disclosed that Ralph Singh's sexual initiation happened incestuously with an aunt, Sally. The complement of his uncle, Cecil's, relations with Ralph Singh's sister simply underscores the endogamy associated with "racial purity," and the prohibition-laced psychological traces that colonialism's experience of it engenders. The subsequent "decadence" that Ralph Singh and the rest of the newly educated and deracinated elite enjoy on their island returns, along with their allies among the new generation of international expatriates, provides the "difference" that they try to use to re-invent themselves as a new class in opposition to an old world from which they feel they have escaped. Ralph Singh does not achieve his complete "mimic" status, however, until he enters politics.[9]

At that point in his story, the confluence of his "experience," characterized by precosity, includes a rapidly successful run as a property speculator and thus the achievement of financial independence. That such security is as short-lived as his political career, however, is the obvious corollary the novel employs to illustrate its central thesis about the apparently ephemeral quality of postcolonial "stability." Thus, in the same way that financial speculation requires an economy that continues to offer windows of opportunities, or the appearance of them, so, too, the novel implies, does a political system depend upon a foundation of its own generation. Herein lies one of the most important areas of disagreement between Naipaul and his more historically informed critics, and between his supporters and detractors. By attributing to the new elite of former colonies an atrophied sense of their own histories, his portrait of Ralph Singh as a mimic man emerges as a capricious shadow of a "whole" person playing at being both historical and political. At this crucial juncture of formation, unfortunately, Naipaul also casts the novel's "historical" analysis in much the same light, reducing the hazards of decolonization to the pat formulae of events that "seem oddly *expected* and dramatically right" (*The Mimic Men*, p. 141). The characters' play-acting, as a consequence, takes on a slightly sinister cast when it continues into adult territory for its incompletion rests in a repetitive stasis rather than in the formation of a realized hybridity. Homi K. Bhabha's critique of the colonial stereotype is chillingly enacted in Naipaul's version of the postcolonial mimic man. While acknowledging that Naipaul's application of "mimicry" is a trope to characterize a particular moment of alienation in the novel, Bhabha nevertheless demonstrates that Naipaul's treatment of the phenomenon cannot wrest itself from the satirical.

The postulate of Bhabha's critique is that "colonial mimicry is the desire for a reformed, recognizable Other, as *a subject of a difference that is almost the same, but not quite.*"[10] Ralph Singh's self-definition characterizes this partial and virtual aspiration towards *authenticity* in the now famous statement, "We pretended to be real, to be learning, to be preparing ourselves for life, we mimic men of the New World, one unknown corner of it, with all its reminders of the corruption that came so quickly to the new" (*The Mimic Men*, p. 146). Ralph Singh's memoir documenting his marginality, therefore, fails to recognize that "What emerges between mimesis and mimicry is a *writing*, a mode of representation, that marginalizes the monumentality of history, quite simply mocks its power to be a model, that power which supposedly makes it imitable" (Bhabha, p. 87). Bhabha's reading, of course, engages Naipaul's fixation on writing and its relation to "knowledge" by implying that the frame of the memoir is Naipaul's way of preventing rather than allowing his protagonist to negotiate his way out of the role into which he has "written" himself. The "knowledge" that is supposed to stem from "self-knowledge" through the agency of writing is, for Ralph Singh, only an existentialist epiphany of marginality through choice. Or, his reclusiveness at the end of the novel stems from choosing to be embarrassed. Mimicry and repetition, therefore, are the two narrative forms that Naipaul locks the colonial and postcolonial characters he creates and their respective situations into. Fiction in the Caribbean, then, apparently originates in self-deception, not self-invention.

A FLAG ON THE ISLAND (1967)

Naipaul's next publication, *A Flag on the Island*, is a collection of stories with the title story as the only "new" piece. The cluster of stories from an earlier stage of his career offers something of a respite from the grim new realism that his publications since *A House for Mr. Biswas* increasingly have delved into. The collection also starts another trend in Naipaul's publishing history, inasmuch as it is the first volume designed to gather together previously published material in a more accessible form. The assumption, of course, is that Naipaul's reputation now merits the recognition of a significant "writer," whose works have secured a self-sustaining readership. "A Flag on the Island," according to Naipaul's prefatory note, was commissioned by a film company which required a specific treatment of the island themes, further confirming the reach of his professional appeal.

The story falls into two main segments: the narrator, Frank, is a former American serviceman whose sojourn during the war was on the island to which the liner on which he is now a passenger is being forced to call due to an approaching hurricane. His ambivalence about his unplanned return is characterized by his drunken and seemingly erratic behavior among an odd assortment of passengers and, after they dock, in the island's tourist facilities, fashioned since Frank's initial sojourn. Mid-way through the narrative, as Frank lies in a drunken stupor, he surveys the changed landmarks of his earlier stay and remarks of the American war presence, "We brought the tropics to the island" (*A Flag on the Island*, p. 169). This recognition allows the narrator a long reminiscence of the conditions of his and the island's past. In settling for a simple dichotomy between a sense of the past and the present, Naipaul creates a narrative frame in which to juxtapose two versions of island "culture." The first is the various islanders' aspirations towards a petty bourgois version of their entrepreneurial enterprises. The second is the manufactured commodification of just those enterprises through the help of the narrator's black market uses of the American military base supplies, an activity that became the basis of the now firmly established tourist industry.

Naipaul's juxtaposition creates a before and after effect where the transformations that occur take on a relief that reveals their equivalent inauthenticities, despite their resulting prosperity. Among Frank's former friends on the island is a stenographer, and aspiring novelist of English romances, Mr. Blackwhite. The transformation of Blackwhite's novelistic style allows the narrator to wryly mock the exploitative use of warped island "themes" such as miscegenation and interracial sexual relations, while also laughing at Blackwhite's earlier attempts at historical romances set in Georgian English milieux. The subsequent wooing between H.J.B. White (formerly Blackwhite) and Leonard (one of Frank's fellow passengers on the ship, who is ultimately revealed to be a fraudulent philanthropist) is a clear occasion for Naipaul's not-so-subtle critique of the skewed "black" and politically correct topics that a quasi-nationalist agenda asks of its literary producers. Leonard, an American, represents the new generation of liberal humanists who under the guise of seeking native authenticity simply continue to feed their prurient fascination with a notion of the "exotic."

Similarly, Henry's place and its elevation into an elite tourist "cultural" nightclub, and Priest's metamorphoses from preacher to insurance salesman to radio announcer and advertiser, all attest to the groundless "mimic" status that each has achieved. Since both their present and their original situations are depicted as delusional, Naipaul's narrator, Frank, with his antipathy on his return, suggests that he is aware of his own complicity in helping to create caricatures of his island friends. They, in turn, also display an awareness of their plastic status, so that the cumulative effect of the story's mood is an odd nostalgia for something that never was. The flag on the island, therefore, is the easy emblem for the made-up, manufactured quality of the island's independent "identity," engaging as it does in a simplistic representation of the multiracial composition of its inhabitants, rather than a culturally authentic amalgam of its locally bred hybrid traditions.

THE LOSS OF EL DORADO (1969)

Naipaul's history of Trinidad is recreated primarily from extant documents and original historical collections of the former colonial overlords of the island, as well as from their imperial correspondence, news reports, court documents, travelogues, dispatches, and letters. It is a formidable undertaking both for the volume of materials required to be sifted through and sorted out, as well as for the method Naipaul chose to adopt in piecing his version of the island's story together: a novelistic compendium of a continuous narrative. Furthermore, as he states in his Preface, he was at pains to ensure that every quoted dialogue or exchange be strictly true to the original, thus appearing to rob himself of the novelist's license with free, direct, and reported speech. The result is a long, dense, and tightly organized structure of episodes, each of which revolves around a principal figure under whose jurisdiction Trinidad once fell. By choosing to frame the narrative with two well-defined events, "the end of the search for El Dorado" (*El Dorado*, p. 17), which contains lesser-known information about Sir Walter Raleigh's exploits in the Caribbean, and, 200 years later, the trial of one British governor, Picton, for the torture of one Luisa Calderon in the early nineteenth century, Naipaul seems to set up thematic guideposts for the larger topics he feels constitute the region's actual history: "El Dorado, slavery, revolution" (*El Dorado*, p. 13).

Critics have long noted that Naipaul's choice of these two framing events creates the illusion of rather than the key to the island's "History."[11] Considering the formidable challenge that *The Loss of El Dorado* must have posed as an act of formal narrative, it is nevertheless soon evident that the telescoping of such selective moments inevitably leads to a quagmire of historiographical pitfalls. To claim that textual evidence constitutes the singular material from which legitimate "History" can be written is to subscribe immediately to the Hegelian methodology developed and valorized by the imperial project itself. Furthermore, to rely completely upon a referent of narrative order in the name of historical reconstruction relies too heavily on the source materials' ability to represent adequately the eras in question. And finally, to undertake to contribute the novelist's touch to such a project bespeaks a disingenuousness, for it trusts that the idiosyncratic and imaginative nature of the undertaking's execution substitutes for a scholarly thoroughness.

Naipaul is fastidious in his attention to his source materials' nuances of expressiveness: the frustrations of administrators, the disappointments they endured and the time-lags their ill-defined roles thrust them into are finely captured. The enduring portrait of Spain's first governor in Trinidad, Antonio de Berrio, the evocations of Raleigh's utopian fantasies, and the narration of the saga of Venezuela's protracted efforts at nationalist definition are painstakingly set against the bitter development and establishment of a slave society. Naipaul's accounts of Trinidad's strategic location in relation to Britain's political and economic competition with Spain, and of the fragmentation of French, British, Spanish, and other European immigrant or militarily indentured populations serve to locate the island in more than three centuries of European historical development, thus allowing Naipaul the discovery that the island of his birth was at least central to the imperial theme, rather than entirely peripheral. Thus, towards the end of the narrative, the almost self-denigrating way in which he casts the island "at the rim of the world" is somewhat mollified by the almost Ptolemaic nostalgia that stems from Naipaul's subtle acknowledgment of the personal excitement that his researches into the history of the city of Port of Spain procured him.

The density of the volume makes its reading difficult, however, for it is punctuated with momentary and too frequent episodes of novelistic suspense that start to cast the social actors into fictional universes, each of which suggests a resolution but ends, always, in disappointment. In the same way that Gandhi is quoted in support of Naipaul's observations of India in *An Area of Darkness* before he is named, so figures such as Bolívar, Burley, Nelson, and even Raleigh are introduced into the narrative. Similarly, Naipaul's careful establishment of the originary role that incidents set in either Trinidad or the Caribbean played in the development of European imperial imaginations – such as late sixteenth-century notions of utopia, Defoe's *Robinson Crusoe*, or the simple but astonishing contradiction between voiced abolitionist sentiments and British colonial constitutional demands – conveys a sense of curious regret that the island, after having participated in "European" events, should then have been so utterly abandoned. His most sustained editorial comments are reserved for the volume's conclusion, allowing him to chart his version of the formation of a colonial sensibility as a consequence of a society's devolution from a state of action to one of inaction.

Trinidad's history, therefore, is made to serve as an exemplary and empirical site for Naipaul's most deeply felt thesis about the achievement of colonial status: an atrophied polity, racialized social stratification, and cultural impoverishment. The disparateness he attributes to its composition is robbed of its potentiality by the severance from each other of the island's several cultural sources. For the colonialists left behind after Britain's relocation of its imperial project to India, for example, Naipaul reads a loss of contentiousness as the cause for a gradually more entrenched belief in racial superiority rather than fully attributing the growth of racial theories and racist ideologies to the irrational complacency bred by a plantation economy and slavery and their attendant rationalizations. For the "negroes" of the island, alternatively, Naipaul is simply damning, for he attributes "fantasy" as the only realm within which something that resembles black communal life manifests itself; this despite the excruciatingly detailed documentation of the brutality of slave penal codification and institutionalization on the island. Naipaul is not blind to the dehumanized conditions of a slave society, but his analysis is deterministic, suggesting as it does that slavery rendered the Afro-Caribbean incapable of rationality.[12]

The limited distribution of Naipaul's survey, therefore, has been justifiably criticized.[13] By piecing together his reconstruction from the single perspective of the literate participants of Trinidad's past, he elides, or leaves unexplored, the nascent

development of the island's creolized resistance to both extinc-
tion and cultural homogeneity. Perhaps the most enduring
trope that Naipaul employs to emblematize his method is also
one that serves to illustrate the historiographical myopia that
his choice of materials results in. The scene of his second
"incident," Luisa Calderon's torture and her subsequent trial,
starts at the prison where Vallot, the jailer, systematically
carries out his duties of discipline and punishment, which
include the sanctioned practice of exacting confessions through
torture. The relative wealth of detail about various tortures
and information on specific incarcerations housed within this
one jail that are available to Naipaul comes in part from the
various records and reports associated with Luisa's case, as well
as the dispatches of Fullarton, the First Commissioner, who
challenged Picton's authority. Nevertheless, the quantity of the
detail is offset by Naipaul's repeated observation that "Vallot's
jail, like the setting of so many court cases, becoming a place of
myth, [is] to be constructed by each man in his imagination.
*No plan exists of the jail; it is known only from its individual, unrelated
rooms*" (*El Dorado*, p. 274, emphasis added). The analogy to be
drawn, of course, is clearly to *The Loss of El Dorado*'s own
historical reconstruction which, in the absence of a "plan,"
nevertheless maps itself out of the *suggested* or plausible contours that are implied by the framing events' metonymic links.
The reliance, therefore, upon spatial narrative constructions
begs the question of Naipaul's temporal recourses, and, by
extention, Luisa's torture's displacement of the manifold and
overwhelming brutalities suffered by slaves. It is here that the
novelist almost undermines his "history" with his narrative
license. Twenty-five years later, in *A Way in the World* (1994),
Naipaul reintroduces several of the historical figures from *The
Loss of El Dorado*, but much more consciously as "characters"
than as personages engaged in history-making. The long "dialogue" between Raleigh (the spelling is modified in the later
work) and the surgeon is conducted as an interrogation of
Raleigh's *The Discovery of the Large, Rich, and Beautiful Empire
of Guiana*, thus allowing Naipaul a more speculative treatment
of his materials than he allowed himself in *The Loss of El Dorado*.

From the outset of *The Loss of El Dorado*, Naipaul is careful to inform his readers that one of the central frustrations, or facts of their commissions, facing imperial and colonial administrators and crown-sponsored adventurers alike was the time-lags that existed between the dispatch, receipt, and response of their correspondence with metropolitan authorities. With the seventeenth-century Spanish Court, furthermore, paper work was apparently often neglected after receipt, and responses to specific requests sometimes arrived some years later, if at all. And, finally, with the various rivalries and enmities between colonial, nationalist, and mercantile interests, interception of correspondence was a constant hazard. Thus the massive effort that Naipaul must have expended in tracing the genealogy of the interlinked correspondences surrounding his two framing incidents is impressive. At the same time, however, the effort is also responsible for an extraordinarily tight narrative seam that almost eliminates all but the "official," rhetorical, and ultimately hollow, often deliberately deceptive, version of affairs and events. While this narrative choice does highlight the haphazard and sometimes accidental nature of Europe's modern forays into empire, it also courts the danger, at least for the purposes of his history, of reinscribing a "silence" to the slave experience, whose massive weight of accumulated presence, over real time, properly underwrites the consolidation of Europe's acutely exclusionary and acquisitive empires. Naipaul is neither indifferent to the sustained brutality of European slavery, nor uninformed about Europe's own confusions about its responsibility for it. Nevertheless, as novelist, his choice to write a European history of Trinidad, or of the city of Port of Spain, is historically skewed.[14]

IN A FREE STATE (1971)

This volume appears to be another innovation in Naipaul's corpus of works, not only because it simultaneously incorporates fiction and non-fiction, but also because the title novella is his first work of fiction with an African setting. The chronological contingency of the publications of *The Loss of El Dorado* and *In a Free State* also crudely suggests that there is a linkage between Naipaul's inability, or choice not, to write the history of Trinidad as other than a European one, and his African story's concentration on the besieged and outgoing *European* expatriate protagonists in a newly independent African nation. Furthermore, it would appear to be a logical progression for Naipaul to now explore the continent of Africa, for it represents the last major world player in colonialism's history, the topic that by this stage in his career seems to overwhelm the local and situated investigations that his personal history had hitherto supplied him. Not surprisingly, therefore, Naipaul's first foray beyond the boundaries of the places that constitute his personal history also carry an historical rather than personal connection since the continent qualifies as a vital referent in the history of the Caribbean.

In a Free State presents itself as a confident but elusive series of narratives that demonstrate the lambent spread of their collective global span. The "Prologue" and "Epilogue" are the non-fictional bookends, and each is set within a "safe" corner of the continent, Egypt. The first story, "One out of Many," traces the migration of an Indian foreign-service official's servant, Santosh, from Bombay to Washington D.C., and the second, "Tell Me Who to Kill," is an internal monologue of an immigrant from the Caribbean who becomes insane in his quest to protect his brother's passage to and settlement in Britain. Taken together with some of the short stories of *A Flag on the Island*, they begin to form their own independent corpus of "immigrant" stories which, more than twenty years later, in *The Enigma of Arrival* (1987), Naipaul claims to have missed as a proper subject for his attention (*The Enigma of Arrival*, p. 141). At the time of its publication, however, *In a Free State*'s geographical sweep signaled more a sense of the author's expanded purview than a thematic consolidation of post-Second World War migratory patterns from the Third World to the First.

The most frequently discussed aspect of the book is its treatment of the themes of "freedom" and "alienation" which Naipaul treats with a many-layered irony.[15] On a simple level, the stories all allow Naipaul to expose the absence of freedom by demystifying the myths surrounding misperceptions that one must be elsewhere to be "free." By establishing situations which involve what used to be called "culture-clashes," Naipaul is able to pinpoint the moments of transference that occur from one form of entrapment to another when his characters make their choices. To compound his new thesis about postcolonial upheaval and rootlessness, Naipaul also charts the role that deracination plays in making the fate of each of the social actors or characters appear so irrevocable: Santosh, Dayo's brother, Bobby, Linda, the Tramp, even the narrator of the "Prologue" and "Epilogue" are each circumscribed by their own choices or actions. Their subsequent despair only surfaces when a self-knowledge reveals itself after they find themselves still entrapped, or entrapped again. This layering of despair and entrapment has been read as an example of a postcolonial generation's existentialist crisis and indeed it is; but while Naipaul is careful to show that part of its origin is the result of misplaced and sometimes misled desire, his acuity in explaining the metropolitan-centered development of colonial identity-formations still cannot wrest itself from an historical determinism.

In the first story, "One out of Many," Santosh's first-person account, for example, opens with a statement cast in the future perfect tense, and then immediately undermines its potential mythic proportions: "I am now an American citizen and live in Washington, capital of the world. Many people, both here and in India, will feel that I have done well. But" (*In a Free State*, p. 21). His subsequent reconstruction of his passage from the streets of Bombay to his employer's closet, and finally to his marriage to an African–American cleaning woman and his life as a cook typically insists upon a class equivalence for the immigrant experience. Santosh's recollections necessarily follow a course of self-awareness as Naipaul allows him a progressive series of recognitions, first of the conditions of his existence, and then of himself. When, in the middle of the story, Santosh tries to make sense of the cleaning woman's interest in him, he peers into a mirror and, "Slowly I made a discovery. My face was handsome. I had never thought of myself in this way. I had thought of myself as unnoticeable, with features that served as identification alone" (*In a Free State*, p. 35). This delayed "mirror phase" that Santosh suddenly has to negotiate at first appears ironic, cutting as it does into the narcissistic moment that supposedly heralds an individualism necessary for "westernization." From the point of view of the narrator's self-consciousness, however, this graduation from subservience to "freedom" is less a Naipaulian moment of "self-knowledge" than an attempt to chart the blindness that Naipaul feels characterizes a subcontinental state of mind.[16]

Similarly, in "Tell Me Who to Kill," the narrator's dementia is designed to illustrate the pathological side of the migratory process, one where a sense of self is lost rather than gained. We soon learn that the narrator is a madman, and that he is Dayo's brother, all direct references to himself being repressed into a third-person address. The actual events that punctuate the protagonist's life are hazy indicators of the obsessive paternalistic concern with his brother's life that develops into the insanity we watch unfold. We learn that the narrator's feelings of having been betrayed, and his subsequent need to find something or somebody to kill, stem from his brother's successful assimilation which has necessitated the narrator's massive disjunction from a sense of his responsibility. By supplying Dayo with a sense of continuity, he has lost his own. The story's dark irony is that Dayo's tale corresponds to the norm of the theme of migration, and that the narrator's casualty is the sacrifice migration often entails. Both "One out of Many" and "Tell Me Who to Kill" explore loss and alienation as the impoverished consequence of having subscribed incorrectly, or carelessly, to an ultimately skewed sense of historical opportunity.

"In a Free State" is a more concentrated study of yet another related postcolonial migratory trajectory. Rather than centralized protagonists representing alternative options in a world no longer bound by a tightly controlling metropole, Bobby, the mildly idealistic British expatriate expert, and

Linda, a disaffected British expatriate wife, represent instead the attitudinal chaos unleashed within the colonialist mentality as it tries to deal with the first stages of decolonization. The other, differently ominous, player in the story is the newly emerging African nation which Naipaul casts in a menacing and heavily symbolic landscape. Finally, in one of his first and most studied explorations of homosexuality as the sexual trope most suited to exemplify a "liberal" colonial paternalism, Naipaul is able to block the action of Bobby's frustrated sexual pursuits of African men as a corollary of the earnest but equally ill-targeted professions of intimacy of a "common wealth."

By choosing to explore an expatriate mentality, Naipaul focuses on a source material most available to a literary endeavor which has schooled itself in the already articulated utterances of developing colonialist perceptions. From the observations of a Froude to the more studied examinations of a Kipling or a Conrad, the habits of an imperial gaze are filtered through the narrower visors of a post-settler perspective that still carries the traces of paranoia about Africa's "evolution." The closed and clichéd conversation between Bobby and Linda as they drive from the capital to their compound in the Southern Collectorate, and which makes up the bulk of the novella, is Naipaul's first sustained protracted fictional dialogue, the course of which allows his characters to voice almost every received assumption ever developed within the lexicon of British colonial Africa. The anchor that the *idea* of South Africa provides Linda, for example, is an acutely replicated moment of an internal colonial register which, in the African context, has always allowed the oddest apologia to white settlers looking for a legislated haven and escape. Naipaul fully compromises Bobby's more idealistic and apparently humanistic stand by casting him as a homosexual first and an administrator second, and then by rewarding his individual commitment with the arbitrary and ineluctable violence of a military checkpoint, where soldiers brutally beat him for no apparent reason.

Despite the novella's emphasis upon Bobby and Linda, the story's sharpest impact remains the menace written into the

"tribal" politics being played out within the newly independent African state. Never named, the country is obviously a
composite of Uganda and Kenya, which is to become, with
Rwanda, Burundi, and Zaire, the even more seamless starting
point and setting of Naipaul's more sophisticated "African"
work, *A Bend in the River* (1979). But where Naipaul creates
distinct nations through which his protagonist travels in *A Bend
in the River*, his unnamed nation in "In a Free State," is
deliberately charted as an amorphous political space. Naipaul's attempt is to create a political atmosphere charged with
all the turmoil and volatility associated with the transfer of
power at the advent of decolonization. In doing so, however,
he condenses the events of several different histories with the
result that his new African nation is unnecessarily overdetermined. For example, even though "In a Free State" was
written after the overthrow of the Kabaka, and then Milton
Obote in Uganda, but before Idi Amin's massive expulsion of
Asians in 1972, Naipaul also grafts the ripe memories of
Kenya's history of its Land and Freedom Army's campaigns,
the so-called Mau Mau emergency of the 1950s, as well as the
1964 revolution in Zanzibar, and the first stages of "Africani-
zation" in Kenya, Uganda, and Tanzania in the late 1960s.
While this tactic may draw upon a rich harvest of post-
independence conflicts, its conflation within a single nation is a
dubious basis for Naipaul's thesis about Africa's and Africans'
preparedness for "independence." The exercise of state power,
therefore, is presented as raw and arbitrary, even while aided
by American and British strategic interests. Thus, Bobby and
Linda's drive through the Great Rift Valley, periodically
dotted with blackface advertisements, runs parallel with the
president's helicopter searching for the hiding king; their stops,
at checkpoints and for refreshments at formerly white-only
safari lodges and an isolated home of an Asian family, are
episodes that conspire to present a picture of a fragmented and
torn social order. The tenor of impending apocalypse, which
will be more fully realized in *A Bend in the River*, is finally
articulated when Bobby is brutally beaten at the last checkpoint. Nowhere does the story suggest a deeper awareness of

the political complexities and economic handicaps created by Africa's colonization. Instead, the portraits of Africans, filtered through the blinkered and distorting colonialist gazes of the non-African characters, are like Natural History Museum displays of evolving "Man."[17]

The "Epilogue" and "Prologue" of the volume constitute the documentary brackets that allow Naipaul to present his stories' fictional rendering of postcolonial "chaos" within the frame of his travelogue persona. The narrator's self-appointed status as strict observer rather than participant of events during his sea approach to the continent foreshadows the study of aggression that is undertaken in varying degrees within each of the volume's stories. In the "Prologue," one of the passengers on board, the Tramp, is ridiculed cruelly by the others, a circumstance the narrator watches, but does not attempt to interfere with. The Tramp eventually retaliates so that the episode narrated manages to reconcile itself without the narrator, as fellow passenger, having to step in. By the time of the "Epilogue," however, when witness to a more diffuse but no less virulent scene of naked attitudinal posturing of tourists in Egypt, where they bait local lads by throwing food at them, the narrator's intervention as he tries to stop the hotel staff from whipping the boys is a sudden and dramatic gesture:

I felt exposed, futile, and wanted only to be back at my table. When I got back I took up my sandwich. It had happened quickly; there had been no disturbance. The Germans stared at me. But I was indifferent to them now as I was indifferent to the Italian in the cerise jersey ... he was ostentatiously shaking out lunch boxes and sandwich wrappers onto the sand.

The children remained where they were. The man from whom I had taken the whip came to give me coffee and to plead again in Arabic and English. The coffee was free; it was his gift to me. But even while he was talking the children had begun to come closer. Soon they would be back, raking the sand for what they had seen the Italian throw out. (*In a Free State*, p. 244)

The almost immediate erasure of the narrator's intervention becomes a parable of despair and can be read, coming as it does at the end of the volume, as the event that solidifies

Naipaul's pact of an existentialist disassociation from the testimony he writes. This disassociation remains a feature of all his subsequent narratives, be they fiction or non-fiction, despite the recent tempering of his singular gaze upon a now older postcolonial world.

The ideological basis for this disassociation, a modulation of his agenda of writing as separation, seems to be the belief that in order to chronicle events that in their sum accumulate into historical movements, the story-teller cannot participate or intervene for to do so is to lose the ignorance of a "stranger's eye." Only with it, Naipaul suggests as part of his conclusion, can the writer approach "the only pure time, at the beginning, when the ancient artist, knowing no other land, had learned to look at his own and had seen it as complete ... Perhaps that vision of the land, in which the Nile was only water, a blue–green chevron, had always been a fabrication, a cause for yearning, something for the tomb" (*In a Free State*, p. 246). Thus the volume ends with a horrified contemplation of what the narrator feels the fabrication of postcolonial history entails, and further suggests that any attempt to represent this process can only take place after a massive repression of context, that which allowed the "ancient artist" to observe his world and to see it as "complete."

CHAPTER 5

The world

I take possession by turf and twig! *Yo corto esta yerba.*
(Domingo de Vera, [*c.* 1592] quoted in V.S. Naipaul, *The Loss
of El Dorado*)

When writing about *In a Free State*, Alastair Niven stated in
1975 that, "I remember commenting after I had read *The
Mimic Men* a few years ago that I doubted if V.S. Naipaul
could write another novel."[1] His prophecy was prompted by a
feeling that Naipaul surely could not take his "self-exploratory
process" to a more distilled degree of "detached observation
and neutrality," than that novel had achieved. Nevertheless,
he continues, reading *In a Free State* not only disproves his
prediction, but also simultaneously reconfirms it because this
new collection of both fiction and non-fiction arrives at an
"un-Forsterian position of *total* disconnection" (Niven, p. 69,
emphasis added). While Niven attributes much of this stance to
a personal investment that has bred a deep despair, what such
an argument also demonstrates is that a lack of Forsterian
connectedness, ultimately, is apt or necessary for readings
that agree that Naipaul's special relation to the Third World
can only be understood as an existentialist urgency. At the
same time, for Naipaul to have arrived at such a posture is
seen as both inopportune and almost adolescent for other
critics who smart from Naipaul's insistence upon this need for
radical separation. For, if Naipaul's disconnection from
"belonging" to the "world" is indeed a sign of his achieved
"objectivity," then what is to be the basis for the *proprietary*
nature of his claim to "authority" about the greater Third
World?

As if to prove just this proposition of objectivity's authority, the decade of the 1970s unfolds with a spate of publications that appear to consolidate Naipaul's command over the intricacies of postcolonial casualty. The publication of the retrospective as well as contemporary essays of *The Overcrowded Barracoon* in 1972, for example, serves as a reminder of the steady development of both his idiom and opinions. The volume is also designed in such a way that each of its sections provides either an update or further endorsement of Naipaul's reading of the places and issues that had figured in all his major publications up to that date. The first section, accordingly, deals with Naipaul the writer and the curious posture his colonial origins imply for that status; the second section, entitled "India," is a mixture of reviews, journalism, and minor travel pieces. Collectively they reinscribe many of Naipaul's already articulated views about India and Indians, but this time with more concentration than *An Area of Darkness* simply because the journalistic nature of the individual essays requires an immediate, sharply defined focus. The third section, "Looking Westwards," takes the reader through a series of interviews and straight reportage as Naipaul tests his eye upon a deluded Japanese visionary, the myth of John Steinbeck in Monterey, and as an observer of Norman Mailer's mayoral bid in New York during the 1969 campaign.

The last essay in this third section, "Jacques Soustelle and the Decline of the West," is perhaps the most extraordinary in the volume because it demonstrates Naipaul's quick-fingered dexterity in being able to intertwine disparate significations. Soustelle's career as an ethnographer in Mexico and his political life in France's Algerian and colonial enterprise obviously lend themselves to Naipaul's project; nevertheless, the mixture of Soustelle's personal narrative does combine to set in place an expanded cartography of "experience" for Naipaul to chart. What is attributed to Soustelle's perspective of the life of empires, therefore, also becomes a rare instance where Naipaul finds a moment of personal and professional affinity:

He [Soustelle] still seems able to survey his experience with wonder; he seems continuously to process and refine this experience as it expands within its defined limits. It is the method neither of the scholar nor of the politician, but of both together; and it comes close to the method of the novelist, making art of egoism, creating a private impenetrable whole out of fragments which from a distance might appear unrelated. (*The Overcrowded Barracoon*, p. 192)

The accident of Soustelle's biographical linkage between Spain's empire and France's, and between the Aztecs and the Algerians, it should be remembered, *is* historically *unrelated* regardless of the comparative frame offered, and despite the similarities of the vicissitudes of conquest.

Thus, when *The Overcrowded Barracoon* ends with the section "Columbus and Crusoe," not only are the source materials of both *The Middle Passage* and *The Loss of El Dorado* rehearsed but they are also realigned to accommodate now Naipaul's more discernible agenda of recording what he suggests his study of empires has alerted him to: the necessary and inevitable failure of modernity in former European colonies. The title essay, a book review, is a short, deft statement upon the "gloss" given to readings of Europe's first encounters with the Americas, and as such it serves to deflate the tendencies towards romanticizing "discovery." However, Naipaul's analysis also allows him to offer his own perspective on "discovery" as the one that correctly places the brutality and accompanying "banality" of conquest within the generic category of all exercises of imperialism. It is encounters with "primitive" peoples, he contends, that gives rise to the need to place "discovery" within a narrative of Romance and that casts the discoverer as hero. When the fiction of a utopia turns to disappointment, Naipaul concludes, then the debased cycle of imperial fantasies is redeployed again and again, thus allowing for a repetitive replay, well into the twentieth century, of an unequal exchange between the "civilized" and the "primitive." This allows Naipaul to neatly conclude his observations with a remarkable conflation of Columbus' discoveries and all subsequent imperial, colonial, and postcolonial metropole-peripheral relations. Whether to praise or condemn the "horror of discovery" – that moment on the cusp of a belief in and fear of "total power" – Naipaul's analysis carries with it a sense of an intractable, fixed posture of historical petrification between colonizer and colonized.

As though to prove his point immediately, *The Overcrowded Barracoon* is rounded out with essays on British Honduras and the political rupture that transpired between the tiny islands of St. Kitts and Anguilla, as well as an account from one of the Indian Ocean's versions of the Caribbean, Mauritius.[2] These four pieces necessarily appear as exemplification of Naipaul's thesis of postcolonial failure because Naipaul's descriptive talents present four narratives that focus primarily upon each country's "shipwreck" status. Set adrift from either an historical or cultural matrix, each place is apparently in search of its own local center, hence each is elected into a Naipaulian universe of partial and absurd "national" definition. Indeed, the psychosomatic malaise that seems to afflict a generation of young Mauritians is presented as more than just an epidemiological phenomenon but also quietly serves as an analagous development or consequence of the obsolescence Naipaul implicitly attributes to socialist experiments of the postcolonial era. It is fitting, then, that in his sketch of British Honduras and the competing Mexican and Guatemalan claims upon it, Naipaul either consciously or not echoes Forster's final exclamation of absurdity and futility when at the close of *A Passage to India*, Fielding declares, "India a nation! What an apotheosis! Last comer to the drab nineteenth-century sisterhood! She, whose only peer was the Holy Roman Empire, shall rank with Guatemala and Belgium perhaps!" (322)

The equanimity with which Naipaul presents his concluding national portraits in *The Overcrowded Barracoon*, however, is quickly transformed into a grimmer, more forbidding determinism in the publications of the next decade. With an eye now apparently trained to perceive damage, or the possibility of it, his two major novels, *Guerrillas* and *A Bend in the River*, each depict situations that chart moments of profound collapse in already fragile social orders. While each of the novels is a carefully fictionalized reconstruction of actual events and political circumstances, their emphases nevertheless make a singular point about an *a priori* futility at the core of each novel's political setting. Furthermore, his study of India during Indira Gandhi's state of emergency, *India: A Wounded Civilization*, his second collection of longer essays, *The Return of Eva Peron with The Killings in Trinidad*, and his survey of the Islamic world, *Among the Believers*, are also insistent and stubborn efforts at reiterating received assumptions established by Naipaul's *own* theses of colonial and postcolonial political pathologies rather than just those of his adopted British colonial precursors. This phase in his career, therefore, not only solidifies his engagement with the troubled modernity of the greater Third World, but also presents itself as the mature signature of his claim that his is now a comprehensive view of the world.

GUERRILLAS (1975)

Despite the preparation for a harsh and bleak realism that *The Mimic Men* and *In a Free State* establish in Naipaul's fictional work, *Guerrillas* nevertheless comes as something of a shock. Its unpleasant tale of a doomed quasi-cooperative enterprise on a Caribbean island between the skewed Black Power initiatives of Jimmy Ahmad and his corporate sponsors, Sablichs, is played out amongst a cast of characters confused by their missions and arrogant in their ignorance. The resulting posturing between the expatriates Roche and Jane and the returned "revolutionary," Jimmy, is from the start fated to abort at the level of a gross theatricality because of their failure to grasp anything but their own misplaced vanities. Against a political climate that remains controlled by outside forces, Jimmy's Black Power commune is like the thwarted and stunted vegetables that they profess to cultivate, while the importation of both Roche's anti-apartheid South African resume and Jane's London-chic Third-World slumming are similarly misallied. All three characters have in different degrees been molded by a metropolitan liberalism that has utterly failed to discern that its attitude to and understanding of decolonization are necessarily blinded by its own guilt-ridden complicity in the prior colonial enterprise. The postures of this liberalism's adherents, therefore, are reactive. The characters in the novel consequently are earnest but vapid and sometimes dangerously deluded, and they act under a license of pietistic political and "moral" self-righteousness. That their efforts cause more damage than anything else is, fundamentally, the thrust of Naipaul's postcolonial thesis. His villains, then, are the careless, self-serving as well as confused expounders of *rhetoric* mouthed by the generation of decolonization.

Thus, these singularly unsympathetic characters and the brutal details of their social disaffection, sexual misadventure, and the eventual murder of Jane are all narrated through a cleverly inflected narrative stance that allows all the figures, rather than the narrative voice, to represent each other as well as present their own version of their disappointments and delusions. Jimmy Ahmad's quasi-novelistic narratives which use his version of Jane's voice to extoll his virile and revolutionary virtues, for example, are only the most overt moments of this technique that mediates between an omniscient third-person narrative and a more implicated first-person voice. The delusional nature of Jimmy's narratives of self-aggrandizement is thus rendered transparent but the narratives are also designed to address directly the phenomenon of a third-person consciousness or subjectivity that characterizes the alienation built into the state of subjugation.[3] Naipaul is careful, at the same time, to extend this same trait to the other, "white," characters, Jane and Roche, though in their cases the reactive casting is more subtle. We learn about each from the other's reflections of their first, and developing, impressions rather than from a distanced narrative's recounting of background detail. Jane speculates about Roche's London persona and its depletion on the island where his fieldwork exposes his agenda as empty. Roche, on the other hand, develops a dangerously non-committal attitude towards what he sees as the basic delusion of Jane's self-serving liberal postures. In both cases, the characterizations are refracted through an already established "stock" image that each seems to embody.

The novel's local island characters are similarly compromised. Harry, the Ridge suburban group's informal social host, has achieved landed immigrant status in Canada, thus calling into question his allegiance to the island's future. Meredith, the local politician and radio journalist who eventually provides the frame within which the political confusions of the principals is set in context, is ultimately fated to a career as incoherent as Ralph Singh's in *The Mimic Men*. In other words, not a single character in this novel emerges as an original or individual figure. Instead, each is an embodiment of either a well-documented stereotype – such as Jimmy's skewed Black Power revolutionary – or a version of a Naipaulian "mimic" character which includes the status of Roche's South African credentials. Jane, perhaps Naipaul's most sustained female voice, is therefore necessarily revealed to us in a similar way as a member of a category – woman – through Roche's, Jimmy's and the narrative voice's objectification of her in their midst. While she is neither mysterious nor compelling, she nevertheless represents a sexual license that within the island setting is both threatening and inappropriate. Thus, towards the end of the narrative Jimmy's act of sodomy upon her is the novel's twinning of her with Bryant, the foundling of the commune and Jimmy's male lover, and serves as the narrative's impelled sexual mirroring, making sex and sexual promiscuity the novel's frame for political misadventure and misalliance.

In the same way that Bobby's homosexuality in *In a Free State* was a symptom of an overdetermined British liberal paternalism towards "black" Africa, so Jimmy's and Bryant's homosexual comfortings are cast as the aberrant basis of Jimmy's false consciousness bred during his sojourn in London. From the moment of his misunderstanding of Jane's allusion to his "playboy" status in London as "plaything," it is apparent that he will operate almost exclusively within a realm of reversed delusion about himself. Bryant, therefore, serves simultaneously as the sexual body upon which Jimmy realizes his domination as well as the politically disenfranchised body whom he manipulates for his cause. The "leadership" that Jimmy represents to Bryant, however, has a rival in the figure of Stephens, a lapsed commune member who, it seems, was not taken in by Jimmy's appeal or stand. While Stephens never enters the action, he nevertheless supplies the novel with the necessary alternative to Jimmy's imported and distorted political stand. The visit that Roche pays to Stephens' mother, just before the

police gun Stephens down, is an important episode in Naipaul's carefully reconstructed portrait of this confluence of
political options within a confined, urban, neo-colonial setting.
The possibility of legitimate political action from the disenfranchised and economically excluded urban proletariat is momentarily suggested when it becomes apparent that Mrs. Stephens
is acutely cognizant of the lie that Jimmy represents to the
community. The repetitive intonation of her discourse not only
underscores her grief, as Roche notes, but also her endorsement
of the fragile but functional rhetoric of redemption and liberation that still exists amongst the island's population.

Roche is also allowed a moment of insight during his visit to
Mrs. Stephens'. Using the same device that characterizes most
of the narrative – namely, letting each figure reflect upon the
other, or attribute thoughts to them – the narrative offers the
following observation: "England, Roche thought: it was so
hard to get away from England here. And there were so many
Englands: his, Jane's, Jimmy's, Lloyd's, and the England –
hard to imagine – in that old woman's head" (*Guerrillas*,
p. 119). While this observation is central to the novel's thesis
about the differently constituted consequences of a marginal
and dependent society's conceptions of its distant center, it also
indicates that Roche is given the chance to acknowledge that
the England in "that old woman's head" will indeed be
explained and revealed. We learn that it is as dangerously alien
as the "sweetness" of Jimmy Ahmad. In other words, Mrs.
Stephens has no illusions about either the promises of immigrant Britain, which one of her sons has opted for, or "revolutionary" upheaval on the island, which kills her other son.
She represents, then, that silent constituency that helps maintain the status quo through its balance between the revivalist
faith of the redemption-minded servant class and a distinct
communal identification, despite the harsh realities of poverty
and abandonment.

The final political analysis takes on an even more cynical
hue, however. After the introduction of Mrs. Stephens a
clearer picture of the island majority as opposed to elites begins
to take shape. The servants on the Ridge, the remnants of the

commune, the streets during the emergency, and the establishment figures such as the police and, finally, Meredith
Herbert, who opts for a political commitment, collectively but
peripherally make up the populace who prevail. But since they
are accorded the same kind of attention as the landscape, into
which they blend and from which they only occasionally
emerge, the larger narrative takes on a panoramic, generalized
view of their situation. In the same way that the island's setting
is repetitively and relentlessly described as a debris-littered and
scorched wasteland, so the majority is pictured as deeply
insulated in their immediate, limited, indeed myopic preoccu-
pations. The idea of a cohesive and "authentic" political
matrix from which an "independent" polity can emerge is
ruled out, first in the depiction of failed collective imaginations
and in the subsequent comparative frame that the novel sets up
in its distinction between "guerrillas" and "gangs."[4]

When Roche is interviewed by Meredith for his radio
program, for example, Meredith's questioning meticulously
manipulates and coaxes Roche into an admission that the
grandiose rhetoric associated with Jimmy's commune is
nothing but a license for the urban anarchy and predatory
inclinations of street gangs. The admission comes as a den-
ouement which exposes the hypocrisy and paternalism of
Roche's role on the island, as well as the deepseated complacency that underscores a baseless political iconoclasm
which his subversive actions in South Africa now appear to
have been. Thus his final complicity in Jane's murder, where
he gives Jimmy Ahmad an alibi by removing any evidence of
her presence on the island, comes as a bitter indictment of a
politics of liberalism whose pathological nature is revealed to
be a deadly carelessness. While Naipaul's novel clearly and
scathingly faults the importation of received ideas into settings
not suited to their application, *Guerrillas* nevertheless still tells a
story that is itself disproportionate to its historical location. In
other words, in condemning outsiders for importing political
turmoil into the island, Naipaul dwells upon a "human"
rather than political symptom and thus minimizes the
institutionalized role played by the agents of the island's

continued dependency, such as the multinational interests of
Sablich's. Even Jane's entry into the island in the company of
Sablich executives, who take her through immigration without
her passport being stamped, and thus her presence not being
officially recorded, becomes a novelistic rather than analytic
device. As a device of the plot it allows for her death to assume
the character of a double erasure whereby both her life and her
"existence" achieve an undocumented status, ironically under-
scoring the banality of her participation. By attributing
"blame" to the inadequacies of individual characters, therefore, Naipaul only indirectly implicates the larger economic
and political circumstances that create the conditions enacted
in the novel. Furthermore, even though the events are crafted
out of an actual case of murder, which is the subject of the long
essay "Michael X and the Black Power Killings in Trinidad,"
the novel's version still endorses an analysis that seems unable
to acknowledge its own neo-colonial sympathies as it obsessively traces human failures and character flaws.

In the penultimate essay of *The Overcrowded Barracoon*,
entitled "Power," Naipaul's stand and the politics of *Guerrillas*,
fall into relief when the tilt of his emphasis reveals itself to be a
deeply frustrated impatience with both the importation or
appropriation of political rhetoric bred elsewhere. Thus the
recourse to an Ethiopian ruler that the Jamaican Ras Tafarians use to equip themselves with an iconography and lexicon
of separatism is to Naipaul the epitome of absurdity. But in the
same way that he accuses the movement of practicing a literalism, he too engages in a similar tactic when he refuses to read
the political text of "black" – the discursive indicator of the
formerly enslaved who now aspire towards enfranchisement –
and instead continues to insist that the issues of "Black Power"
in the Caribbean revolve around a fallacious literalism about
skin color. For example, after citing the local efficacy of "Black
Power" in the United States, where African Americans constitute a disenfranchised minority, Naipaul faults Caribbean
movements for failing to realize that a local variety of "black"
power is already in place inasmuch as the local governments
are mainly staffed by and led by Afro-Caribbeans. While he is

correct to point out the necessary difference in political situations between the two areas, Naipaul will not acknowledge that the greater Caribbean's relation to the Euro-American metropoles is not so dissimilar from the dependent minority status of African Americans in the United States. Furthermore, it is not merely accident that informs the histories of alliances between Afro-Caribbeans and African Americans in the formation of black nationalisms in the early decades of this century, nor is it coincidental that the Pan-African movements, including the different manifestations of negritude, either stemmed from or were inclusive of the multiplicity of "black" articulations in the Caribbean region.

Naipaul's indictments, therefore, operate in a profoundly restrictive, almost blinkered, universe where the fate of decolonization can only be read in an immediate, hasty fashion. *Guerrillas*, as a consequence, purports to tell a postcolonial morality tale that is universally representative of a political malaise that necessarily prevails when former colonies fail to realize that an ascendancy to stability requires more than gestures towards it. He attributes the failure of "independence" to the debilitating effects of slavery, the survival of which has only bred the propensity to "fantasy" in the imaginations of its descendants. It is exactly the same recourse to fantasy that Naipaul identifies in *The Loss of El Dorado* when accounting for the underground and night life of the slave populations during the late eighteeth and nineteenth centuries in Trinidad. The resulting activities of Carnival, therefore, are for him less the sublimated expressions of an historical experience than an escape into fantasy that has subsequently inhibited the emergence of any collectively productive, active, rational, and original political imagination. The fabulist aspect of *Guerrillas* is even more evident, furthermore, when read in conjunction with Naipaul's detailed reconstruction in "Michael X and the Black Power Killings in Trinidad."

Here, the events leading up to the murder of both Gale Benson, the visiting English woman, and Joe Skerrit a commune member, involve many more players than the novel. There are two principal "outsiders," Jamal (with whom Gale arrives) and Kidogo, who were both African Americans involved in Black Power movements in the United States. In the novel, they are refashioned into the character of Jimmy as well as a white South African, Roche, thus placing in perspective the span of the composite *ideas* that the creation of that character is designed to embody. The Jimmy Ahmad figure, Michael X or Malik, is indeed fueled by a skewed liberalism in Britain, including its media, and much careful attention is paid to that period of his life. And while there is also much more exchange and commerce between commune members, according to the court documents Naipaul draws upon, overall, his reading dwells with much more ferocity upon the criminality of the opportunism exercised by both Jamal and Michael X. That their movement in Trinidad enjoyed any support or legitimacy at all is a circumstance that Naipaul attributes to the pathology of the island's economic composition of consumerism and dependency. The chances of the situation happening again, Naipaul suggests, are built into the Fate, as it were, of such former colonies. Naipaul's "despair," or "anger," at these circumstances has been duly noted as has his contention that the situation of "borrowed cultures" and "half-made societies" is irredeemable.[5] What results, of course, is a picture of postcolonial political situations wherein events are doomed to repeat themselves endlessly since the economic and historical factors dictating their existence are fixed in time, or for as long as the communities involved continue to imagine themselves as other than what they are.

INDIA: A WOUNDED CIVILIZATION (1977)

Time, memory, historical participation, accomplishment, and collective self-knowledge or definition continue to be the categories within which and through which Naipaul tries to make sense of an India experiencing the emergency of Indira Gandhi's rule. The visiting persona of this volume relies less upon the "stranger's eye" and cultural memory of the narrator in *An Area of Darkness*. Instead, the intervening journalistic pieces on India, many of which are collected in *The Overcrowded*

Barracoon, coupled with the publication and reception of *An Area of Darkness*,[6] provide Naipaul with both a better-defined audience and a professional rather than personal mandate to fulfill. Nevertheless, the testament that the volume tries to become is still littered with familiar tactics of representation that force the reader to engage in an exercise of social Darwinism where the social structures and historical processes signifying "India" are constantly rendered as historical organisms in a state of decay, and its people as tainted specimens of either genetic degeneration or arrested intellectual development.

While this assessment may appear harsh, indeed damning, it must be borne in mind that Naipaul's habits of evaluation still rely upon the historically unreliable synecdochal narrative techniques of reporting random interviews, surface observations, and clippings from newspaper accounts as well as local novels and political biographies. All of Naipaul's readings in this volume consequently carry the mark of a compendium critique that appears to have the advantage of an overview which he insists Indians cannot share. The positioning of his personal history remains the base from which he starts:

India is for me a difficult country. It isn't my home; and yet I cannot reject it or be indifferent to it; I cannot travel only for the sights. I am at once too close and too far ... A hundred years had been enough to wash me clean of many Indian religious attitudes ... An inquiry about India – even an inquiry about the Emergency – has quickly to go beyond the political. It has to be an inquiry about Indian attitudes ... And though in India I am a stranger, the starting point of this inquiry – more than might appear in these pages – has been myself. *Because in myself, like the split-second images of infancy which some of us carry, there survive, from the family rituals that lasted into my childhood, phantasmal memories of old India which for me outline a whole vanished world.* (*Wounded*, pp. ix–x, emphasis added)

The massive play with disproportion whereby Naipaul pits himself and his perspective against entire and non-commensurate social phenomena that comprise the Indian nation state is again in place. Similarly, the quasi-mystical category he still attributes to the traces of his cultural memory fail to accommodate the migrant's loss; namely that with the passage of time the place of origin cannot remain the same place that the migrant left, or was taught to remember.

After establishing the bases for his observations, Naipaul proceeds with his customary descriptive reportage about areas visited, people encountered, projects he inspects, and, of course, critiques of novels he feels capture or illustrate the Indian "attitudes" he is explicating. "Hinduism," and "Gandhianism" are the belief and ideological systems he uses as referent frames within which to chart the passivity and defeatist sensibilities he feels he encounters and the "depleted intellects" that have resulted on a national scale. From the peasants in Bihar and Rajastan to the middle-class professionals, as well as workers and activists in cities, and in the pronouncements and platforms of political leaders, Naipaul finds again and again the same "attitudes" manifesting themselves in the face of civil turmoil and country-wide economic chaos. In a move that is reminiscent of mid-nineteenth-century "medical" rationales used for racial ranking, Naipaul enlists the observations of an Indian psychoanalyst, one Dr. Sudhir Karkar, who attributes the Indian "underdeveloped ego" to the habit of "withdrawal" encouraged by Hinduism's meditative practices of negation and inner consolidation. Quoting liberally from his correspondence with the doctor, Naipaul carries this analysis into his critique of Gandhi's autobiography and the subsequent icon he and his political strategies became in India.

In a fascinating continuation of his use in *An Area of Darkness* of Gandhi's observations about India which Naipaul had introduced to bolster his own, initial, perspective upon the subcontinent, he now adds a self-distancing wrinkle. Where the earlier references had celebrated Gandhi's "South African eye" as being the feature which allowed him to see India as Indians could not, thus matching Naipaul's Trinidadian equivalent, the present reading now adds a "defect" in Gandhi's vision which hitherto had remained more or less hidden. By noticing the lack of physical description in Gandhi's account of his sojourn in England, and through the fleetingly peripheral presence of "Africans" in the South African chapters of his book, Naipaul concludes that Gandhi too engages in the overdetermined "Hindu" practice of self-absorption that ultimately inhibits the development of a perception and habit of observation necessary for a vigorous political overview. However, since Gandhi has also been "made" in important ways by influences from non-Indian worlds, his particular "individuality" carried to the end a self-awareness too. Hence, the semi-deification that Gandhi initially used as a means for political coalescence was fated to atrophy into an impotent rhetoric even during his life-time because, according to Naipaul, "he has nothing to offer except his presence, and he knows it ... At this terrible moment his thoughts are of action, and he is magnificent" (*Wounded*, p. 118). Gandhi's successor, Vinoba Bhave, and his insulated "mimicry" of Gandhi in Naipaul's opinion, is more than illustrative of his thesis that "When men cannot observe, they don't have ideas; they have obsessions. When people live instinctive lives, something like a collective amnesia steadily blurs the past" (*Wounded*, pp. 119–120). The observation cements Naipaul's analysis of India's inherent, self-afflicted vulnerabilities.

In 1983, well before the publication of Naipaul's third book on India, *India: A Million Mutinies Now* (1990), Ashis Nandy's study, *The Intimate Enemy: Loss and Recovery of Self under Colonialism*, appeared.[7] In the first of two long essays, "The Psychology of Colonialism: Sex, Age and Ideology in British India," Nandy provides a far more exhaustive and soundly scholarly analysis of the philosophical trajectories, both eastern and western, that comprise the politically strategic thinking of "Gandhianism." Drawing on both psychological and philosophical categories, he is able to contextualize the "mysticism" and "spirituality" of Hinduism in a way that quite devastates Naipaul's efforts. Rather than either attacking or debunking Naipaul, however, Nandy is more concerned with contextualizing the view that Naipaul's represents in the discourse generated by India's colonial experience. In the second long essay of his study, "The Uncolonized Mind: A Post-Colonial View of India and the West," Nandy observes that India "invites one not only to project onto it one's deepest fantasies, but also to

reveal, through such self-projection, the interpreter rather
than the interpreted. All interpretations of India are ultimately
autobiographical" (Nandy, pp. 79–80). Both *An Area of Darkness* and *India: A Wounded Civilization*, according to Nandy,
easily fall into the category of "those who 'see through' Indian
spiritualism and find underneath only second-class materia-
lism" (Nandy, p. 83). Likening Naipaul to Nirad C. Chaudhuri,[8] Nandy continues by explaining their disdain as a form of
self-protection where "They provide 'secondary elaborations'
of a culture designed to hide the real self – the deepest social
consciousness of the victims – from outsiders. The determinate
is not the determined after all" (Nandy, pp. 84–85).

It is not surprising, then, that *India: A Wounded Civilization*
concludes with a swirl of more direct assessments of political
figures and the poverty of their ideologies as well as with a
seemingly closer look at the state of emergency itself. For good
measure Naipaul focuses on India's "science" and scientists as
a gauge of modernity and offers a scathing debunking of the
policy of "intermediate technology," associated with improving bullock carts and the hapless tutelage at a National School
of Design. Naipaul, however, is ultimately more interested in
offering the kind of diagnosis of India's ills that rings with an
overweening certitude, the weight of which is contained in his
insulated security about the ways of the world: what he calls
India's need to develop a "racial sense," or "racial consciousness." In a series of rapid and extraordinarily transparent
moves, Naipaul reintroduces Gandhi's "South African eye"
and then goes on to argue that that perception also accounts
for Gandhi's experientially confirmed but unexpressed knowledge that he belonged to an Indian "race." The lessons of
South Africa, where all Indians are subjected to the same
racial laws, is, according to Naipaul, the origin of Gandhi's
initial nationalist genius. What is astonishing, of course, is
Naipaul's uncritical acceptance of the verity of South African
"racial" designations. Such an acceptance does not negate the
truism that modern nationalism requires an encompassing
unitary myth around which to coalesce, but it does suggest
strongly that Naipaulian terms carry with them the blindly

deterministic ferocity of nineteenth-century taxonomies of Man.

It is fitting, and perhaps predictable, that Naipaul's last reference in *India: A Wounded Civilization* should be from his own, prior, work. He quotes from the penultimate paragraph of a 1967 journalistic piece entitled, "A Second Visit," where he first identified India's problem as one of a "decaying civilization."[9] It is not Naipaul's supposed prescience that is interesting, however, but the section that precedes the concluding portion of the article. In a conversation about "aboriginal Africa," Macaulay is brought up, and, writes Naipaul, "Later it occurred to me, for the first time, that Macaulay had not been disproved by the Indian Revolution. He had only been ignored. His statement can be reaffirmed more brutally today ... India is simple; the West grows wiser" (*The Overcrowded Barracoon*, p. 96). Naipaul's confidence in his referents by this stage in his career is also a measure of how deeply internalized the received assumptions of his explorations are, fully confirming Nandy's analysis. Nowhere is this more apparent than in the most pure fiction of his career, his next major novel, *A Bend in the River*. Before considering the novel, however, the publication in 1980 of another collection of his longer essays, *The Return of Eva Peron with The Killings in Trinidad*, offers some more useful insights into Naipaul's fully developed theses about the greater Third World.

THE RETURN OF EVA PERON WITH THE KILLINGS IN TRINIDAD (1980)

Even though this volume of collected essays appeared in the early 1980s, thus serving as a capstone to the prior decade's fictions and second-round travelogues, the individual essays that compose the volume appeared through the 1970s at much the same time as those same full-length publications. There is an obvious relationship that exists between the publications, especially between the essays "Michael X and the Killings in Trinidad" and *Guerrillas*, as well as "A New King for the Congo: Mobutu and the Nihilism of Africa" on the one hand,

and on the other, *A Bend in the River*. Additionally, the title
essay, "The Return of Eva Peron," is a further refinement of
this symbiosis in that it too is a collection within a collection of
articles, thus creating both a more global span to the now
established Naipaulian commentary, as well as an oasis of
self-referentiality where the last sections turn back to the first
for confirmation that its central thesis endures through time.
Finally, Naipaul's "Author's Note" acknowledges that the two
longer pieces "bridged a creative gap: from the end of 1970 to
the end of 1973 no novel offered itself to me. That perhaps
explains the intensity of some of the pieces, and their obses-
sional nature." He then continues, "The themes repeat,
whether in Argentina, Trinidad or the Congo. I can claim no
further unity for the pieces" (*The Return of Eva Peron*, no page).

The suggestion, of course, is that the realms of fiction and
non-fiction only differ in degree, are unified in a register more
aligned with responding to experience than to historical circumstances. That the themes repeat regardless of location and
history, therefore, is disingenuous rather than considered, for
Naipaul's examinations in the three regions continue to be
formulaic despite their intensity. Where "Gandhianism" in
India is essentialized as an ultimately vapid political rhetoric,
so Peronism in Argentina is reduced to an arbitrary program of
state misdirection. Similarly, Mobutu's "nihilism" is offered as
the key to understanding post-independent African politics,
while the hideousness of the crime committed by Michael X is
diagnosed as the symptom of the even bleaker disease of
liberalism's consequences. Intent on uncovering villains within
the ranks of Third World governing elites, Naipaul tends to
focus upon the process of political deification as though it were
the manifestation of the warped talent of only preternaturally
ignorant people, who, of course, overwhelmingly populate the
formally colonized world. In so doing, he asserts that the
difference between the north and the south is as much an
intellectually as an economically imbalanced one. Thus his
observation that "the social–intellectual diversions of the north
are transformed, in the less intellectually-stable south, into
horrible reality" (*The Return of Eva Peron*, p. 106), carries with

it a tone of unassailability simply because he believes that everything he encounters in the "south" is nothing but reactive.

As in *The Loss of El Dorado*, the essays in this volume all practice an almost arbitrary selectivity in what Naipaul chooses to focus on, and are then offered as synecdochal of the whole. As a result, while appearing to give an analysis of the current political status of the countries visited, he instead constructs a hugely partial synopsis of what appear to be their national features which he sees as varied confirmations of his own theses about flawed political endeavors that result from hubris and ignorance. "Attitudes," for example, are always a Naipaulian indicator. So, when Naipaul states that, "Magic is important in Argentina: the country is full of witches and magicians and thaumaturges and mediums," by way of then explaining that Argentinians function in a fictional realm, he does not seem to realize that an equivalent point could be made, say, about Nancy Reagan's astrologer and the mighty edifice of the "universal civilization" of the United States. What he calls the "diversions" of the north being translated into the "horrible reality" of the south, in other words, is not an astute comment upon the vicissitudes of metaphoricity, but an arrogant dismissal of the massive legacy of obstructionist economics that prevails in the Third World's forced relation with the industrialized north.

Naipaul also dismisses the vital fact that Argentina's relation to Europe, historically speaking, is with Spain as part of the Spanish American empire, and not Britain and its empire, despite their late nineteenth-century monetary and trading alliance. While this bias is finally redressed in two recent articles describing Argentina in the early 1990s,[10] the intervening two decades do not seem to have changed his mind much about the political viability of the nation. Indeed, Naipaul cites Conrad's *Heart of Darkness* with unwavering confidence to help explain a "missing moral idea" that, like the Belgians in Marlow's Congo, he feels the Argentine national idea still lacks: the recognition that "work" redeems the "idea" implicit in the "civilizing mission" of imperialism's spread.[11]

Not surprisingly, then, Naipaul also attributes this failure to an essentialized understanding of the "cruelty" of Spanish conquest, "that cruelty of the sixteenth-century, living on at the end of the twentieth," which continues to inform "the old Argentine-Spanish idea of blood, the enemy" ("The End of Peronism?", pp. 47–48). Nevertheless, Naipaul continues, recent signs of the abondonment of formally entrenched nationalist (Peronist) economic policies do herald the beginnings of a change in attitude, and conflicts such as the Malvinas/Falklands war, extraordinary inflation rates, and a sustained repetition of civil strife appear to have broken down a national delusion that the country was engaged in "revolution."

While this project of reassessment, more fully realized in *India: A Million Mutinies Now* (1990), displays a new spirit of receptivity to profound changes in the world order in the late twentieth century, Naipaul's return visits are still as deeply invested in validating his initial observations as they are in recording signs of change. In "Argentina: Living with Cruelty" (1992), for example, his account of being detained by police while traveling in the north, during the government's "dirty war" of the late 1970s, acknowledges the sublimation of the tension of that experience into the novel he was soon to write, *A Bend in the River* (1979). The practice of affective memory that is suggested here helps underscore the continued liminality of his constructions of the greater Third World. Thus, the essay "A New King for the Congo," when coupled with *A Bend in the River*, is subtly reinvested with a Naipaulian moment of near escape. "A New King for the Congo," therefore, can continue to be read by ignoring Zaire's point-zero situation in terms of a national personnel made ready for the transfer of power at independence. The nation's lack of preparedness is deliberately cast as a symptom of the Zairois' inadequacies rather than the willed aggression of Belgian colonial practice.[12] Not only does this contradict Naipaul's continued reference to *Heart of Darkness* and Marlow's indictment of Belgian colonial practices as a paradigm to help explain the consequences between Spanish imperial legacies and British varieties in Argentina, but it also cleverly allows Naipaul to reinscribe the sense of nationalist play-acting in *A Bend in the River*.

Historical facts and competing analyses aside, Naipaul's non-fiction at the time of the publication of *The Return of Eva Peron* is replete with a sense of awe and horror in its ability to see a dysfunctional pattern of human and political behavior. The observer's high ground from which he speaks therefore suggests that he has discerned a truth, the empirical evidence of which stands before his and his readers' eyes. It is appropriate, then, that the volume closes with the essay, "Conrad's Darkness," a piece that traces Naipaul's debt and divergence from his literary precursor. Inaugurating the autobiographical inflection that will come to full measure in the next decade, Naipaul's reflections are a mixture of literary critique and professional self-definition. Naipaul charts the imaginative formulation of his awareness of fiction through Conrad, which leads him to observe, "When art copies life, and life in its turn mimics art, a writer's originality can often be obscured" (*The Return of Eva Peron*, p. 233). Observations such as this speak directly to the nature of the investment that a writer such as Naipaul puts into the act of representation *after* having lost the faith that *what* is represented is the issue.

A BEND IN THE RIVER (1979)

In a sense, Naipaul has remained true to one aspect of his experience: the careful nurture of his "outsider's" status always translates into his fiction as characters who, for one reason or another, do not "belong." Like *Guerrillas*, *A Bend in the River*'s principal players have arrived at the scene of the action from elsewhere. They are either Asian (the generic term adopted for Indian subcontinental immigrants in East and Central Africa), European settlers and expatriates, members of distant groups (for Naipaul, "tribes"), or people of a mixed ancestry that denies them full status as any kind of "authentic" group member. Thus, even while this displacement has always been one of Naipaul's "themes," it also serves as a plot device that allows Naipaul to narrativize the events from the "outside," looking "in." Not only does this device lend itself to an often full exploration of existential questions, it also seems to give Naipaul's fiction the license of "experience" in the guise of "history." In other words, the political action of *A Bend in the River*, against which the characters are pitted, is only presented as a series of brutal but tangential developments witnessed but not participated in by the protagonist, Salim. Thus, the pitiless first-person voice actually functions with the veneer of a guarded neutrality normally associated with a *third*-person narrative. Thus, the events depicted impinge upon Salim's existence rather than emerge as an integral form of action consequent upon the character's participation. The political events of a postcolonial "Africa," therefore, appear to operate with the sinister force of a ghostly, disembodied specter of power imaged solely as a Conradian "immensity."

Thus, where *The Middle Passage* provided Naipaul with a non-fictional verification for his Caribbean fictions, *A Bend in the River* relies upon the 1975 essay, "A New King for the Congo: Mobutu and the Nihilism of Africa," as a "factual" base from which to establish a sense of historicity for the novel. Mobutu, for example, the "Big Man" of the novel, and his cult of self-aggrandizement which serves as the fulcrum of his "African authenticity" drive towards nationalization, is filtered through his chimeral reputation and the proliferation of his photographs in public places as well as the impact of his policies in the novel. In this way Naipaul's attempts to humanize him by referring to his lowly origins, his mother, and the patronage of Raymond the imported Belgian historian, is constantly undercut by the fabulist aura of a parodic but sinister political deification. The parallel development of Ferdinand as the evolving "new African man," furthermore, only serves to reinforce Naipaul's thesis of postcolonial mimicry rather than explicate an acceleration into modernity that the novel as a whole finds so astonishing. Already, as we have seen, "In a Free State" stands as an already articulated statement about a tightly constructed *composite* "African" postcolonial state. Consequently, Salim's origins in the coastal region of this adjacent

East African state, where political stability appears uncertain and arbitrary, draw upon the earlier work in its replication of the journey into the interior and the road blocks that litter Bobby's and Linda's trip. So it is Naipaul's own textual universe about "Africa," therefore, that is used to supplement, or, rather, further his already established theories about empire and its aftermath.

In an extraordinarily crafted fiction that uses the frame of recollection already developed in *The Mimic Men* to mask its amalgam of sources, *A Bend in the River* is Naipaul's most "pure" creation because of its very constructedness. His first-person narrator, for example, operates through a filter of disingenuousness and naiveté so embedded in his discourse that his overview of the events of his "African" life is always couched in the discoveries of his ignorance. That he first learns to "see" his home setting after dhows are depicted on a postage stamp manufactured in Britain is only the first acknowledgment of many that Salim makes about Europe's role in discovering the world for him. This perspective of an insight into how someone else views his familiar world is less a moment of defamiliarization than it is a wholesale adoption of Eurocentric frames of reference. His admiration for European books, mainly popular science magazines and children's encyclopedias, carries the residues of Mohun Biswas' romance with the Word, but in an unmediated, humorless, and less imaginative vein. Ultimately, it is the displacement of his own sense of cultural impoverishment onto his "African" setting that seems to rescue Salim from the repetitive cycle of "Africa's" metamorphoses. Perhaps the most persistent trope of Naipaul's image of Africa is related to *misreading* represented in the deliberate misquotation of Virgil used on the commemorative plaque at the Steamer service dock: "*Miscerique probat populus et feodera jungi*" (*A Bend in the River*, p. 62). Rather than disapproving of a mingling of the peoples of Rome and Africa, the gods in the new Africa now approve. While Salim is staggered by this adaptation, Naipaul leaves his readership either amused at the playful audacity, condescending towards the "error," alarmed at the blithe arrogance it may represent, or, one suspects, confirmed about the suspicion of Africa's mimicry.

The other image Naipaul employs to illustrate the aborted novelty of his version of Africa's postcolonial birthings is the water hyacinth which is gradually but relentlessly claiming the river for itself. As Salim explains, "The tall lilac-coloured flower had appeared only a few years before, and in the local language there was no word for it. The people still called it 'the new thing' or 'the new thing in the river,' and to them it was another enemy" (*A Bend in the River*, p. 46). Here, in addition to providing a symbol for the history of invasion and incursion of the region, the water hyacinth also stands as a kind of fluid border between the "old" Africa and the "new." Its particular beauty is an ironic counter to its self-seeding and self-perpetuating capability which carries with it an inevitability of complete takeover. The river dwellers' losing battle against the water hyacinth's spread also suggests the eventual entropy of their historical struggle. The plant's appropriation of the river echoes another, equally pernicious thesis about "Africans" that Naipaul uses the novel to explore. The Africans' "Africa," the "old" one, the plant imagery implies, belongs to an ill-equipped discursive realm, for the safe haven it represents in times of political upheaval only has recourse to a "magic" that is too self-contained and therefore inadequate for negotiating the events of the "new."

Zabeth, the river trader, epitomizes this incapability. Even though she is of the region, she too is an "outsider" in her setting because of her status as a medicine woman. Rather than acknowledge that her "powers" stem from a well-documented function, belief in her abilities is skeptically dismissed by Salim as a kind of "magic" that she and her adherents subscribe to. He rests his case with his discovery that it is the odoriferous potion she wears that keeps people at bay, and not some inexplicable power. While her difficult dugout route to the markets of her trade are accorded the admiration of the skill required to navigate it regularly, the acknowledgment is made only to be undercut by Salim's observation about the zero-growth of the trade's dividends. Thus, even though her request that Salim serve as patron or guardian to her son, Ferdinand, is depicted as the act of a shrewd and prescient mind preparing for the future and its changes, Zabeth displays no more than a passive acknowledgment of the futility of the endeavor, when Ferdinand's government career begins to become vulnerable to the volatile political climate of the times. Towards the end of the novel, for example, when Ferdinand is due to return as the commissioner, Zabeth's assessment of the Big Man's power and her son's ultimate powerlessness within its orbit is described by a clever melding of perspectival foci. Commenting on the presidential photographs, she uses a single-dimension reading of the spatial proportion his person commands in all newspaper pictures as evidence of his control. She then reveals that his emblematic stick is neither a fetish nor functional and finally attributes his political acumen to the white man who always goes ahead of him. Even though her analysis carries a symbolic truth, it does not suggest that she and all she is representative of can make the conceptual leap necessary to engage in challenging the situation or offer an alternative. It is as though her character is invested with a "natural" intelligence but not the discursive and analytical sophistication necessary to deal with the modern world.

Naipaul's attempt to represent an African point of view is an interesting comment on his criticism of Gandhi's failure to do so in his explanation of his politicization in South Africa. In *India: A Wounded Civilization* Naipaul responds to Gandhi's account as follows: "The adventure [of Gandhi's politicization] never ceased to be internal: so it comes out in the autobiography. And this explains the most remarkable omission in Gandhi's account of his twenty active years in South Africa: Africans ... they are the motive of a vow, and thereafter disappear" (*Wounded*, pp. 104–105). Similarly, Salim's dealings with Africans, including Metty, his sometime servant from the family compound on the east coast, appear as affected by but as unengaged with them as Naipaul saw Gandhi's to be. Rather than equate Salim with Gandhi, however, Naipaul's novel is actually more concerned with trying to offer an explanation or analysis of the state of Being and historical location of

African Asians, as emblems of a forced deracination, within the tightly played political turmoil of Africa's postcolonial emergence. It is as though Naipaul's novel is a confirmation rather than examination of the tenuous place and accommodation in the modern world of displaced Indians like himself. Africa, then, provides Naipaul with a setting within which he can further ascertain and develop his propositions about Third World collapse and, in particular, the political failure that cultural and "racial" disruption visits upon the world.

The canvas that Africa offers is at once fortuitous inasmuch as its demography reflects similar global migratory irruptions seen elsewhere in the former colonial world – such as the diasporic spread of subcontinental Indians – so that its setting provides Naipaul with what appears to be another testing ground for his theories. Added to this is that Africa's textual existence within European colonial discourses is far more singularly dense, though less extensive, than that of either the Caribbean or India. Conrad's *Heart of Darkness* is of course the most overt of Naipaul's intertextual engagements within this novel, but others include Virgil's *Aeneid*, Shakespeare's *The Tempest*, and studies such as the Belgian missionary and early colonial anthropologist Father Tempels' *Bantu Philosophy*.[13] This latter work, never referred to directly, but embodied nevertheless in the character of Father Huismans, who is the head of the *lycée*, serves as one of the subtexts of Salim's education. Tempels' romanticizing of "Bantu" systems of belief while also trying to establish a means with which to "open" it to Christian proselytizing represents a key moment in Europe's "anthropological" engagement with Africa. Salim's admiration for Huismans' appreciation of African religion and culture intuits the nature of Huismans' Tempelean engagement when he recognizes that the priest "was [not] concerned about Africans in any other way; he seemed indifferent to the state of the country." When the narrator continues, however, that "I envied him that indifference; and I thought after I left him that day, that his Africa, of bush and river, was different from mine. His Africa was a wonderful place, full of new things" (*A Bend in the River*, pp. 61–62), it becomes clearer that what Huismans introduces Salim to is the category of official "knowledge" where Salim's impressions and responses to his setting can find definition in the set paradigm of "History."

This development in Salim's "education" helps put into perspective his initial explanation of his own family's "relation" to Africa, which he describes as *attitudinal*:

Africa was my home, had been the home of my family for centuries. But we came from the east coast, and that made the difference. The coast was not truly African. It was an Arab–Indian–Persian– Portuguese place, and we who lived there were really people of the Indian Ocean. True Africa was at our back. Many miles of scrub or desert separated us from the upcountry people; we looked east to the lands with which we traded – Arabia, India, Persia. These were also the lands of our ancestors. But we could no longer say that we were Arabians, or Indians or Persians; when we compared ourselves with these people, we felt like people of Africa. (*A Bend in the River*, pp. 10–11)

Without using the term, Salim characterizes the East African coastal "Swahili" society as a Creole one, centered, again without mention, in the Omani Sultanate of Zanzibar. In broad descriptive terms this is the case; however, the implication of cultural homogeneity that Salim suggests is not. Even though he goes on to distinguish his family's "special" status, "My family was Muslim. But we were a special group . . . in our customs and attitudes we were closer to the Hindus of north-western India, from which we had originally come," he does not use the occasion to elaborate because, he states, the means to do so do not exist: "When we had come no one could tell me. We were not that kind of people . . . we seemed to have no means of gauging the passing of time. Neither my father nor my grandfather could put dates to their stories . . . the past was simply the past" (*A Bend in the River*, p. 11). Salim then credits his own reading "from books written by Europeans," as having provided him gradually with a sense of a *textual* rather than cultural context.

Perhaps because Africa is too vast and varied a continent to characterize as having been "shipwrecked," Naipaul instead invests his protagonist's language with another image with which to understand its relation to "History": "Without Europeans, I feel, all our past would have been washed away, like the scuff marks of fishermen on the beach outside our town." He then concludes, "All that had happened in the past was washed away; there was always only the present. It was as though, as a result of some disturbance in the heavens, the early morning light was always receding into the darkness, and men lived in a perpetual dawn" (*A Bend in the River*, p. 12). The echo here, of course, is of Hegel: "Africa proper, as far as History goes back, has remained – for all purposes of connection with the rest of the World – shut up ... the land of childhood, which lying beyond the day of self-conscious history, is enveloped in the dark mantle of Night."[14] Rather than shipwrecked, then, Salim's Africa, even in its postcolonial aspect is "still involved in the conditions of mere nature ... as on the threshold of the World's History" (Hegel, p. 99).

Against this backdrop, then, Naipaul can construct a universe within which the immigrant community of both Indian subcontinentals and European settlers as well as expatriates enact a Naipaulian version of a generic postcolonial experience. The diminution of cultural significance that characterizes these "outsiders," which constitutes the bulk of the detail in the novel, is offset by the studied distance that separates them from the Africans, who, whether back in their villages during political unrest, or in the town during a boom period, are always somehow just outside the action of the plot. And, perhaps because the place is Africa, origin of the Atlantic slave trade, and the major source of the subsequent peopling of the Caribbean, Naipaul, curiously, also grafts his already articulated slave depositions upon these players too. His version of *attitudes* bred by a slave past are lifted wholesale from his Caribbean reflections and forcibly imposed upon the history of Arab slave trading as well as the African interior's role in providing slaves for both the east and the west.

What I have outlined as Naipaul's broad canvas, nevertheless, is still crafted with the brilliance of his descriptive writing, where an acute eye for detail is executed within a tightly domestic and subjective world of the protagonist. The bulk of the novel is a combination of observed description and Salim's reflections upon it. Even as his journey to the interior is a version of Marlow's in *Heart of Darkness*, repeated by Metty when he arrives from the coast, it also serves as the narrative conduit that allows for the history of the Arab penetration to be acknowledged. In doing so, Naipaul not only allows his protagonist to chart his own personal history, but also to open the continent to an historical trajectory that connects it to Asia, thus balancing Conrad's imaginary realm by aligning it with the world-historical divisions Hegel recommends. The novel's first section, "The Second Rebellion," establishes both the Hegelian paradigm of Salim's understanding of Africa, as well as introducing a portrait of the first generation of postcolonialism's political and cultural refugees.

In the second section, "The New Domain," Salim is introduced into the prefabricated world of expatriates in Africa – "Europe in Africa." Ensconced as advisors and experts for the ruling regime, the community is dominated by Raymond, a Belgian Africanist whose academic credentials and friendship with the Big Man appear to place him at the drafting table of the new nation's political design. What quickly becomes apparent, and what would have been the object of satire in Naipaul's earlier fictions, is that Raymond, for all the respect he commands, expounds a dangerously sentimental and romantic thesis about African leadership that will eventually undermine his own position as well as allow the president to justify later his increasingly authoritarian rule. In addition to exposing the artificial and insecure role that a generation of expatriates played in several newly independent African countries, Naipaul is also reconfirming his thesis in *Guerrillas*, where he credits the importation of carelessly liberal ideas with helping to create political chaos.[15] The purpose Raymond serves in the novel, however, is more than just as the mouthpiece of received liberal attitudes. Rather, his failure also illustrates the efficacy of "the lie" that Salim identifies towards the beginning of the novel: "black men assuming the lies of white men. If it was Europe that gave us on the coast some idea

of our history, it was Europe, I feel, that also introduced us to
the lie . . . the Europeans could do one thing and say something
quite different; and they could act this way because they had
an idea of what they owed to their civilization" (*A Bend in the
River*, pp. 16–17). While appearing to lay part of the blame of
post-independence political turmoil upon the former colo-
nizers, Salim is actually endorsing Marlow's lie to Kurtz's
Intended.

Salim gains access to the world of the Domain only through
the introduction of Indar, his childhood friend and compatriot
from the coast. In *The Mystic Masseur* as well as *The Mimic Men*
the name "Indar" belongs to two characters who return to
Trinidad and Isabella after educations in England. Both discover that politics exists as one of the few pursuits available to
them, and they pursue it accordingly. In *A Bend in the River*,
however, Indar ostensibly does not have a country to return to
and instead finds he can gear his education towards returning
to a neigboring country as an intellectual. Naipaul's postcolonial intellectual, then, is offered both to contrast Salim's vision
of Africa as well as provide a demystification of the false hopes
of settlement that the idea of a European education offers to
characters in Salim's position. Indar's eventual casualty,
reported to Salim by Nazruddin's daughter, is conveyed as a
failure of imagination bred of not being able to overcome the
eventual existentialist crisis of his rootlessness. From the self-
assurance of having said to Salim "I exploit myself. I allow no
one to exploit me . . . I carry the world within me" (*A Bend in
the River*, p. 155) to the public knowledge that "it was time for
him to go home, to get away . . . 'From time to time that is all
he knows, that it is time for him to go home. There is some
dream village in his head'" (*A Bend in the River*, p. 244), Indar's
passage represents a bleak fulfillment of Naipaul's belief in
cultural atrophy.

While Indar functions as a kind of alter ego for Salim,
Mahesh and Shoba, together and each alone, supply a view of
the imperceptible but gradual degeneration of the narrator's
Asian community. As with the image of the water hyacinth
gradually covering the river, the reader is presented with a

portrait of a couple consumed by their narcissistic desperation. Their entrapment is less a foil for the narrator's sense of incarceration than it is emblematic of the complete disconnection with a functional context within which their presence in Africa can make any sense. Completely isolated in the end, Mahesh and Shoba's extreme dependency on each other arises from an experience of "Africa" as an historical space that disallows an interchange between character and context. Ultimately, then, the character of Salim is made to function as a litmus test for the efficacy of *personal* power in the face of Africa's seeming ability to resist "outsiders."

In examining a transfer of power from a state of dependency to one of "independence," therefore, Naipaul crafts personal encounters within the novel to serve as allegories. One of his repetitive frames for such encounters remains that of the master/slave relationship. Salim's position in relation to both Metty and Ferdinand is as former master turned benefactor for the one and patron for the other. Benign though these designations appear to be, Salim is only able to focus on them at those moments when each displays a resistance to the "duty" the relationship asks of them. The process whereby Metty settles into Salim's flat is characterized by the chores he agrees to perform, as well as by the information he begins to supply Salim as he becomes more a part of the local surroundings. Other than deducing its existence, Salim cannot concern himself with Metty's other life, and only Metty's "betrayal" at the end indicates the narrator's recognition of what Metty's bondage may have been. Meanwhile, Ferdinand's almost phantom-like metamorphoses from lost child into new African man is charted exclusively through Salim's bemused and sometimes irritable characterizations of his mimic-phases. The narrator follows these transformations closely only when he somewhat triumphantly matches his own knowledge or insights against Ferdinand's posturings as he goes through the *lycée* and university.

Africa as a textual/sexual site is simultaneously played out as well. Following *Guerrillas*, Naipaul seems impelled to depict the betrayal of postcolonial history in stylized scenes of sexual humiliation between men and women, or men and men, of different races. The particularity of the representation of Salim's affair with Raymond's wife, Yvette, is that it draws so self-consciously on the language ascribed to the colonizer and colonized. Until his first encounter with Yvette, for example, Salim tells us that, "my fantasies were brothel fantasies of conquest and degradation, with the woman as the willing victim, the accomplice in her own degradation. It was all I knew" (*A Bend in the River*, p. 174). What follows is a literalization of fantasy where the brothel and the imperial project are indistinguishable. The twist within Naipaul's allegory is that the white woman, Yvette, becomes an image of the conquerability of Africa, while the Indian Salim assumes all the anxieties and glee of the conquering European. "She was the experienced one," Salim declares "I was the beginner" (*A Bend in the River*, p. 176), thus rehearsing the colonial wonder with the hidden – erotic – historical experience that "Africa" represents.

That Yvette is Raymond's wife, who himself is the specter-like and expendable European authority of the Big Man, only confirms Salim's unquestioned deference towards Europe's part in discovering the world for him. Naipaul's narrator tells his story with the self-consciousness of a Marlow, but finally exits like a latter-day Kurtz, to take refuge in a union with his "Intended," the daughter of Nazruddin, who lives, of course, on Gloucester Road in London. By this stage in Naipaul's complicated relationship with Conrad as his literary precursor, the question which begs an answer is whether Naipaul is playing Marlow to Conrad's Kurtz, or, more disturbingly, whether Conrad is Marlow to Naipaul's Kurtz.

AMONG THE BELIEVERS (1981)

If Naipaul's reputation with a significant sector of the western and western-oriented literati had become one of an intrepid and brutally honest chronicler of the Third World, the publication of *Among the Believers* now stood as a kind of test for some and confirmation for others of his ability to also provide a comprehensive and rigorous assessment of a major and historically rooted global phenomenon shaping twentieth-century politics: Islam. Neither a country, nor an ideology, the "Islamic world" had for some time begun seriously to interfere with the tidy categories of First- and Third-World encounters, and the advent of the Iranian revolution only consolidated the growing chasm between a newly defined east and west. Capitalizing on a timeliness that the fast unfolding global events seemed to demand, Naipaul undertook an intense seven-month journey through Iran, Pakistan, Malaysia, and Indonesia. But, as one critic has pointed out, Naipaul's Islamic journey is neither inclusive nor comprehensive, and its selectivity is framed almost entirely by his own "range of interests" and established "ways of looking" (Weiss, *On the Margins*, p. 148). Nevertheless, during the course of his travels, American hostages were taken in Tehran, Afghanistan was overrun by the Soviet Union, and with the new influx of massive US aid in response to events in Afghanistan, Pakistan's martial rule of Zia-ul-Haq was solidified, and the program of Islamization initiated.

Continuing with the pattern of focusing upon the details of his personal encounters with hotel staff, guides, interpreters and his travels against the backdrop of larger political events, the travelogue has both a typical Naipaulian tenor and, because of the unfamiliarity of his terrain, a more exposed and therefore more openly sustained posturing of his traveling persona. Quick to set the Iranian revolution within an empirical context that reveals its ideological poverty, Naipaul's political analysis from the start undertakes to cast recent events into an accessible frame of reactive behaviors towards the west. In this way he introduces a single formula wherein each of his commentaries is posed as illustrative of how the regions traveled have turned to Islam, or some version of it, as the single panacea against their multiple failures with modernity. Rather than immediately casting twentieth-century Islam as a monolith, as much of the western media had begun to do by affixing the prefix, "fundamentalist," Naipaul starts by appearing to be a little more careful to distinguish between the major branches of the faith and their historical divergences. But, because of the magnitude of events in Iran, Shia Islam is accorded a special attention which gradually evolves into a referential frame which his analysis can draw upon. Attributing the rise of the Shiite faith to "political–racial" differences in the eighth century, the question of succession in the Caliphate, over which the Shiites broke away, offers itself as a modal instance of resistance to a prevailing hegemonic mode. Consequently, Naipaul's understanding of the historical origins of Shia Islam provides him with a central referent for Islam's resurgent function in its challenge to the west.

Early in the narrative, for example, Naipaul draws attention to a habit that he considers self-evidently absurd in its contradiction: his encounters with anti-western rhetoric even while the west's technological resources are being employed to voice this same resistance. From the telephone to Phantom fighters, the benefits of what Naipaul cites as the prevailing "universal civilization" remain the means whereby a resurgent Islam makes itself known. The calls for a return to a polity based upon the religion's "pure" time of either the Prophet's life, interpreted through various *hadith*, or its codification and institutionalization during the period of the first four Caliphs, the last of whom, Ali, the Shias pay obeisance to, are all exercises that Naipaul charts as historically capricious. The literalism that the Iranian clerics, the proposed Pakistani *sharia* courts, the proselytizing youth movements of Malaysia, and the Islamic educational programs of Indonesia all espouse are, in Naipaul's historical and political estimation, attempts to deny history but not the benefits of modernity. Or, rather, the benefits of modernity are not recognized as such, but are assumed to be the ground-base for re-establishing the past. That such a "past" never existed is Naipaul's basic proposition. Thus, even though he reads the willful and insistent denial of metaphoricity and history by adherents of a revealed religion as having given the designation "fundamentalist" a ferocious power, he is not persuaded by "fundamentalism's" inherent counter-hegemonic plea. In other words, he bypasses the opportunity to critique the masculinist/patriarchal thrust of these resurgent Islams' offering of a *unitary* coalescence as opposition to the social, cultural, and economic hegemony of the west.

In Iran, Naipaul's principal guide and interpreter has socialist leanings and represents those who viewed the revolution in secular terms and who were therefore still awaiting its eventual promise. That the guide's political connections, such as a leftist publication, and his nascent political party are systematically silenced during the span of Naipaul's travels becomes emblematic of the rapid consolidation and control the new force exercises. The culturally proscribed and socially repressive program which Naipaul traces from his observations and during a visit to the center of Islamic learning at Qom, strike him as replicating a high medieval orthodoxy that is by definition resistant to any mode of secularization. In this way, Naipaul's theories of empire allow him to acknowledge the imperial pasts of the Arabian, Persian, and Moghul expansions because he can also fix their respective civilizations in the time warp of a completed and dissipated cycle. While Islamic history meets his criteria of the rise and fall of political and economic creativity, the faith's intellectual obsolescence is now revealed by modernity. The new wealth of oil, and the post-colonial redefinition of cheap industrial and export labor are inadequate sources for the development of autochthonous political structures. Thus, according to Naipaul, the return to Islam is a defensive rather than participatory movement.

Naipaul arrives at this general formulation in a more tentative fashion than that of any of his other travelogues' pronouncements upon their respective terrains. As Peggy Nightingale has astutely observed, this is in part because of Naipaul's handicap with the languages of the countries he visits, and his subsequent dependence upon interpreters (Nightingale, *Journey through Darkness*, pp. 222–228). Consequently, he never seems able to penetrate beyond an observational level with any of the issues, concepts, or agendas he would like to engage in or raise. Unfamiliar languages as well as unfamiliar histories of colonialism and civilizations unrelated to the west's all conspire to force Naipaul to have recourse

in a writerly stance that records his individual encounters with
the precision of a diarist. He looks to the press, educational
institutions, official agencies, locally well-known writers, and
his guides and interpreters for insights. The result is a personal
odyssey, unlike his previous quests, for this Islamic journey
intrudes upon his sense of personal identification, a feature
hitherto essential to his previous investigations. While the
array of young men who guide him – Behzad in Iran, Masood
and Nusrat in Pakistan, Shafi in Malaysia, and Prasojo in
Indonesia – are all asked to provide autobiographical information that Naipaul starts to relate to his own, he is eventually
forced to leave them to speak for themselves as transitional
figures of a different era. It is Naipaul's generational difference
that fills the subtext of his interpreted and translated conversations.

That Naipaul encounters few women is immediately an
unspoken acknowledgment that Islamization is often synonymous with an institutionalized subjugation of women.[16] Each
of the encounters he does have reflects random confirmations of
an array of these restrictions upon women. Behzad's girlfriend,
whom Naipaul realizes is the reason for his guide's self-
censorship with him on the trip to Marshad, and thus the
indicator that his access is circumscribed, is elusive despite her
gestures of defiance on the train, when she leaves her socialist
pamphlet on the seat for all to see. She enters a novelistic realm
as Naipaul speculates on her slight deformity and Behzad's
protective but elliptical characterizations of her. Similarly, the
"Brave Girls" he interviews in Malaysia seem to inhabit a
universe consisting of a meld of passionate romance formulae
and their own disembodied relation to "Islamic" corporeal
prohibitions, such as whether a woman may show her feet in
public. The lady guide who is briefly assigned to Naipaul by
the Pakistan Information Service is equally ephemeral in her
allegiance to her dead husband and her almost fatalistic grasp
of her minority status. It is not coincidental, then, that she
should be his introduction, amidst his other conversations with
eventually elusive Pakistani contacts in Karachi, to the beleaguered Ahmadi community. A latter-day Islamic divergence

that reflects but is unrelated to the Shiite history of internal division and messianic deliverance, Ahmadis in Pakistan, somewhat like the Bahais in Iran, constitute a domestic religious minority whose persecution has been sanctioned by the state. Naipaul's curiosity about them, which leads him to seek out their headquarters, is stimulated by the fact that as a community, Ahmadis are heavily represented in professional, international, and intellectual fields.[17]

Revivalist Islam's deeply troubled relation to issues of gender, therefore, is unconsciously played out in Naipaul's pursuit of or non-premeditated encounters with members of migrant or minority groups in several of the countries visited. The Bahai traveling companion, Behzad the communist, the Indian Shia newspaper editor in Iran, Africans in Karachi, the female government official, the nomads of the north, the Shia doctor and his family and the Ahmadis in Pakistan; making sense of the ethnic and class stratifications between Malays and Chinese –almost as a game – with Shafi in Malaysia; and, finally, the odd quietude that descends on his appreciation of the complex but harmonious cultural hybridity that Indonesia still enjoys despite the brutal violence of its recent history: all these encounters and reflections are narrated with an uncertainty about whether Naipaul has found the key to their definition. The potential feminist critique that would have provided a theoretical frame for identifying the Islamic essentialism he seeks is therefore missed. Instead, he insistently employs "racial" and class divisions. Where his identification of class is classicist in its agrarian, pre-industrial, and urban categories, his "racial" demarcations are less safe. When, for example, so many of the people in Naipaul's journey appear to him to be of one or another racially "pure" stock, to the extent, indeed, that the nomads in northern Pakistan evoke near fantasies of the Aryan or "Caucasian" he uses his "racial eye" as a substitute for a cultural and political frame.

Among the Believers stands as a sort of personal interlude in Naipaul's career of discovering the world. In his search for "Islam on display," the people he encounters do not sit easily with the ideas he formulates, leaving him with a less than certain view about group identifications and ideological allegiances. While revivalist Islams can be dismissed for their intellectual intransigence and anachronistic orthodoxies, the amelioration that they nevertheless supply, on a scale that even Naipaul recognizes as profound, seems to suggest that more complexity exists in the world than his theories of empires is equipped to explain. As a result, Naipaul's ultimate recourse to his traveling persona, and the care the narrative takes in recreating the frustration of failed conversations as well as the pleasures of surprise revelations, leads him inevitably into a reinforced reliance upon his narrative facility and its now public subjectivity. Rather than having to will a separation between himself and his world, in other words, his encounters with "Islam" offer a resistance he chooses to ignore rather than contend with.[18]

CHAPTER 6

Right of abode

British citizens have the right of abode in the United Kingdom. No right of abode in the United Kingdom derives from the status, as British nationals, of British Dependent Territories citizens, British Nationals (Overseas), British Overseas citizens, British protected persons, and British subjects.
(from Item 2, "Notes," Passport of the United Kingdom of
Great Britain and Northern Ireland)

In *The Enigma of Arrival*, Naipaul's most autobiographically transparent working fiction, the first-person narrator recounts two occasions in his adult life as a writer when he fell seriously ill. The first malady precipitated a fever that was immediately reminiscent of childhood fevers in Trinidad, where the bodily senses of disorientation and heightened sensation were also associated with the comfort and security of being looked after and protected. The second, more serious affliction he associates with adulthood and intimations of mortality and as such its occurrence functions as a narrative indicator to one of the themes the novel constantly rehearses: mutability. It is the first illness, however, that of "battle fatigue," which obliquely acknowledges a more enduring closure. Manifested as recurring dreams where the narrator's head explodes, the condition is diagnosed as the stress of work: the work of writing and the work of travel. Part of what the novel documents, therefore, is the record of the narrator's life-long negotiation between his writing subject's dialectic of first- and third-person addresses, where the irruptions of postcolonial anxieties have revealed his pursuit of a unified subject to have been imaginary.

Not surprisingly, rather than achieving an equanimity brought about by the process of disalienation, the ramified self-consciousness that Naipaul's novel is the embodiment of is more in the nature of a rediscovery of the repressed where the constituted subject remains the same as it always was, only now its function is more clearly defined. It is the novel's writing itself, then, that is its proper focus, and its project of self-discovery as object lesson is less a topic than it is a realization of a narrative achievement. Like Salman Rushdie's narrator in his novel *Shame*, Naipaul's voice is at "a slight angle to reality,"[1] but where Rushdie's referent is the historically and problematically constituted nation of Pakistan, Naipaul's is the equally fraught composition of his own writing life. The genre of autobiography as a consequence immediately becomes a more complex undertaking than a formalist reflection on oneself or one's life, for it also includes the exercise of consolidating – through the claim of fiction – the narrative base of a life-in-writing that stands in lieu of or as a necessary alternative to belonging to a single already articulated cultural tradition.

The primary grounding of his cultural base at this stage of his career, then, is neither the old anxieties of the Caribbean and Indian amalgam of his origins nor the canon of an adopted Britain; instead, the need that, once fueled, his ambition has been unexpectedly met by the disappointment of its realization, wherein, of course, most enigmas and paradoxes are usually housed. Ramified disappointment, however, does not necessarily pose a danger when it is also understood that its consequences ultimately delineate the boundary between theory and practice, or, in Naipaul's words, "abstract education" and "experience." Thus the novel's quietly ironic allusive gestures to the tradition of *domestic* nineteenth- and twentieth-century British literature, stands in a relation of correspondence to its autobiographical origins in a colony. The existential crisis of an individuated postcolonialism that the narrator as a young man stumbled upon and nurtured, therefore, is precisely the material that produces the territory-as-metaphor so necessary to the development of an idiom that defines itself as unaligned to anything but itself. The displacement brought about by Naipaul's diasporic location, in other words, is no longer an unaccounted space in which a writer has to search for cultural bearings; this discovery – and its concomitant disappointment – is neatly encapsulated in the trope of arrival summed up in the novel's title. Thus Naipaul's most recent phase, starting with the publication of two essays under the title *Finding the Centre*, maintains a mood of confident reflection that replaces the registers of urgency and dismissal so characteristic of his work during the 1960s and 1970s.

FINDING THE CENTRE (1984)

The juxtaposition of Naipaul's new mood and his characteristic skepticism towards the greater Third World is nicely posed within and between the two essays in *Finding the Centre*. "Prologue to an Autobiography" and "The Crocodiles of Yamoussoukro" are, according to Naipaul, "about the process of writing. Both pieces seek in different ways to admit the reader to that process" (*Finding the Centre*, p. vii). The first is a much-quoted source for Naipaul's theory of writing where he recounts his own struggles with composition and retraces the genesis of the stories he considers his first viable attempts at fiction. The struggles are twofold: they constitute his first effort at drawing upon the life he thought he had left behind in Trinidad and which he had hitherto not understood as appropriate material; and the actual act of writing fiction demonstrably illustrates for him textuality's self-generating capability. The lesson, it seems, was the revelation that the relationship between writing and the experience that informs it is a far less reticulated one than he had supposed. By way of exemplification, then, he recounts the experience of seeking and finding the figure who served as a loose model for one of the early characters, Bogart, and in so doing provides a link between the impulse of his early fiction and his subsequent travel writing.

Similarly, while "The Crocodiles of Yamoussoukro" dwells deliberately upon the dissonance between Naipaul's anticipation about a francophone African nation and the situation he actually finds in the Ivory Coast, the essay is also almost indulgently preoccupied with describing its own methods of gathering information that have little if anything to do with informing him about the country visited. By his own declaration, he is more engaged by how his method affects his record of the setting and experience than in whether it is illuminating about the place. In this way, then, the two essays together offer an extraordinary testimony of Naipaul's swings between being able to elucidate a complex and involved process of representation and his inability, or reluctance, to distinguish between opinion and analysis. In an attempt to trace the development of his ambition, for example, "Prologue to an Autobiography" wends its way through a precise but nevertheless moving reconstruction of his father's role in nurturing a love and respect for reading and writing in his son. There is, however, nothing particularly benign about the paternalistic authority the younger Naipaul responds to; instead, it is in the interstices of their relationship – through witnessing and learning about the humiliations, disappointments, frustrations, and mental strains of the father – that Naipaul builds his allegiance towards his father's aspirations. Thus, after having established that the father's ambitions represent an aspiration equivalent to an unavailable Hindu brahmin ideal of the pundit and its attendant caste anxieties, Naipaul's assessment of his own career acknowledges with a limpid lucidity the source of his own desperation in his need to become a Writer.

The contrast with "The Crocodiles of Yamoussoukro" is all the more dramatic after this admission of transference that Naipaul makes, for his account of his sojourn in the Ivory Coast is more than what Nixon calls, "vintage, predictable Naipaulia"; (Nixon, p. 159) it borders upon parody. In attempting to use the trip to explain how and why he writes his travelogues, Naipaul's account is quickly transformed into a metatext where the careful foregrounding of his method, as well as an unabashed display of his travel persona, combine to produce not only a receding view of the country (where he focuses almost exclusively on the expatriate community, or local opportunists), but also an inexorable resurfacing of his most abiding formulae and clichés about postcolonial situations.

Because he encounters expatriates from the Caribbean, for instance, he cannot help but recycle his pat analyses of West Indian bourgoisie and racial mores; and when he addresses the possible function of the crocodiles on the grounds of the president's palace, he cannot help but resort to his theses about "magic." Then again, when pursuing an audience with a *féticheur*, a kind of seer, the unconscious bias of his own racial perception is never questioned:

I asked whether there would be any trouble because I was a foreigner. He said no; then he said yes. I was a Hindu, wasn't I? Hindus had a great reputation as magicians, and a *féticheur* might see me as a rival and try to hide things from me. It would be easier for a European, easier for someone like Philip, though Philip and I were the same color.

This last was an extraordinary thing to say; it was far from being true. But it was true for Djedje. He still had the tribal eye: people who were not Africans were simply people of another color. (*Finding the Centre*, p. 101)

Used as evidence that "Africans" do apparently operate with a different – the implication is "flawed" – sense of reality, this exchange is actually more illustrative of Naipaul's failure to recognize a particular social dynamic. Because the *féticheur* does not subscribe to Naipaul's "racial" distinctions, should not presuppose that the *féticheur* does not try to accommodate and even play upon its social register and its proclivities.

Even though he makes no pretense that his travels are conducted for anything other than the narrative exercises they demand and the personal income that this aspect of his career generates, the essay still functions within a parodic realm that undercuts its presumed status as "knowledge of the world." When explaining why he chose the Ivory Coast, for example, Naipaul's apparently random, almost arbitrary reasons immediately register as astonishingly, indeed embarrassingly, anachronistic. He cites a personal boyhood fantasy loosely tied to the romance of the notion of "France in Africa." While this acknowledgment of a boyhood fantasy is closely parallel to Conrad's, and Conrad's incorporation of it into Marlow's narrative towards the beginning of *Heart of Darkness*,[2] Naipaul fails to distinguish that Conrad's depiction of adolescent romanticism is one of his postulates about the aggression of the imperial imagination when faced by the absence of knowledge: only when that imagination ceases to be adolescent and is tempered by "restraint" can it hope to become a productive force. Thus, despite a tone of mild self-mockery, Naipaul's admission of fantasy immediately becomes the opportunity for a veritable litany of versions of imaginary Africas, Africas that proliferate dizzingly, but Africas that eventually dissolve behind a façade of modernity to be gradually exposed by Naipaul's unrelenting eye. By focusing only on what he sees, hears, and experiences from which to assess the Ivory Coast's development since independence, therefore, Naipaul represses what in Conrad is the development of the acquisition of "knowledge," by simply ignoring the larger historical perspective that would have provided a context for the economic and political history of the nation. Instead, Naipaul's account frames its observations of the Ivory Coast so that the events depicted appear to parody themselves because they seem to exist in as phantasmagoric a realm as a boy's fantasy world. From the elaborate monuments and tourist facilities to the earnest Afrocentric arguments of a "drummologist," the essay liberally grafts ideas developed in earlier essays onto its selective Ivory Coast setting to create a national portrait barely distinguishable from those that emerge from *The Middle Passage, The Overcrowded Barracoon*, and *The Return of Eva Peron*.

So while the two narratives are indeed about the process of writing, writing itself is not a topic that can rest as a topic alone. Offered as synecdochical of a generic "writing process," *Finding the Centre*'s narratives are pieces that profess to demonstrate how this particular writer arrives at, first, the intention he conceives – a "particular truth" – and then the new discoveries that he makes – "adding to his knowledge of the world" (*Finding the Centre*, pp. vii–viii). If this is the case, then a consequence that is not acknowledged in these prefatory statements, and not addressed within the essays themselves, is under what aegis Naipaul's "truths" and "knowledge of the world" are truths and knowledge at all. For Naipaul and many of his readers they obviously operate in and of themselves and in their relation to the role his work has played in discovering just those truths and just that knowledge for them. However, even while the essays tackle two different spheres of experience, their alliance in his overall design of "looking for the centre" actually brings into sharper relief a key narrative tactic of Naipaul's work which belies a comfortable acceptance of his stated intentions. Since the self-consciousness of the first-person address gives it the tenor of a third-person relation to itself, his deliberate moments of self-reflexivity, such as the writer reflecting upon his earlier work and the traveler explaining that place almost does not matter for the kinds of reflections and knowledge he seeks, create narrative universes that are dominated by a multiply refracted egocentrism. The issue is not simply whether Naipaul's subject is always directly or ultimately himself so much as to what end, for whom, and against what measure are his truths and his knowledge deemed significant enough to merit attention?

Questions about the *ethics* of Naipaul's representations of the greater Third World and, by extension, about the valorization of his ways of seeing, resurfaced with some energy among intellectual circles after the publication of *Among the Believers* and *Finding the Centre*. In an ongoing discussion about "Intellectuals in the Post-Colonial World,"[3] for example, Edward Said's assessment of Naipaul's position succinctly sums up a prevailing view among what can be loosely defined as the Left. While identifying the often unaccommodating reception that postcolonial intellectuals' ideas receive in both their home countries and in the metropoles, Said observes that:

The most attractive and immoral move, however, has been Naipaul's, who has allowed himself quite consciously to be turned into a witness for the Western prosecution. There are others like him who specialize in the thesis of what one of them has called self-inflicted wounds, which is to say that we "non-Whites" are the cause of all our problems, not the overly maligned imperialists. Two things need to be said about the small band whose standard bearer Naipaul has become ... in presenting themselves as members of courageous minorities in the Third World, they are in fact not interested at all in the Third World – which they never address ... their accounts of the

Indian darkness or the Arab predicament – is precisely what is weakest about it: with reference to the actualities it is ignorant, illiterate, and cliché-ridden. Naipaul's accounts of the Islamic, Latin American, African, Indian and Caribbean worlds *totally* ignore a massive infusion of critical scholarship about those regions in favor of the tritest, the cheapest and the easiest of colonial mythologies about wogs and darkies.[4]

While Said's indictment could be understood in solely ideological terms, especially within the debate about culpability,[5] it is in fact his observation about Naipaul's willful recourse to an overdetermined *personalization* of his views that exposes his work about the greater Third World to be irresponsible as long as it professes to be knowledgeable, or is granted an authority by others who profess it to be.

Whether Naipaul's work breaches a moral boundary in its elision of material analysis, or whether it meets an ethical standard in its personal testimony, questions of veracity and integrity have always dominated debates around his work. In a response to Said's condemnation, for example, Conor Cruise O'Brien's defense of Naipaul is illustrative. Claiming that Naipaul does not pander to western intellectuals, O'Brien points out that, "Naipaul is not a strident collector of injustices ... His principal concern is not with injustice, or justice, but with truth. He is not bothered as much by the prevalence of injustice as by the prevalence of untruth. He is deeply concerned with the rhetoric of those who address public issues. And he wishes that not only more Easterners but also more Westerners were concerned with the ethics of rhetoric" (O'Brien, *et al.* p. 68). O'Brien's substitution of "truth" for "justice," here, is key to understanding that these debates do not operate in a complacent plane of competing sophistries, but are crucially engaged in maintaining their respective holds on their assumptions of authority. For those who feel like Said, Naipaul has been deliberately elevated to a position he does not deserve; for others, Naipaul serves as the conscience of a humanistic enterprise that calls a spade a spade. O'Brien's view, for one, closely echoes one of Naipaul's when, in "Prologue to an Autobiography," while remembering the strength of the sentimentality of O. Henry stories combined with the pathos of their association in his mind with his father, he recalls that, "From the earliest stories and bits of stories my father had read to me, before the upheaval of the move, I had arrived at the conviction – the conviction that is at the root of so much human anguish and passion, and corrupts so many lives – that there was justice in the world" (*Finding the Centre*, p. 31). Both the tone and nature of this recollection carry with them the same kind of conviction for the current essay: that there is no justice in the world, and that to either look for it or its absence, and propagate its cause, it seems, is an impulsion bred of youth, naiveté, and groundless idealism. The writer's proper pursuit, Naipaul says he has learned, is truth; initially and ultimately a self-knowledge from which other knowledges can be acquired.

The issue, then, comes down to a question of social responsibility against, or in conjunction with, personal responsibility. It also comes down to different political inclinations as well as differences in conceiving what the political is. Since both function within the bounds of human responsibility, and within the realm of writing with the attendant complexities of representation and aesthetic forms, disagreements about the kind of writer Naipaul is are doomed to continue. It is probably more productive, then, to shift the focus back to the discursive exercises Naipaul repetitively practices in order to see how he himself has continued to couch his ideological affiliations deeply within his narratives' public and private spaces.

Naipaul's use of his own writing persona, mainly as a traveler in his non-fiction and in most of his fiction as narrators or characters whose backgrounds reflect colonial and postcolonial compositions similar to his own, has allowed him to invest the public expression of his works with the aura of a private, personalized, sometimes self-critical subjective presence. While this equation between the public and the private is a central dialectic of writing itself, Naipaul's particular conflation has been unusually intense, in part because his explorations have been almost exclusively into how a unique cultural phenomenon generated by modern European imperialisms finds its voice. He is his own best example, and so his life as a writer has necessarily been offered up for all to see. In this respect the autobiographical emphasis of his most recent decade of writing does carry with it the maturity of a realized goal and as such does stand up to the scrutiny of what its first promise was. *The Enigma of Arrival*, therefore, is a resolution, and its theme of mutability more an allegory than a conclusion. What its writing allows, it seems, is a release for Naipaul, not only into parts of the First World he had hitherto not deemed appropriate to his kinds of investigation, but also into a "state of mind" freed from its need to find any anchor other than itself.

THE ENIGMA OF ARRIVAL (1987)

"Prologue to an Autobiography" establishes the basis for the enterprise of *The Enigma of Arrival* because it necessarily presumes that the career of which it speaks has already assumed something of a canonical status that merits or can sustain such an inquiry into its composition. The thread of this presumption rests in the groundwork of his first major novel, *A House for Mr. Biswas*, but the subsequent self-exploratory aspects of the travelogues *The Middle Passage* and *An Area of Darkness* carry a resonance which later works such as *India: A Wounded Civilization* and "Conrad's Darkness" capitalize upon. In addition to this sustained preoccupation, the collective weight of his multiple publications, and the debate that his opinions generate between his diverse audience, all conspire to grant Naipaul a visibility commensurate with the importance, in literary studies, that now attaches to writing from former colonies, minorities within the metropoles, and late twentieth-century migratory spreads.

To have cast *The Enigma of Arrival* as a novel, therefore, allows Naipaul the license of fiction-making, most obviously manifest in the severe repression of personal details such as his marriage, but just as importantly in the illusion created that his life has indeed been like a book – a novel – of his own making. This makes *The Enigma of Arrival* Naipaul's most self-consciously modernist text. For example, its modernist moment surfaces when it becomes evident that the ideological and moral tension between an "ideal" and "experience" that Naipaul created for himself in the sharp polarities of his earlier work must now be redefined to accommodate his awakening to the knowledge that his idea of England was always an impossible one. This revelation is gradually developed in the formalism of the novel's self-reflexivity, where its self-referentiality and its intertexuality with both his own works and its English nineteenth- and early twentieth-century literary echoes, are all strategies that allow the act or art of writing to dominate all the intersecting themes. The "Writer's Life," as a result, takes on the character of an organism whose mutability is in its metamorphoses which, "book by book," eased him "into knowledge" (*Finding the Centre*, p. 34).

The novel reiterates its understanding of this graduation in the narrator's several reflections on decay. Close to the beginning of "Jack's Garden," for example, while surveying the driveway near his cottage, he makes the following observation:

and the taut lines of barbed wire made me feel, although the life of the valley was just beginning for me, that I was also in a way at the end of the thing I had come upon.
... But already I had grown to live with the idea that things changed; already I lived with the idea of decay. (I had always lived with this idea. It was like my curse: the idea, which I had had even as a child in Trinidad, that I had come into a world past its peak.) Already I lived with the idea of death, the idea, impossible for a young person to possess, to hold in his heart, that one's time on earth, one's life was a short thing. These ideas, of a world in decay, a world subject to constant change, and of the shortness of human life, made many things bearable. (*The Enigma of Arrival*, p. 23)

Where "decay" had once evoked a sense of regret at having missed something, "change" now assuages the disappointment with the knowledge that what he sought never existed. The catalogue of deaths that are subsequently announced during the entire course of the novel helps illustrate this cycle of mortality so that 200 pages later, the narrator can affirm, "I lived not with the idea of decay – that idea I quickly shed – so much as with the idea of change. I lived with the idea of

change, of flux, and learned, profoundly, not to grieve for it . . .
Decay implied an ideal, a perfection in the past" (*The Enigma
of Arrival*, p. 210). What appears to be a demythification of the
narrator's early imaginings about the British imperial past,
however, does not cancel their role in the shaping of his writing
career; instead, the "change, flux," of Britain's dismantled
empire is what allows for his current right of abode.

Divided into five sections, *The Enigma of Arrival* begins with
"Jack's Garden," which deals with the narrator's move and
settlement into a cottage in Wiltshire. As he acquaints himself
with his surroundings, the narrator also observes his various
neighbors and the way their lives begin to help define his daily
walks around the manor grounds and beyond. What is striking
about "Jack's Garden" is the overwhelming, indeed hugely
overdetermined, description of the environs. From meticulous,
detailed accounts of routes, pathways, clusters of vegetation,
views, panoramas, the relation of one habitation to the next, of
neighbors, bus rides, and passing traffic, the cumulative impact
of what is seen merges with the passage of time into an illustrative orchestration of one place undergoing the slow turn and
transformation of its seasonal cycles and, by extension, its
historical ones too. While this orchestration is underway,
Naipaul also undertakes a fascinating reconstruction of the
way his narrator slowly acclimatizes to a sense of local bearings
after having initially had to rely on art history and his linguistic and literary knowledge to provide reference for his new
setting. In doing so, the narrator casts himself as a stranger, a
foreigner in the Wiltshire countryside.

The close to the twelve-year period that the novel spans not
only qualifies the narrator as a resident, but it also roughly
encompasses the time it takes for a stranger's eye to be
replaced, not by that of the local, but by the eye of the newly
constituted social order. Thus, when one of the novel's discoveries turns out to be that, unnoticed by him, complementary material had been accumulating alongside the narrator's
thematic obsessions – what he calls "that great movement of
peoples . . . between all the continents," including the "flotsam
of Europe" into Britain – he is better able to place his own

presence in the English countryside as part of this larger, already defined historical phenomenon (*The Enigma of Arrival*, p. 141). The second section, "The Journey," therefore, engages in a dual rehearsal, that of his initial passage to the west when, unbeknownst to himself, he was already a sign of the end of empire, and his subsequent journey through his writings, the reflections upon which take him back to this same knowledge that he had not at first grasped. This duality of the narrator's life allows him to see the time present of the novel – his settlement in Wiltshire – as a second life, one that has come about through his recognition that settlement itself is as subject to change and as self-willed a state of being as was his "first" life as a colonial.

The narrator's first life, the one that reaches consciousness through its articulation in his novels, travelogues, and his history, is reproduced in "The Journey" through his diagnoses of the various neuroses that attended the writing of each. While providing fascinating "background" information to the composition of works that resemble Naipaul's major publications,[6] the retrospective gaze is also a device which he uses to make a comparative study between the nature of the insights of his earlier work and the present project underway. He begins by alluding to his title, which he stumbles upon in a book of paintings by Giorgio de Chirico, where one painting catches his eye by its title: "The Enigma of Arrival." That the picture was named by Apollinaire only adds to its appeal, for the poet's short life is immediately emblematic of the loss of promise. The story that comes to the narrator's mind, a parable about journeying in a vacuum, or a full circle, appears at this stage in the narrative as a link between the two lives he now understands himself to have lived. Where the second life, in the Wiltshire of "Jack's Garden," is documented as a developing perception of setting that grows to match the intimacy and familiarity of place already achieved in the first life, the dialectic of these two lives prepares the ground for the novel's other major theme: the end of empire.

"The Journey" ends while the narrator is writing a volume not unlike "Among the Believers." He uses the project as an excuse not to respond to a letter he has received from a woman who supervised the boarding house he stayed in during his first weeks in London as a student. His inability to respond serves as a marker of the distance the narrator has traveled. To a young colonial migrant in London for the first time, the woman, Angela, had represented an appeal and sophistication that was part of his introduction into the First World. Now, however, as a well-known writer who appears on television, the narrator's reluctance to reconnect with that life reveals the sensitivity he still harbors towards that era. Accordingly, just as Angela's memory must remain in the narrator's tidy archeology of his past, her letter now must become submerged under a pile of papers. What is more interesting about this anecdote, however, is that it is a class as well as a racial anxiety that is revealed. This becomes evident in the positioning of the anecodote rather than in its actual account. By serving as a transition between "The Journey" and the novel's following section, "Ivy," the class stratification among his neighbors that the narrator gradually discerns as part of his newly acquired familiarity with a late twentieth-century settler's England locks firmly into place. It allows "Ivy" to be an examination of post-imperial Britain through a pitching of the narrator's arrival – at middle age, at a late stage in his journey – against his landlord's declining health and fortunes.

That the owner of the manor upon whose grounds the narrator's cottage stands gives orders that no ivy on the property is to be disturbed, because he likes it, is as overdetermined an image as any Naipaul could invent. The parasitical plant not only supplies a comment on the anachronistic economics of a landed gentry and aristocracy, but its status within the iconography of class is also unparalleled. Nevertheless, "Ivy" is just as interested in examining another, more personal dynamic of empire. When the narrator is assured that he is free to roam the manor grounds, for instance, his initial forays are conducted with the tentativeness of an unsure trespasser, a visitor who is uncertain of his welcome despite assurances to the contrary. The feeling that disturbs the narrator's sense of welcome is the historical irony he reads into his entry, as a former colonial, into his landlord's domain, empire's very heart itself: "I was his opposite in every way, social, artistic, sexual. And considering that his family's fortune had grown, but enormously, with the spread of the empire in the nineteenth century, it might be said that an empire lay between us. This empire at the same time linked us ... But we were – or had started – at opposite ends of wealth, privilege, and in the hearts of different cultures" (*The Enigma of Arrival*, p. 191). Thus, all transactions between them take place through sightings, correspondence, messages, and gifts rather than a face-to-face encounter, so that Naipaul can extend his allusion to *Heart of Darkness* to accommodate his own modified Marlow to his landlord's Kurtz. Their relationship of landlord and tenant must express itself in a minuet of inverted imperial images.

Perhaps the best characterization of the narrator's relationship with his ailing landlord is Suleri's:

Each time the narrative focuses on the physical helplessness of the landlord as a synecdoche for imperial devolution, the narrator is somehow able to situate his own body as a racial presence in the text. This presence becomes increasingly strong in a directly oppositional relation to the landlord's disablement, and the postimperial narrator learns to acknowledge that his imperial counterpart is a secret sharer in his own progress toward bodily stability. (Suleri, "Naipaul's Arrival," p.171)

The new social order which he has learned to see himself a part of, in other words, has come about through a curious transfer of power, a rewriting of the imperial configuration. It is at this point in the novel that the fictional dimension slips into a comic mode. Whether Naipaul's actual landlord sent him samples of his poetry, fiction, and sketches or not, their rendering in the novel achieves a playful irony that tugs at the narrator's own career. The universalizing tendencies of the Hindu deities in the landlord's poetry and the African parable of a woman missionary harboring fantasies of sexual assault but ending by stewing in a pot allows the narrator to heavily invest his own parable with something resembling self-parody. Without adopting a parodic tone, the narrator concludes that:

This was the joke knowledge of the world the young boy of eighteen had arrived at; this was the knowledge (which would have appeared like sophistication) that had been fed by the manor and the grounds. And perhaps later knowledge had not gone beyond the joke: outside England and Europe, a fantasy Africa, a fantasy Peru or India or Malaya. (*The Enigma of Arrival*, p. 282)

Having already offered examples of his own juvenalia in "The Journey," the category of "joke knowledge" that he identifies as the enduring trace of imperial myth-making becomes the measure of the narrator's quality of distance his own graduation has effected within the same general theme. However, as Naipaul's rendering of the Ivory Coast in "The Crocodiles of Yamoussoukro" reminds us, a "joke knowledge" still informs his own work despite his identification of it in someone else's. As Suleri points out, "To have a 'joke knowledge' of the world is of course a double-edged issue, for if Naipaul obtains a certain quiet satisfaction about witnessing the imperial body placing itself in a cannibalistic pot and stewing in its own juices, he omits to take note of the fact that his postcolonial critics are quite willing to let him enter the canonical pot, and watch what happens to his body" (Suleri, "Naipaul's Arrival," p. 172). Suleri's observation is not merely a reference to critics hostile to Naipaul's representations, but is more crucially about the inflection within the "joke" that plays self-parody off against parody of the other. As though to create a buffer between his initiation into his landlord's "joke knowledge," then, Naipaul's narrator also focuses on two other figures in "Ivy": Pitton, the last of the gardeners, and Alan, the writer friend from London and a relation of the landlord.

Midway through the section, another writer friend, Tony, observes to the narrator that the impression and image of Pitton "proves something I've long held. People get to look like their employees" (*The Enigma of Arrival*, p. 230). Already introduced as someone who "was socially scrupulous, knowing how in England to look through both the caricature and the self-caricature," the narrator is nevertheless not convinced by Tony's thesis, preferring instead to see the latent mimicry between classes as a symbiosis bred by a militaristic hierarchy.

Pitton is the only member of the servant class who has this regimented obeisance and to the narrator it distinguishes him from the caretakers, the Phillipses, Bray the car-hire man, and the dead Jack. Thus what is compelling about him is his independence from a nostalgia for the grounds whose gradual decay he oversees, for his allegiance appears more abstract, more faithful to what his position allows him to do than to what it represents. The narrator's subsequent friendship with Pitton, such as it is and while it lasts, is also premised on the Wordsworthian status that the image of Pitton, as solitary, supplies. Even more so than Jack's father-in-law in "Jack's Garden" and Mr. Phillips' father in the next section, "Rooks," Pitton's solitariness becomes the occasion for the narrator's recollection of and reconnection with figures from his Trinidadian childhood and later travels in far-away places who also projected the same image. The potential for parody introduced by Tony, therefore, is abated in the narrator's own embrace of Pitton.

When Pitton is fired, the abrupt change to the narrator's routine is marked with the same irreversibility that all other records of change in the narrative note. Their final encounter on a street in Salisbury can only be described in terms of erasure, a willed forgetting that must eradicate a sense of the past: "One day in Salisbury, in that pedestrian shopping street where he had tried to fill me with his own panic, one day he saw me. And then – the new man – he didn't 'see' me" (*The Enigma of Arrival*, p. 284). Where the narrator's resistance to Angela's letter at the conclusion of "The Journey" bespoke his own panic at bridging the distance he had covered with such difficulty, Pitton's similar gesture of resistance denies any communion he had had with the narrator. The gesture acts as yet another kind of release for the narrator so that "Rooks," the penultimate section and "The Ceremony of Farewell," the novel's *envoi*, are each able to bring to a close the culmination of the inverted imperial theme. In order to accomplish this, the narrator finally offers a direct comparison between his journey as a writer and that of an English contemporary. Where the narrator has already documented his own corpus, Alan's remains unwritten. Likening Alan's adult ambition to that of the narrator's twenty-five years previously, Naipaul suggests that the elusiveness or repression of Alan's material lies in part with his historical location, that is, at the end of empire. Like his relative the landlord, Alan's writing block is described as an atrophied ambition, stuck at the point of its conception and corrupted by its failure to acknowledge the present.

Alan's death is attributed to an inner turmoil, a childhood trauma that figuratively accounts for his failure to achieve the necessary synthesis between his experience and ambition; his death also coincides with a larger, more diffuse changing of the guard at the manor as the old order of the narrator's familiarity begins to crumble. Mr. Phillips the caretaker dies; vagrants begin to appear; preparations are underway for the narrator's move to another location in the vicinity, where his renovations destroy an old lady's memories; itinerant workers are substitutes for the manor staff; the once independent Bray succumbs to a cultish spirituality; and the narrator falls ill only to recover and find middle age. The changing of the guard occurs without ceremony. The gift of the walking staff from the older Mr. Phillips provides the narrator with the symbol of the transfer of memory, whose power of course is to be the record of the present text. The full transfer, however, cannot be realized until the narrator is forced to reconnect with his own generative sources. Thus, finally, it is the news of his sister's sudden death in Trinidad that provides the final experience from which the writing of *The Enigma of Arrival* can begin.

In "The Ceremony of Farewell" the narrator finds solace in the answer, or confirmation, to his persistent query into the contours between the metaphor of decay and the philosophical category of change, of flux. Having already arrived at a preference for the concept of change, the issue of grief is understood by the purpose that change, not decay can suggest. The loss that grief tries to grapple with – be it of a fantasy of a "perfect time" such as the young writer sought on his first arrival, or of a person – is for the narrator finally personalized and therefore codified in his witness of the ceremonies attending his sister's funeral. Arriving in Trinidad days after the cremation, the narrator recreates the scene of his brother's arrival in time to stand over the last embers of the pyre. The scene almost replicates the earlier occasion of their father's death, when this same brother at the age of eight stood in lieu of his absent brother, the narrator, at their father's funeral pyre. The narrator's absence on these two occasions serves as an oblique reference to another of the novel's overtly autobiographical facts: its dedication to the memory of the author's brother, Shiva, who died while *The Enigma of Arrival* was being written. The novel itself, however, refers to the sister's death as the "real" one; the one needed within the internal design of the narrative to provide the link between death and generation.

Her death is "real" to the novel because she represents that part of the narrator's family which did not leave Trinidad. The ceremonies surrounding her death therefore also represent a cultural practice that has undergone a transformation not dissimilar to the one the narrator records with such faithfulness in Wiltshire. Listening to the pundit conduct the rituals, the narrator's description closely resembles Naipaul's early fictional versions of pundits in Trinidad, such as Ganesh in *The Mystic Masseur*; nevertheless, the practice of this Hinduism and its continued application within the community provides the narrator with his last elegiac note in a novel that has recorded so many deaths:

Sati's husband said, "I would like to see her again." His voice sounded whole; but there were tears in his eyes.

The pundit didn't give a straight reply. The Hindu idea of reincarnation, the idea of men being released from the cycle of rebirth after a series of good lives – if that was in the pundit's mind, it would have been too hard to pass on to people who were so grief-stricken.

Sati's son asked, "Will she come back?"

Sati's husband asked, "Will we be together again?"

The pundit said, "But you wouldn't know it is her." (*The Enigma of Arrival*, p. 349)

Reincarnation, however imperfectly it is described or interpreted by the pundit, nevertheless supplies Naipaul's narrator with the last conceptual link he needs to confirm his own continued regeneration as a writer.

A TURN IN THE SOUTH (1989)

Well towards the end of Naipaul's account of his journey
through the southeastern United States, he offers his readers an
editorial comment on travel writing and the particular constraints that writing about the United States imposes upon
those who try. Quite apart from a new and slightly odd
jauntiness of tone, Naipaul's observations are deliberately provocative, for they claim that the present task at hand requires a
different criterion of observation than that called for by less
familiar settings – such as Africa. The resistance to "casual
inspection" that the United States poses to its travelers has to
do with the familiarity, through the media, that a readership
already possesses. Settings such as Africa on the other hand
usually provide a foreign background against which the writer
can define himself. Naipaul's solution therefore has been to
pursue "themes" and, relying on "luck," to have imposed his
own focus as the accidents on the way have allowed him. But
readers familiar with any of Naipaul's other travel writing, the
chronologically most proximate being "The Crocodiles of
Yamoussoukro" and *Among the Believers*, are also familar with
the same place that "accident" is given in those works, and the
same struggle for "theme" they both exercise. *A Turn in the
South*, therefore, may be a smoother journey but is no less
charged with the writer's need to make his setting accommodate his persona.

Rather than prefacing this journey's account with his customary evocation of his Trinidadian background, *A Turn in the
South* distributes its associations with Naipaul's childhood and
his knowledge of Trinidad throughout the text. His childhood
in Trinidad, therefore, is one of the referents that allows him to
claim a thematic focus, which not only provides a comparative
basis for his reflections, but also a narrative continuity with
some of his other work, namely *The Middle Passage* and *The Loss
of El Dorado*. In an important review of *A Turn in the South*,
Arnold Rampersad also acknowledges that "the South ... does
represent some additional illumination of [Naipaul's] larger
mission to the Third World."[7] Thus, as Rob Nixon has argued,

A Turn in the South can rightly be read as the final volume in Naipaul's "slave society trilogy" (Nixon, *London Calling*, p. 166), so that his recorded anxiety about looking for his theme in the United States is not without its precedents. The volume starts with contacts with African Americans in New York and a trip to Harlem followed by a preliminary excursion to the home of one of his hosts, Howard, in North Carolina. It is here that Naipaul is provided with a schema that eventually serves as a ground plan for his subsequent investigation. While being shown the environs, southern demography is suddenly essentialized by Hetty, Howard's mother: "Black people there, black people there, white people there. Black people, black people, white people, black people. All this side black people, all this side white people. White people, white people, black people, white people" (*A Turn in the South*, p. 10). The litany, which is repeated twice more in the book, is in many ways the final truth the travelogue confirms, and the course the confirmation takes also defines quite plainly where the author's fascination lies: black people, black people, white people, white people, white people, and white people.

Naipaul of course is allowed his sympathies, and in the end his fascination with the "white" south does provide the most interesting material. The dichotomy that the southern United States has always presented is a fitting paradigm for his well-established obsessions with "race," historical memory, and cultural homogeneity, even though the First-World setting severely mutes his ordinarily cutting need to match these categories against their nationalist implications and uses. Questions about the "past," on both a personal and communal level, predominate in most of his interviews, which are further characterized by less editorial intervention and more direct quotation than in his previous travelogues. Perhaps in deference to his sense of his readers' familiarity, and from a sense of obligation towards the decorum of a liberal and "free" society, Naipaul begins his journey in search of truths about the "race issue," but his real pleasure of the trip is with "that other South – of order and faith, and music and melancholy" (*A Turn in the South*, p. 25). In Naipaul's analytical lexicon this becomes a journey from black to white; it need not have been, but the focus of the "race issue" as the only lens for his interviews with southern African Americans makes it so, and places his understanding within a white-dominant view of the south.[8] His early reflection in Atlanta, while still searching for an elusive "black elite," for example, equates black politics in the United States with "many black or backward or revolutionary countries," where the cult of leadership forecloses the possibility of anything but a derivative political action (*A Turn in the South*, p. 31). He stops at precisely the point where he could have begun, and lapses instead into extended, correctly representative queries of identity politics and orchestrated political action.

Even though Naipaul receives much of the information about racial identification among his black interviewees with a degree of personal identification – one Michael Lomax's account of being black in Brazil is close to Naipaul's account of the panic of being Indian in India in 1962 – he refuses to examine the political dimension of such a reaction – it seems to be understood – and is content instead to let the existentialist dilemma of cultural atrophy speak instead. Similarly, even though he grows to admire the black activist Hosea Williams and his organization, the Forsythe County incident, where protest marches had been organized to challenge an early-century ordinance against black residency, is rendered as exemplary of an obsolete political action despite the "human" faces of Williams and the pragmatic Forsythe County sheriff. It is not that Naipaul is carelessly dismissive; on the contrary, his ploy of transcribing, seemingly verbatim, huge portions of his interviews allows readers to assess many of the social actors' attitudes for themselves. Instead, it is in his newly constituted persona which apparently does not have to define itself anymore, that the measure of his "racial" perception reveals the depths of its sentimentalities about "black" capability and "white" achievement.

After having established the still-difficult status of civil rights in the contemporary setting of Atlanta, for instance, Naipaul moves to the circles of southern white aristocracy in Charleston,

South Carolina. It is only from there that he starts to offer an overview of the history of slavery, recreating a comparative base of Caribbean and American slave conditions from a tour of an old, newly renovated slave plantation. However, despite a foray into the ecomonic exigencies of the two systems, it is a chance encounter with someone with ancestral connections to a white claim to Trinidad that sparks Naipaul's immediate, self-authorized imagination. Recourse to his own, "white" history of Trinidad, *The Loss of El Dorado*, and his first travelogue, *The Middle Passage*, is taken, and his subsequent record of typically paternalistic attitudes towards blacks by his hosts, also helps to re-authorize Naipaul's already articulated views; that is, the rationalizations he records serve to set his own critique of slavery's irrationality into a sharp focus. The inscriptions of the Confederate Memorial in particular, with their complete repression of the fact of slavery, plus the renovated plantation house's absence of slave quarters, further offsets Naipaul's vantage point. But rather than offered with any customary condemnation of the irrational, his South Carolina excursion instead becomes the occasion for his discovery of the intensity with which white southerners nurture their imaginary past, despite its practice of slavery.

This intensity proves to be seductive to Naipaul. But before it finally culminates in Naipaul's uncharacteristic excited celebration of "rednecks" and "redneck culture" in Mississippi, and his meeting of minds with the poet John Applewhite in North Carolina, "the past as religion," encountered in South Carolina, has still to be screened through Naipaul's sightings of "the black experience." Accordingly, he is careful to meet as many spokespeople of the black experience as he can muster. After the still unsatisfactory interviews with politicians and activists in Atlanta, Naipaul looks for a sense of the past from a female preacher, a musician of spirituals, and a parole officer in Tallahassee, Florida, and, finally, with a trip to Tuskegee in Alabama. In the chapters entitled, "The Truce with Irrationality–I" and then "–II," Naipaul's encounters range from individualized portraits that are often moving personal histories, to a series of associational reflections that place "the black experience" within a heavily reticulated frame of his own dimly remembered encounters, as a child, with references to it. He attributes the difference of the historical experience of slavery between African Americans and Afro-Caribbeans to the escalation of sustained violence and brutality and segregation in the United States. Quoting from James Baldwin, Naipaul prefaces his two chapters with a suggestion that the African American past as such has yet to coalesce into a sustaining referential matrix, imaginary or otherwise, because the "reality" with which African Americans live – with which "to effect some sort of truce" – is still defined by the irrationality bred by slavery: the racism of today (*A Turn in the South*, p. 120).

Individual achievement rather than collective action, therefore, becomes his yardstick for assessing the African American south, and in Florida his three major interviews each illustrates personal battles won and workable compromises reached. However, the achievement that Naipaul reads into these struggles does not transcend the despair he also reads as part of the African American "reality," and ending the trip with a visit to a detention center, he momentarily evokes his dreadful thesis, from *The Loss of El Dorado*, of the slaves' inability to move beyond fantasy; but, in the United States, it is now "vacancy." While not exactly "blaming the victim," this attitude of ascribing "damage," more fully explored in *India: A Wounded Civilization*,[9] is a much-used and facile response to the still active and socially sanctioned brands of American racism. It also serves as an instance of the sophistry of looking for "truth" rather than "justice." Additionally, the observation provides a typical Naipaulian segue into the next chapter by suddenly quoting from Booker T. Washington: "We shall constitute one-third and more of the ignorance and crime of the South, or one-third of its intelligence and progress; we shall contribute one-third to the business and industrial prosperity of the South, or we shall prove a veritable body of death, stagnating, depressing . . . the body politic" (*A Turn in the South*, p. 135). By focusing on the rhetorical style favored by Washington, Naipaul's sudden invocation juxtaposes statements from the nineteenth century with accounts of a contemporary social situation, allowing him to suggest the realization of a self-fulfilling prophecy: spoken by a black leader himself.

Tuskegee, consequently, becomes the occasion for one of Naipaul's most novelistic ruminations. The grounds, the campus, the very elderly retainers and residents, and most importantly the associations with his own introduction to Booker T. Washington's *Up From Slavery*, all allow for a textual play between the symbols of the past, and symbols of the present. Does present dereliction belie past promise? Or, was it dialectically inevitable that from segregation would come integration, and hence present dereliction? An engagement with the underlying ideologies about "black uplift," therefore, is introduced when Naipaul refers to the well-publicized disagreements about vocational education for blacks between Washington and the young W.E.B. Du Bois at the turn of the century. By siding with Washington after dismissing Du Bois' lack of program in *The Souls of Black Folks*, and reducing the subsequent twists and turns of his unusually long career to his burial in, by Naipaul's estimation, a failing "independent" Ghana, Naipaul's added admiration of Washington's dexterous accommodation of his "reality" finally heralds a confirmation of a deterministic, even fatalistic prognosis about African Americans in the south. Little distinction is made between the late nineteenth century and the present time, nor does he mean to make one. Thus, when he travels to Mississippi, he sets out to look for the white point of view.

The last three chapters are the most self-expository despite the careful mapping of personal association and comparative information about the history of slavery in the western hemisphere that informs the first half of the book. Dutifully recording his last meetings with black Mississippians (one of whom is wearing a bath cap and has shaving cream on his face when he drops Naipaul off at his hotel), Naipaul leaves the black south behind when his search for the white point of view stumbles upon an explanation of rednecks. Naipaul's enthusiasm, sparked by his introduction to rednecks and redneck "culture," grows to dominate the rest of his journey. Part of the charm rednecks hold for him has to do with the embodiment of some fierce, individualistic pioneer spirit they insist upon and the subsequent class stratification their apparant indomitability helps maintain. Naipaul complements his new understanding of rednecks with a relatively detailed foray, through the ex-governor, into the needs to change the state's 1890 constitution, which, it seems, has helped Mississippi maintain its resistance to industrialization. While a stasis in social innovation has resulted, the discrepancies in financial parity with the rest of the region now need to be addressed. Through a cast of varied, and in themselves differently informed, informants, then, a steady investigation into the fundamentalist basis of southern churches, (throughout the journey God speaks directly to both blacks and whites), compels Naipaul to celebrate the sentiments and professions of collectivity and faith that he finds he so admires about Mississippi. His enthusiasm is such that even his comparisons with Shias and Islamic fundamentalists fail to remind him of the disdain similar protestations of faith evinced from him during his Islamic journey, *Among the Believers*.

After Mississippi, nevertheless, the trip to Nashville, Tennessee, leads Naipaul unaccountably, or perhaps logically, to delve into country music and examine the iconic status of one Elvis Presley. While few could argue with the magnitude of the Presley phenomenon, its ideological measure leaves little to explore if taken out of its "black" cultural context. So it is a little disappointing, especially during what purports to be an investigation into the foundation of a culture, when his reading of a Presley poster deifying the icon settles for a mild admonition: "Redneck fulfillment – socially pathetic on one level" (*A Turn in the South*, p. 225), and is willing to overlook the full, political implications of the social and cultural aggression it represents. Instead, he reads the adulation as an equivalent of Caribbean-style "black political adulation," even equating a performance at the Grand Ole Opry to "a tribal rite," conducted in a foreign language. What this analogy fails to capitalize on, despite his own observation that a class equivalent to the redneck could not have developed in the Caribbean, is that its race-consciousness is deployed for ends quite contrary to political enfranchisement. Ultimately, Naipaul is content to accept country music's valorization of the simplistic and the sentimental. The folk status he grants it, which of course is valid in itself, hardly satisfies a "search for truth." That it fulfills an entrenched nativist ideology seems to be its validation.

Further investigations in Tennessee take him to a Nissan assembly plant and an extended interview with Church of Christ members. The connection between automobile assembly plants and three different kinds of witness of fundamentalist faith is the change that they bring to the contours of redneck culture. Like the long and involved scrutiny of the permutation of "tradition" in *The Enigma of Arrival*, the tributaries that feed white southern sensibilities are read with a wistfulness for an era forced to adapt to differently constituted economic and political demands: more women in the workforce; secular education and new missionary agendas; the epiphany of faith that moves a pastor to succor Klaners after a career fighting racism. The return to Chapel Hill, North Carolina, in the last chapter "Smoke," seals the mood with which the previous chapter, "Sanctities," ended. And as a record of the journey's end, its sense of a return is much in keeping with Naipaul's habitual method of summing up: the measure of how an intervening trip has transformed the place and time of departure into the new awareness of arrival at its end.

Naipaul's sojourn with the poet James Applewhite, and his lesson in the special appeal of tobacco culture, with all its appropriate emblematic value of a hazardous narcotic supporting a now dying way of life, is symbolically very neat. It also allows a new contextual equanimity for more comparisons between Naipaul's past travels and the present one. Thus, in a long and detailed interview with an avid supporter of Jesse Helms, what could be, and usually is, dismissed as a brand of anachronistic fanaticism on the part of certain chapters of white southern Christian fundamentalists is reworked here into an appeal for the maintenance of universalist humanistic values in the face of modernity. And modernity, as Naipaul

allows his interviewee to infer, encompasses the social consequences of slavery and segregation, the "race issue." Again,
Naipaul mutes his nascent criticism with acceptance: "The
past transformed, lifted above the actual history, and given an
almost religious symbolism: political faith and religious faith
running into one ... But in this flat land of small fields and
small ruins there were also certain emotions that were too deep
for words" (*A Turn in the South*, p. 296).

The feeling and empathy that Naipaul can now express, at
the end of the journey, for Applewhite's poetry carries with it
the timbre of familiarity, of immersion, that bespeaks an affinity of understanding between Naipaul and a southern history,
connected as it is with a hitherto unlooked for and unacknowledged chapter of an older and larger colonial history. That his
amble through the south should have provided Naipaul with
this connection is only to his readers' benefit; that it should also
allow him to grant its internal contradiction a sanctity where
his explorations of other, commensurate if not equivalent,
histories did not, still begs questions.

INDIA: A MILLION MUTINIES NOW (1990)

Naipaul's third book about India is his longest in any genre
and his most extensive attempt to represent and accommodate
the greatest number of views about contemporary life in the
subcontinent. The scale of the book more or less meets the
agenda of Naipaul's introductory explanation about the
fruition of the nation's secular–democratic experiment. Even
while faced with sectarian and secessionist eruptions on many
fronts, he can still affirm:

The caste or group stability that Indians had, the more focussed view,
enabled them, while remaining whole themselves, to do work –
modest, improving things, rather than revolutionary things – in
conditions which to others might have seemed hopeless ... Many
thousands of people had worked like that over the years, without any
sense of personal drama, many millions: it had added up in the 40
years since independence to an immense national effort. (*Mutinies*,
pp. 8–9)[10]

This uncharacteristically positive affirmation is juxtaposed to the volume's other referential register, that of Naipaul's first visit to India in 1962 and the subsequent book recording that trip, *An Area of Darkness*. To help to account for the contrast between these two references, consequently, the more than five hundred pages of *India: A Million Mutinies Now* are densely studded with interview after interview, a veritable string of planned encounters which are each balanced with acutely, sometimes exquisitely, detailed descriptions of the interviews' settings, be they of past splendor or present squalor. The book's physical density matches in degree the density of *The Enigma of Arrival*, where description crossed the line between background and foreground; it lends *India: A Million Mutinies Now* an evocative visual appeal that is calibrated with the volume's auditory tone which, as in *A Turn in the South*, seems to be Naipaul's newly modified travel narrative mode. While retracing many of the areas traveled in *An Area of Darkness*, the present work also concerns itself with identifying the focal points in India's political landscape, points where sectarian concerns seem to be eating at the nation's secular edifice.

Having said as much, it also needs to be noted at the outset that *India: A Million Mutinies Now*'s length and massive record of detail in no way actually offers an historical or analytical overview or insight into the manifold complexities of India's present; it remains within the category of commentary identified by Ashis Nandy in *The Intimate Enemy*. The book's method of interviews, what Akeel Bilgrami calls "a very specific kind of phenomenology – a personal voice telling a personal but representative history,"[11] interspersed with Naipaul's descriptions and framing comments, instead reads more compellingly like a series of *family* histories. Offered as representative, especially those interviews conducted with people actively engaged in political dissent such as one Gurtej Singh's involvement with the events leading to the storming of the Golden Temple in the Punjab, the family stories ultimately reveal less about the larger political picture and much more about the curious but inevitable telescoping of time that two, sometimes three, remembered generations have experienced. Thus the more sympathetic attitude that Naipaul displays towards India, including the more or less optimistic conclusion about the country's future, is not enough of an adjustment to mitigate the still habitual recycling of his prejudices and the now muted arrogance of a particular kind of deliberate ignorance.[12]

The formula that Naipaul developed in *A Turn in the South*, where he more or less allowed his interviewees to speak for themselves, is further refined in this book. By appearing not to interfere, or by seeming to narrativize as little as possible but still blend reported and direct speech, the kind of authority he banks on is that of testimony where each witness not only vouches for his or her family history but also for himself and herself as its voice, its articulation. The "truth" that this method achieves is necessarily insular to the parameters of the *category* of knowledge under investigation or sought, in this case familial. Thus, *India: A Million Mutinies Now* cannot pass as either an historical inquiry or a political analysis of contemporary India. What it does accomplish and further illuminate are the extraordinary and differently manifested accelerations into modernity that individual families have experienced during the onset and development of India's nationhood.

Bombay is the first area visited, and it is the city's creativity with space that dominates all the interviews conducted and observations made. The sense of constriction coupled with the entrepreneurial fervor, be it legitimate as with the Jain stockbroker, or outlawed as with the gangster figures, combine to create an impression of density that amounts to a novelistic rendering of multitudinousness that India is fabled for. Rather than endorsing a cliché, Naipaul's first chapter manages to redraw and then repopulate an urban setting distinct unto itself. This becomes especially clear when his visit to Calcutta, in the fifth chapter, similarly evokes an urbanity charged with its own special spatial contours, but one which he also sees as "dying." The Bombay of the first chapter, however, is where he also begins his forays into the newly politicized communities expressing their "particularities" in organizations such as the Shiva Sena and the Dalit Panthers. The caste-enfranchisement and militant revivalist Hindu bases of these groups also serve as an introduction to the volume's other loosely connected theme: namely, a search for something like a Hindu essentialism.[13] Thus the chapter also includes a visit to the Muslim "ghetto" area of Mohammed Ali Road, where the miniature-like residential layout helps offset the proportional composition of a Hindu-dominated country, where a "minority" status necessarily helps define the secular urgencies of the polity.

Nevertheless, it is the brief, almost wholly transcribed personal history of Rajan, a secretary who remembers meeting Naipaul during his first trip in 1962, that sets the tone and inclination for the bulk of the volume. "The Secretary's Tale: Glimpses of the Indian Century," traces Rajan's grandfather's, father's, and his own career through the employment corridors of the late nineteenth century to the present as a continuum of a classed professionalization among Indians from British colonial institutions to their postcolonial adaptations. What is startling about Rajan's family story is its linear progression: "I started off as a secretary, and am still a secretary, and shall probably end as a secretary. I haven't risen beyond what my father and grandfather could rise to, at the beginning of the century" (*Mutinies*, p. 135); nevertheless, it also contains the story of regional migration initiated by British rule, and the survival of familial codes of responsibility within a tightly knit kinship communalism. The same pattern, with of course individual variations, is repeated in almost every subsequent life story that Naipaul elicits from his subjects, regardless of the ostensible reason for arranging the meetings.

Thus, whether the issues involved are the sectarian politics of caste- or fundamentalist-specific movements of the Tamil, Dravidian, or Shiv Sena groups, or the programmatic divisions of the communist movements of Bengal, or the separatist–secessionist Sikh campaigns, or the defensive–reactive Muslim response to its minority status and the idea of Pakistan and partition, Naipaul demands that all be refracted through the filter of family and life stories. The humanizing of larger historical events that this tactic in part allows still does not bring those larger events into a sharper focus, though most of the personal and familial dramas contain fascinating sociological information that in itself is illustrative of, but remains unprocessed as, cultural description. The assumption that Naipaul's modified method rests on remains his faith in the ability of *narrative*, once initiated, to almost magically transform the speakers' experiences and recollections into an authoritative *analysis* when framed by the interviewer's apparatus of asking the same questions of each. Thus the apparently democratizing impulsion of allowing a hundred flowers to bloom –to momentarily mangle a metaphor – declares an intention while simultaneously cutting the stems off at a uniform length. For example, in Mysore, after a long reconstruction of the life of the last maharaja's pundit and his service to the court, Naipaul expresses some fascination with the old man's mode of representation: "The story we had heard came out with much trouble; it had taken many hours . . . the story of his life and his service with the maharaja existed in his mind as a number of separate stories, separate little stories. He had never before, I think, made a connected narrative out of those little stories" (*Mutinies*, pp. 201–202). Naipaul then rounds out the chapter with a detailed physical desciption of the palace and its remains of past opulence. The description serves as a demonstration of the old man's powers of repression, where the singular selectivity of his recollection completely eliminated any representation of material facts. Naipaul's surprise suggests which narrative form meets his measure of complexity and "development."

Similarly, his frustration when interviewing two former Maoist rebels in Madras has less to do with the recitative, formulaic nature of their story about assassinating a landlord and more to do with his need to place them within a domesticated frame. When he states that "I didn't know what to make of what I had heard. There were so few word-pictures in what they had said, so few details," he needs to recycle one of his own theories of "primitive" peoples: "simple people . . . receiving messages simple enough for their capacities and needs." Having done so, he poses a question to fit this "simplicity" – about religion – and elicits a response that satisfies him: "The older man said they weren't religious, but their women were.

Though even the women had begun to do without brahmins in their ceremonies ... This sounded genuine. So, right at the end, I began to feel that the two men, whatever their relationship with the police, might have been what they said they had been" (*Mutinies*, pp. 278–279). It is difficult to ascertain what status Naipaul would have granted these men had he not asked the "right" question – paid police puppets to please an interviewer? The differences of narrative modes these small examples demonstrate serve as reminders of the premium Naipaul places on a specific tradition of narrative authority. The ability to articulate a connected narrative after all is the basis of his own discovery of writing's role in the process of self-realization; the necessary predicate of achieving knowledge.

The discrete layers of Naipaul's narrative, which function through the filter of translation, interpretation, direct and indirect speech, narrative description, and corroborative commentary, therefore, become the textual arena upon which the volume's other framing device exercises its connectedness. The references to Naipaul's first trip twenty-seven years prior to the present one not only allows him to measure in a somewhat superficial way the level of overall development and coalescence achieved in the country, but it also provides him with the opportunity to reconnect with the historical authorities of his apprenticeship as a traveler. His passage through Goa to Bangalore and Mylapore, for example, brings to mind the first of modern Europe's forays into India. The poet of Portugal's imperial heights, Camoens, is quoted for the fourth chapter's epigraph. The reference not only corroborates Naipaul's non-Indian eye viewing Indian ways, but it also helps him register Europe's longevity in the subcontinent. And what it also places in perspective, of course, is the relatively recent ascendency of Muslim power in a much older Hindu India. But it is with greater emphasis that Naipaul introduces the writings of one William Howard Russell, a foreign correspondent for *The Times* of London during the nineteenth century. In one of the very few moments when Naipaul's ongoing narrative voice interrupts its immediate progression from place to place and interview to interview, he alludes to his return to England and his reintroduction to Russell's book, *My Diary in India in the Year 1858–9*. One of a legion of works recording eye-witness and other kinds of accounts of the 1857 "Mutiny," Russell's narrative had, in the past, proved difficult for Naipaul to read. It only becomes accessible to him after his own visit to the sites of Lucknow. The avenues of Naipaul's new accessibility are interesting: Russell's dispassionate and Victorian–complacent account of the massacre and looting of the Muslim strongholds in Lucknow opens a channel of empathy he feels towards the sense of historical loss one of his Muslim interviewees in Lucknow, Rashid, expresses; the proximity of place and time of Russell's travels to the region from which Naipaul's own ancestors migrated to Trinidad gives him a sharp jolt of unmediated, direct personal association with the events described. Thus Russell, from the articulation of his nineteenth-century British perspective on Indian affairs, enables a coalition of response between the Trinidadian Hindu Naipaul and the Shia Muslim Rashid. It is a coalition similar to the "human association" that British rule in India ironically engendered among India's disparate and competing groups, leading of course to India's (and Pakistan's) realization of national independence (*Mutinies*, pp. 392–395). While there is a general historical truth to colonialism's role in creating twentieth-century nationalisms, a far greater variety of analytical tools are required to read their subsequent developments and fractures.

For Naipaul, however, this dialogically wrought chapter in an Indian negotiation with the legacy of British rule in which he finds he is a participant is not a nationalistic one. Instead, the historical humiliation that touches his own murmuring group feeling is sublimated into another kind of "human association." Offering a quick synopsis of the philological breakthroughs in the late eighteenth century of the Orientalist scholar Sir William Jones, Naipaul pledges his debt to the circuitous path whereby Jones' work with Sanskrit texts ultimately played a key role in a wider Indian access to its own cultural wealth. In Naipaul's formulation these historical vicissitudes contained a perilous alternative had they not developed as they did:

It fills me with old nerves to contemplate Indian history, to see (perhaps with a depressive's exaggeration, or a far-away colonial's exaggeration) how close we were to cultural destitution, and to wonder at the many accidents which brought us to the concepts – of law and freedom and wide human association – which give men self-awareness and strength, the accidents which have brought us to the point where we can in a way meet William Howard Russell, even in those "impressions made on my senses by the externals of things," not with equality – time cannot be bent in that way – but with something like lucidity. (*Mutinies*, pp. 398–399)

With a sudden flash of emotive weightedness characteristic of Naipaul's non-fictional persona, this gesture, or appeal towards *lucidity* reveals again his perpetual need of a dialogic network that can position him in a direct, almost face-to-face encounter with players in the nineteenth- and twentieth-century colonial and nationalist orchestration of his diasporic dispersion. Thus he can only arrive at this moment by forming a series of novelistic spatial, temporal, and intellectual connections: the span of Russell's long career covering the nineteenth century's wars is a symbolic link between Sir William Jones and Gandhi. The former validated the base civilization, the latter made it face modernity; the intermediary, Russell, represents the brute record of the height of British rule that created the dialectic in the first place. It is not history that Naipaul addresses, but rather the role that figures like Russell were able to fill in the documentation of a process that was larger than any one person or any one people.

This interlude in Naipaul's narrative is actually a prelude to a chapter about a woman's magazine, entitled "Woman's Era." The connection is of course a textual one, and rather than even approaching anything resembling a feminist analysis or an investigation into women's issues, it instead describes a male-edited, and -centered, helpful-hints-and-fables tabloid for lower-class working women to more easily participate in maintaining the status quo. The loose, non-comprehensive survey of publications for women is soon superseded by Naipaul's fascination for *The Woman's Era*'s editor, and his ideological contradictions and love of printing. The juxtaposition of the chapter's opening reconciliation with the imperialist journalism of Russell coupled with its celebration of British Indian scholarship, and this example of contemporary Indian journalism, is stark, but it also heralds a dropping away of the narrative's preoccupation with finding India's past in its present. The penultimate chapter, set in the Punjab amidst Sikh agitation, resembles Naipaul's political journalism of an earlier time. The personal stories of the various social actors remain personal, despite the brutal cast of recent events. So Naipaul's close to essentialist conclusion comes as no surprise. His return to Kashmir, which makes no mention at all of its internal political turmoil, is a deliberately anti-climactic reunion with the hotel and staff of his 1962 visit, and nicely subverts the temptation to create a nineteenth-century narrative resolution. The final reported scene in the book is of a Bombay movie set's slums being dismantled. It is Naipaul's last acknowledgment to the powers of repression of a people whose overwhelming reality, he believes, has again become the source of their now active imaginations.

The optimism of Naipaul's final prognosis for India is a somewhat welcome contrast to the sense of depletion and frustration that characterized both *An Area of Darkness* and *India: A Wounded Civilization*. While Naipaul's Latin America seems to be undergoing something of a reassessment, or at least an updated look, his Africa, as well as his Caribbean have undergone a revised scrutiny that seeks to accommodate or look for the distance the regions have traveled since he first formulated his theories about mimic men and half-made societies. But it remains to be seen whether any equation between his indictments of "fundamentalist" Islams and his subsequent encounters with "fundamentalist" Christianities and Hinduisms will ever be made.[14] But the change of heart or broader view he seems to exercise now is in many ways only a modification of his terms. The "Universal Civilization" of his new optimism can still be traced in part to his continuing engagement with the imperial theme, whose aftermath he no longer sees as simply decayed but rather as the rich fodder of his own incarnation. Thus *The Enigma of Arrival*'s renegotiation with the anxiety of a Conradian influence, coupled with the Forsterian reconnections in *India: A Million Mutinies Now*, strongly suggest the arch but ongoing reissuance of Naipaul's first- and third-person addresses, which *A Way in the World* (1994) continues to confirm.

CHAPTER 7

One way

> There was no ship of antique shape now to take us back.
> We had come out of the nightmare; and there was
> nowhere else to go.
>
> (V.S. Naipaul, *The Enigma of Arrival*)

Just prior to the publication of *India: A Million Mutinies Now*,
Naipaul spoke at the Manhattan Institute in New York. The
talk, entitled "Our Universal Civilization," partially diluted
the response that the longer publication was to enjoy: acknowledgment of Naipaul's more receptive view of a world and a
country hitherto criticized for its failure with modernity. The
title of Naipaul's address, we are told, issued from the questions
posed to him by a fellow of the Institute: "Are we – are communities – as strong only as our beliefs? Is it enough for beliefs or
an ethical view to be passionately held? Does the passion give
validity to the ethics? Are beliefs or ethical views arbitrary, or
do they represent something essential in the cultures where
they flourish?" ("Our Universal Civilization," p. 22). Understanding the rhetorical inflection in how these issues were
offered, Naipaul states that he "couldn't share the pessimism
implied by the questions ... that the very pessimism of the
questions, and their philosophical diffidence, defined the
strength of the civilization out of which it issued" ("Our
Universal Civilization," p. 22). Hence, Naipaul goes on to
explain, the civilization which can accommodate the boundaries of another's intransigence is the one that can claim
universality.

Naipaul starts to illustrate the "strength" of this civilization
by comparing its capacity for accommodation with that of

another, less elastic view of the world. He cites an encounter in Java with a young poet who is helpless in the face of his "culture's" belief in its already-achieved completeness, which makes mute any attempt to enrich itself beyond the achievements of its ancient, sacred texts. The young poet, therefore, exists in a vacuum between "ancient tradition" and modernity; a cultural vacuum that Naipaul can identify with since it resembles the conditions of the world into which he was born. His subsequent negotiation from what he calls the "periphery, the margin" – the stasis of an ancient identification – to the "center" – of a self-exploratory and self-conscious habit of inquiry, is marked by Naipaul's ambition to be a Writer and the journey that was required to find the "cultural" territory that allowed a writer's "sensibility" to flourish. The collective pronoun, "Our," therefore, becomes the measure whereby Naipaul's achievement illustrates the *inclusiveness* of such a civilization's compass, thus addressing his interlocuter's pessimism, and the Javanese poet's dilemma.

Only during his encounters in the non-Arab Islamic world, Naipaul continues, did his formulation of this universal civilization begin to take shape. The area of his research for *Among the Believers*, therefore, is the territory that Naipaul revisits for the bulk of the essay, obliquely suggesting that "return," as in *India: A Million Mutinies Now* and *A Way in the World*, is the logical textual space that now replaces his long agenda of travel and discovery. Rather than just an historical landscape upon which cultural encrustations are embedded, the territories Naipaul now seems to be charting are more overtly the intellectual spheres of the *ideas* that appear to have governed the world and which Naipaul's investigations have exposed in their variety. In "Our Universal Civilization" the secular and the sacred are pitted against one another, with the "fundamentalist" Islamic world appearing as the intransigence that resists modernity because it resists the secular. Naipaul goes on to attribute the historical causes for this "Philosophical hysteria" to the double colonization enacted on the non-Arab Islamic world: that of the Arab faith and that of a mercantile Europe. Being "doubly colonized," such people are "doubly removed from themselves." The Islamic faith, furthermore, "abolished the past," because "To possess the faith was to possess the only truth" ("Our Universal Civilization," pp. 23–24).

What is unsettling in this formulation is Naipaul's extra-ordinary selectivity and reductionism. His isolation of the "Islamic" world to an array of politicized agendas of dictatorial leaders mobilizing disenfranchised populaces, and his reduction of Islamic monotheism to a fixed category ignores the lessons of the historical processes – including colonialism – that allowed for a secularization of Christianity in the seventeenth and eighteenth centuries. Consequently, his reification of the Enlightenment's near-deification of rationality[1] – a philosophical formulation essential to the secularization of Faith – itself abolishes the recent past and its economic divisions of the world that would help explain why the current posture of "our universal civilization" may have engendered a counter-hegemonic stance. The apparent contradiction that Naipaul's personal celebration tries to side-step is clearly explored in the intellectual question exposed by the *fatwa* condemning Salman Rushdie and his novel, *The Satanic Verses* (1989). Gayatri Spivak outlines the complexity enjoined when such a debate is taken out of the easy binarisms of secularism/fundamentalism, and freedom of speech/terrorism:

We can sometimes be released from the claustrophobia of the post-Enlightenment bunker if we acknowledge that we also want to be snug in it. What is punishment is also nourishment. It is only then that we can sense that the spectacular promise of democracy – those rational abstractions coded as Human Rights – is desirable precisely because those abstractions can be used as alibis to deflect critique. In fact, it is only then that we can begin to suspect that the ethical, without which any hope for civil society or social justice must crumble, and which must therefore remain eminently desirable, bases itself upon what might be the lowest common denominator of being human, objectivity, and the universal, and yet *must* code itself as the highest. *Neither* radical alterity *nor* universal ipseity is an unquestionable value.[2]

Where it could be argued that both Spivak and Naipaul arrive at roughly the same space – a desire for an inclusive participation of the human – their paths not only differ, but in their difference radically diverge. The point is that Naipaul still seems content to divide the world into essentialized categories that pay lip-service to historical factors, and he still achieves this by offering his personal and familial odyssey as an historical exception rather than the rule. He is able to do this by not sufficiently differentiating between the postcolonial categories he has himself claimed, such as migrant, exile, refugee, displaced, homeless, cosmopolitan, and rootless. Even his exercise of "return" still seems premised on the belief that what he must look for are "attitudes" rather than the circumstances that dictate historical, political, social, and cultural changes. For example, if the two essays on Argentina, "Argentina: Living with Cruelty" and "The End of Peronism?" published in 1992, do suggest that Naipaul's new agenda has already begun a reassessment of Latin America, then the earlier piece, "A Handful of Dust: Return to Guiana," which appeared a year earlier, may serve as the initial indicator of the kind of rediscovery he seeks. Where *India: A Million Mutinies Now* still constitutes his most dramatic move from pessimism to optimism, Naipaul's reference to Evelyn Waugh's *A Handful of Dust* (1934) in his 1991 essay nevertheless heralds another kind of return. The allusion is qickly dealt with and is used to serve as the ironic literary model for Cheddi Jagan, the current as well as the once and future premier of Guyana. In the same way that Waugh's hero is captured and forced to read aloud from Dickens again and again, so, Naipaul suggests, has Jagan's political life recycled its marxism until it has lost all dealings with reality. Rather than merely unkind, however, Naipaul's update is more focused on trying to read the Jagans as curious survivors of an obsolescent ideology that now, thirty years after his first visit, recorded in *The Middle Passage*, falls more clearly into the fully articulated understanding he has of postcolonial casualty.

Nevertheless, the essay is also interested in reaffirming the categories of analysis that Naipaul was beginning to formulate, in 1960, during his travels for *The Middle Passage*. Rather than acknowledge the obsolescence of his own referents at that time – his Victorians – Naipaul instead recalls that:

As a political observer I was uncertain and diffident. I thought that in this kind of writing I had to take people on trust. I cast aside – as belonging to another form – my novelist's doubts. So in my book I wrote more romantically than I actually felt about the African or black racial movement of the late 1950s. I allowed myself to see it as it was presented to me, as a kind of redemption. I supressed my fears about its glibness and sentimentality, and its element of viciousness. ("A Handful of Dust," p. 16)

In addition to surprising many readers that his assessment of black movements were self-censored, this recollection also contains another kind of reaffirmation. Naipaul credits his younger self with a "diffidence" akin to the diffidence of his interlocutor from the Manhattan Institute, a philosophical stance that he cites as the sign of strength of the "universal civilization" he now sees himself to have been embracing. And finally, as he provides a survey of Guyanese policy over the last thirty years, he directly implies that the migration of a third of the population, the Jonestown horror, and the nation's failed economy are all home-grown consequences rather than factors necessarily linked to larger economic and political developments.

While Naipaul credits Jagan with both integrity and lucidity – though politically anachronistic – he nevertheless understands the Guyanese failure as also having been a failure of literacy. Reporting a conversation with a Guyanese poet, Martin Carter, he concurs that "socialism" in the local context remained "somewhere between ... pidgin ... and the vague set phrases of Marxist lore" ("A Handful of Dust," p. 16). Naipaul's measure of failure, ultimately, then, still lies with the levels of literacy achieved, where misreadings and the absence of a literary imagination and a tradition of inquiry remain the chasms that separate one world from another. Thus the Peronism of the two later essays is seen to have been an ideological smoke screen for the practice of "cruelty" initiated with Spanish rule; Borges' Argentina belongs to the imaginary; Naipaul's brief detention in the north of the country generates emotions and responses his fiction can only accommodate in his own imaginary Africa. Similar fixations haunt Naipaul's most recent publication, a novel or "sequence" or "work of the imagination"[3] that not only revisits earlier texts, but also attempts to reiterate the centrality of Naipaul's literate participation in his constructions of both historical and contemporary human affairs.

The flurry of review and publicity activity that customarily accompanies the publication of a new book by Naipaul, has, with *A Way in the World*, also been coupled with a longer than usual interview with him in the *New Yorker*.[4] In it, Stephen Schiff attributes some extraordinarily self-authenticating statements to Naipaul, including his response to his detractors, "How can I be concerned about people who don't like my work? ... I don't *read* these things ... I'm nervous about being made self-conscious. I've got to remain pure. You've got to move on to the next piece of work in a pure spirit." Naipaul follows with a formula that could be called cultural introspection that he claims has allowed him "a higher global understanding of things" ("The Ultimate Exile," p. 62). Secondly, when further challenged with the possibility that his latest publication could be read as a response to "some of his critics' accusations," Naipaul, after dismissing the question again, states that "The thing is, I am not a simple man. I have an interesting mind, a very analytical mind. And what I say tends to be interesting. And also very true. I can't lie. I can't serve a cause. I've never served a cause. A cause always corrupts" ("The Ultimate Exile," p. 62). These two statements, about "purity" and "truth," suggest the talismanic nature of Naipaul's writing anxieties which have long shielded him from any interference to his claims for a *personal* authority. Thus, when the interview concludes with Naipaul's much-repeated reiteration of writing-as-definition as the very core of his place in the world, his statement that "I had to become a writer very fast. I had to learn it. I had nothing else" ("The Ultimate Exile," p. 71) necessarily leaves the reader with the impression that Naipaul's *literacy* is actually a synonym for "cause," rather than either "purity" or "truth." With this formula in mind, then, *A Way in the World* unfolds as a series of narratives that test the parameters of his previous attempts to find the transitions between colonial historical actions, the Caribbean experience, and the consequent ideas embodied within his textual composition of the late twentieth century.

A WAY IN THE WORLD (1994)

The nine narratives of *A Way in the World* have a loose geohistorical connection, allusive links to earlier works such as *The Middle Passage*, *The Loss of El Dorado*, *In a Free State*, and *Finding the Centre*, and each employs narratological exercises, such as the use of the present conditional tense, or the structure of a screenplay, that allows Naipaul to play with the notion of reworking older materials into hitherto unmentioned ones. The first narrative introduces the tenor of the book when it establishes its close to essentialist thesis about "inheritance," that condition of our humanity whereby "we go back and back, forever; we go back all of us to the very beginning; in our blood and bone and brain we carry the memories of thousands of beings" (*A Way in the World*, p. 11). The occasion for this observation is a reconstructed monologue of a teacher who the narrator meets on one of his returns to Trinidad. Her story is about one Leonard Side, a local Muslim who acts as the judge at the school's annual flower contest. The teacher's account centers around her distaste for Side's "aesthetic" sense, a sense that allows him to dress corpses in the morgue as well as demonstrate pastry decorations for the Women's Association. Between the narrator's supply of contextual information and the teacher's recollections, the portrait of Side that emerges within just a few pages is of a man in motley whose apparently incongruent activities jar the teacher's sensibility, and by extension that of the narrative's two normative registers: that which is Caribbean, and that which is not. Side, it transpires, is emblematic of all the principal figures of the subsequent narratives who at different times and in different situations also emerge from the hybridity of their cultural compositions – be they historically constituted or the result of developments during their life-times – as ultimately deluded by their philosophical subscriptions. The narrator closes the narrative with a speculative moment: he pits his own, acquired knowledge of the area against a quick rundown of Side's probable historical genealogy, much of which he speculates Side himself is unaware of; he then concludes, "Sometimes we can be strangers to ourselves" (*A Way in the World*, p. 11).

The exploratory discursive space that this prelude opens for the other narratives is vast. Not only has Naipaul deftly suggested an asymmetry to Caribbean cultural and social developments, but he also erases the ellipses of cultural disjunction by supplying historical probability that in its articulation establishes both the *idea* of a homogeneity of lineage, and a sense of historical determinism.[5] The "blood and bone and brain we carry," in other words, whether we are aware of it or not, has the determinist power to condition our existence. Inheritance rather than history lies as a kind of cultural unconscious so that "learning" – history – can be the agency whereby consciousness is achieved. The nascent essentialism of Naipaul's use of "inheritance" carries a Cartesian urgency, its postulate moving from "I learn, therefore I am" to "I write, therefore I am." The license of this reconstructive formulation lies in the multiple referents that it allows the author to draw upon. History and inheritance serve as propositions which Naipaul can imaginatively locate, and play off against each other, while the present tense of the lived experience he either reports or creates always operates with the option of the conditional. Thus, whether the principal figures are historical personages such as Sir Walter Raleigh, imaginative constructions such as the narrator in "New Clothes: A Unwritten Story," or portraits of Naipaul's Caribbean contemporaries such as the characters Blair and Lebrun, *A Way in the World*'s narratives are each exercises in exploring relative levels of cultural, historical, or political "consciousness."

The second narrative, entitled "History: A Smell of Fish Glue," is autobiographical, with Naipaul focusing on the time just prior to his first trip to England and entry to university, as well as his sporadic return trips in the subsequent years. As in *The Loss of El Dorado*, the "History" of the title refers to Port of Spain, the first city of the narrator's experience, and the focal site of Trinidadian political developments. Unlike the previous book, however, this chapter charts the developments within the narrator's life-time, so that the transformation depicted is the gradual political awakening of the black population, through what the volume as a whole will consistently describe as a politics of "racial redemption." Even before the chapter embarks on a description of the narrator's clerkship in the registrar-general's department in the Red House, which is also home to all the island's official records, the politics of race is introduced with the narrator's meeting with the lawyer father of one of his school friends. A man of local fame for being self-made, the lawyer nevertheless discomforts the narrator when he mistakenly attributes his name to Homer rather than Virgil. What is discomforting to the reader, however, is the kind of error the narrator sees: "But this flaw in his character, so casually revealed, was worrying" (*A Way in the World*, p. 17). This worry is then immediately compounded by the narrator's next recollection of their conversation, when the lawyer declares himself for "The race! The race, man!" Declining inclusion in the lawyer's gesture of invitation to the seventeen-year-old, the narrator shuns what he feels is the sentimentality of the appeal.

What is interesting about Naipaul's account of one of his first encounters with a politicized "race" consciousness is that he implies that it ultimately stems from a flawed consciousness, because the emerging phenomenon, as he describes it, develops out of a repressed reservoir of political disenfranchisement that is only manifested as an anti-intellectual religiosity. Even as he describes the political rallies that he witnesses over the course of his return visits, the narrator cannot help but characterize the events as sacramental thus stripping the political of a rational basis. In addition to making statements to this effect, Naipaul also imposes a measure of his own distance from the events depicted, so that the growth and spread of a different political allegiance within the island's social composition belongs to both an era and a place with which he has little or no connection. This is cleverly done, mainly by adopting a view from afar which gives him a perspective that sees the political transformation from the colonial to the postcolonial as the changes that the landscape undergoes as urbanization encroaches on the older, pre-industrial demarcations between the country and the city. The symbolic realm of the landscape – the *look* of the place – is as one-dimensional an indicator as the color codes of social stratification are. It allows him a moment of chiasmus when he can state that:

It was as though, with the colonial past, all the colonial landscape was being trampled over and undone; as though, with the past, the very idea of regulation had been rejected; as though, after the sacrament of the square, the energy of revolt had become a thing on its own, eating away at the land. (*A Way in the World*, pp. 37–38)

As if to confirm his thesis about local political awakening in Trinidad, *A Way in the World* focuses on two important figures, Blair and Lebrun, both of whom are used to exemplify the seductive and ultimately corrupt power of a politics of "race." Lebrun, who is apparently modeled on the historian C.L.R. James,[6] is indirectly introduced in the second chapter in its reference to the 1937 oil field strikes, a fuller account of which is explored in the fourth chapter, "Passenger: A Figure from the Thirties." Used as a kind of prelude to the modern political awakening that the book as a whole is concerned with, Lebrun's role in the oil field strike is only fully explained gradually during the course of "Passenger," and the narrative devoted to his life, "On the Run." Blair, on the other hand, is one of the senior co-workers in the Red House, where the narrator fulfills his apprenticeship. The registrar-general's office serves as a microcosm of the social stratification of the larger island composition, where Naipaul provides portraits of *opportunity* rather than character or traits amongst his fellow government employees. Thus his own status as scholarship recipient is the gauge against which such opportunity is measured. There are those for whom the circumstances of their government employment represents the culmination of any ambition; others who have resigned themselves to its stasis even at a young age; and very few for whom it may become a springboard for further aspiration. Blair is among the last group and represents as such the only alternative to the narrator's scholarship opportunity for advancement in a larger, more intellectually challenging world.

After his introduction as the one person who appears to transcend the limitations built into the island existence, Blair's political career recedes from the narrative's immediate attention and is only alluded to as an unexplorable domain that his death, years later in Uganda, may explain. The implication is that the intervening studies – the other chapters – will contain enough reflection to allow for an assessment by the end of the book. Blair's death does eventually serve as the book's final meditation in the last chapter, "Home Again." The third chapter, "New Clothes: An Unwritten Story," is a fictional reconstruction of impressions and the ambiance Naipaul partially experienced during his travels for *The Middle Passage*. Framed within a self-consciously arch attempt at narrative presence, where the present tense encases the third-person developments of events, Naipaul tries to make transparent the process whereby impressions from an actual personal experience can be wedded to historical information to provide the matrix for an imaginative projection of what a moment of cultural encounter and affect may be like. The subsequent narrative emerges as pristine Naipaulian fiction. He casts his narrator – a character rather than the story's voice – as a mercenary of sorts whose journey into the Amazonian hinterlands is sponsored by a conspiracy about to be orchestrated by a faction of a now-racialized political sector. As the framing narrator states, "Such a situation wouldn't only echo the truth of more than one country in the region. It would also hold certain historical ironies" (*A Way in the World*, p. 48). The composite reductionism is particularly Naipaulian, as in "In a Free State," and *A Bend in the River*, and the historical ironies lie with the role that Amerindians are made to play in a political game that has remained unchanged for them since the era of the first European incursions.

The human details of the story are also familiar. At the first encampment the other missionaries/mercenaries provide a milieu of displaced persons whose activities invest them with a power that in their familiar contexts they would not have.

Similarly, the two Amerindian boys guiding the narrator-character to an inner village display a combined child-like and unpredictable compliance with the protagonist, so that the hint of homoerotic bonding between him and Mateo, one of the boys, carries with it the suggestion of a kind of potential miscommunication that their context forces on them. Arriving at the village, Naipaul's protagonist learns that the villagers still operate in a mythical temporal zone, inasmuch as they have telescoped almost four centuries of occasional encounters with outsiders into a fixed anticipation of a promise of domestication first issued by seventeenth-century European explorers. The thesis of inheritance in this instance is an immobilized temporal sense developed by an isolated community unable to discern the passage of time until the promise is fulfilled. The protagonist realizes that his subversive activity will help perpetuate, well into the twentieth century, the lie offered to the villagers by the first of the European visitors.

The fourth chapter, "Passenger: A Figure from the Thirties," most lends itself to the speculation that Naipaul's latest book does address some of his critics. Returning to the topic of Trinidad, the chapter looks again at the way the island has figured in European travel writing. Almost as a playful, provocative exercise, Naipaul focusses on the inter wars era that Rob Nixon's study, *London Calling* (1992), identifies as the most proximate to Naipaul's initiation as a travel writer, despite his allegance to the Victorians. Thus, where Nixon focuses on Naipaul's disagreements with the writers of the 1930s, Naipaul now resurrects a book about Trinidad by one Foster Morris, a contemporary of Graham Greene. Before examining Morris' book, however, Naipaul first describes the difference of perception that attends the associations which a viewer may invest in the look of any place. Using a descriptive name attributed to Columbus' view of a bluff in Trinidad, Naipaul tries to reconstruct both how and why Columbus saw what he thought he saw when sighting the island. By speculating on the kinds of changes the landscape has undergone as well as the kind of mood Columbus might reasonably be expected to have been in on his third trip to the Caribbean, Naipaul manages to illustrate an archeology of perception that then becomes the conceit upon which his examination of foci develops.

Comparing his own vision with Columbus', Naipaul reads a dialectical necessity into the location of the island's place in the world. Only through "foreign witness," we are told, could Trinidadians conceive "of where and what we were." The rub, however, lies with the misperception later exercised by such foreign witness when the peopling of the island is overlooked so that what the foreigner sees is attributed to the wrong circumstance. The historical layering already developed in the first three chapters, therefore, moves from the physical to the intellectual, but now with an awareness that what is seen and what is thought are neither reliable nor constant. Naipaul's subsequent examination of Foster Morris' book about the 1937 oil field strike in Trinidad, *The Shadowed Livery*, is conducted as an illustration of how a habit of perception and its habits of writing can result in precisely such misrepresentations, which, despite themselves, still manage to act as reference for the situation represented. Naipaul's initial criticism of Morris concerns his misreading of both the situation at the oil field strike and the temper of the local players in that drama. With a typical Naipaulian twist, Morris is faulted for not realizing the extent of the local Trinidadians' lack of sophistication about politics as well as communal responsibility.

Nevertheless, Morris continues to be an important figure, graduating from Naipaul's early association of his "foreign witness" to becoming the author's mentor at a time when Naipaul was learning to be a writer in England. The reintroduction of Morris in the author's life heralds two important moments: it steers Naipaul into a more programmatic course of self-instruction, and a casual racist epithet suddenly alerts the young Naipaul to the nature of Morris' self-censorship in the writing of *The Shadowed Livery*. The "white nigger" of Morris' inquiry, we later learn, is the figure of the next chapter, "On the Run," Lebrun. Yet to be named, the incremental introduction of a setting for Lebrun is a careful preparation for an assessment of a life and career that is historically closer to Naipaul's than any other in the corpus of his work. The linkage between these two chapters constitutes some of the most interesting moments in the volume, for they establish a connectedness in Naipaul's Trinidadian origins that his semi-autobiographical writings have tended to elide in the past. Jointly, and on their own merits, Lebrun and Blair stand as two figures whose professional careers are paradigmatic of alternate developments to the course that Naipaul's has taken. More than anything else, the divergence lies in the political and ideological affiliations pursued, thus these recollections at the present time contain a comparative assessment that while unsurprising is nevertheless fascinating.

The connectedness remains mediated, however. Both Morris' work and mentoring act as mediators that enable Naipaul to articulate the difference that he has long pursued. And it rests, of course, with the kind of intervention that writing has exercised and has continued to exercise in his life. The role that Morris takes on in Naipaul's early writing career, then, has as much to do with his early advice as it does with the milieu and reputation he represents. In the same vein as Naipaul credited Conrad with having gone before him in "Conrad's Darkness," Morris is described as having offered Naipaul an example from which he was able to graduate rather than emulate. The sporadic patronage of the older man, along with Graham Greene's comments about him during an interview Naipaul conducted in 1967, all suggest a debt to that generation of writers, but one that is reflected in Naipaul's gradual disdain of Morris. The chapter ends with another typically Naipaulian gesture. By placing Morris' Trinidadian book within the tradition of "the great chain of changing outside vision of that part of the world" (*A Way in the World*, p. 105), Naipaul manages to catalogue the necessary "foreign witness" into a tidy paragraph, indirectly enveloping four centuries' worth of what he calls "a fair record of one side of a civilization" with his own.

Morris' casual reference to Lebrun, the subject of the fifth chapter, "On the Run," both introduces Naipaul to an aspect of the 1937 oil strike he had been unaware of, and reminds him of his first awareness of Lebrun – as a forgotten author of a forgotten book on his school bookshelf. After inquiring about him, Naipaul reports his own incredulity that a local man could be a "revolutionary" and reputed. Thus, while acknowledging his own limited comprehension as a schoolboy, Naipaul nevertheless impresses upon his readers that Lebrun was little known at that time in Trinidad, let alone considered. What is curious here is that Naipaul is quick to challenge Lebrun's subsequent reputation within the academy, where, assuming that one is referring to C.L.R. James, he is indeed credited with having written one of the first books of the Caribbean revolution, *The Black Jacobins* (1938). When Naipaul states, "people doing research in university libraries, where everything is accessible, sometimes see progressions that didn't exist at the time" (*A Way in the World*, p. 108), he pits the trajectories of intellectual history against an extraordinarily localized moment, despite the fact that they operate within different temporal and spatial fields; then, when reporting on the speeches given by Lebrun at political rallies years later, Naipaul acknowledges the fluency, outlines the argument, but credits them as an ego-centered rather than political gesture. He finally dismisses Lebrun's standing as a local force because he never entered local politics. This dismissive gesture, so early in the chapter, sets the tone for what will develop into a curious study in ambivalence. It seems that Naipaul must characterize Lebrun's long career as ultimately flawed, indeed dangerously flawed, because the consistency, patience and lucidity with which it has developed, as well as its global span of influence are so closely parallel to his own, though the dimension is so different.

"On the Run" is the first of the three longer chapters in the book. Its length suggests the first resolution in the sequence of Naipaul's examination of differing perceptual representations of Trinidad and its place in both colonial and postcolonial registers. The distillation it offers are the poles that he and Lebrun represent, so that the narrative seeks to pair the two as their professional lives navigate the same territory but "on different tracks" (*A Way in the World*, p. 121). Naipaul's organizational strategy is familiar. He begins by recollecting his first awareness, be it by reputation or hearsay, then his own acquaintance and the nature of its impact on him, and he rounds out the comparison with a return to the occasion of a previous work of his own, "The Crocodiles of Yamoussoukro," where he finds Lebrun had been before him. Each segment highlights the capital Lebrun appears to be able to extract from the materialist perspective he espouses: his reputation for being a "revolutionary"; the romanticism of being "on the run"; the patronage of a segment of the Euro-American intelligentsia; and the deference of national leaders in Africa. The disappointment Naipaul expresses about the older Lebrun's apparent lapse into a form of racial politics does little to lessen the opportunistic cast Naipaul adopts to characterize his life as a whole. Thus, even though he credits Lebrun's critique of one of his early novels, most probably *A House for Mr. Biswas*, with providing him with an insight that remains of value even today, the extent of his disdain for both Lebrun's marxism and his apparently subsequent politics of racial redemption is soundly played out in the chapter's last segment.

Returning to his trip to the Ivory Coast, Naipaul reintroduces one of the social actors from his account of that journey, Phyllis, an expatriate originally from the Caribbean. In "The Crocodiles of Yamoussoukro," Phyllis' anomalous status fascinates the narrator and she is allowed to become one of his main informants, her story illustrating a moment of displacement that helps Naipaul draw analogies between his own Caribbean "knowledge" and the setting he finds himself in. In "On the Run," Phyllis is remembered for her personal story which did not belong to the earlier work. During the course of her account about her husband, from a neighboring African country, Lebrun's visit to the region is described, and his advice is acknowledged as the source of a new policy of socialization adopted by the government. It turns out to be a repressive, tyrannical policy, typical of Naipaul's thesis of postcolonial casualty. Hence, the indictment against Lebrun could not be greater. Ultimately, this narrative meeting, in Africa, of three Caribbean players, Lebrun, Phyllis, and Naipaul, consolidates a textual drama that between their wanderings covers major portions of the globe. The enlarged story of Phyllis leaves the reader familiar with both the narratives she appears in with a bleak picture of a failed adventure despite her tertiary migration. Lebrun is depicted in the devolution of a double betrayal, that of his mission, and that of his "inheritance" which seems to claim him in the end, and which his admirers, apparently, have never understood. Only Naipaul as narrator survives, thus reiterating one of the earliest obsessions of his writing life: the escape, release, that writing has granted him.

"On the Run" serves as an intellectual half-way point in *A Way in the World*. The chapter following it, "A Parcel of Papers, a Roll of Tobacco, a Tortoise: An Unwritten Story," resembles the narrative departure that the fictional "New Clothes" first introduced: namely, casting the events depicted as a screenplay where the framing narrative operates in the present conditional. Also like "New Clothes," this chapter represents a fictional impulse that Naipaul claims to have had for many years, but which never really materialized, thus accounting for the "Unwritten Story" designation, which, of course, suggests that the ideas embodied by the stories are also original. The main figure of "A Parcel of Papers," is Sir Walter Raleigh, already referred to in *The Loss of El Dorado*, who reappears here as one of the conversants in a long dialogue with his surgeon. The bulk of the narrative consists of their conversation conducted during Raleigh's last, ill-fated expedition to Trinidad to look for El Dorado. The scene unfolds as the surgeon questions Raleigh's written account of his previous expedition twenty-two years prior to the present one. The other principle figure is Harry, or Don José, an Amerindian, or part Amerindian, whom Raleigh had taken with him to England, but who had returned fourteen years later, after having spent much time battling homesickness by facing a wall in silence. The Harry figure is, of course, the ancestor of the villagers in "New Clothes" who returned with the promise of domestication in the seventeenth century.

Naipaul's purpose in animating this historical scene is an excercise in testing his own powers of reconstruction, the measure of which is the amount and quality of humanness he can evoke. And, since it is a Naipaulian sensibility which encases the account, the humanness in question necessarily highlights the passionately delusional, quixotic, and dangerously careless nature of Raleigh's quest. Standing as it does at the start of consolidated British interests overseas, Raleigh's ambitions are emblematic of the transitional quality of the time he lived in when an empirical basis for an historical rationality was still forming. The surgeon serves as interrogator, trying to sift through the fact and fiction of Raleigh's book and, as such, also serves as Naipaul's surrogate since his queries are in the interests of a version of history that is thoroughly grounded in empirical and verifiable documentation, most notably Spanish records of the same era, and the growing body of travel literature written by Raleigh's contemporaries, and from whom Raleigh appears to have borrowed surreptitiously.

The last portion of the chapter involves another interrogation, but this time of Don José by an historian, Fray Simon. Don José's account addresses ellipses in Raleigh's, with the result that the whole chapter looks at the same events from a series of different perspectives. By closing this narrative with Don José, Naipaul also appears to be deliberately trying to invest the Amerindian past of the area with both a voice and a representation usually absent from the literature of the region. Don José's last reply resonates with the kind of vulnerability that is indicative of Naipaul's implicit thesis about "simple" societies and their absence of an intellectual tradition vested in a sense of purpose larger than their immediate concerns. As Don José is credited with saying, "And I think, Father, that the difference between us, who are Indian, or half Indians, and people like the Spaniards and the English and the Dutch and the French, people who know how to go where they are going, I think that for them the world is a safer place" (*A Way in the World*, p. 211). This is Naipaul at his most sympathetic, and yet it is still tinged with an almost Rousseauesque vision about social potentiality. Don José's response also closes out with a modicum of elegance a narrative that is surprisingly awkward, stilted, and uncomfortable in its reconstructive endeavor. The dialogues are a cross between Naipaul's latest travel-writing mode of allowing his informants to speak verbatim, and a screenplay which blocks out the frames in a sequence that forms a plot. This chapter in particular contributes to the volume's overall feel of narrative disjunction.

A short chapter, "A New Man," separates "A Parcel of Papers" from the volume's third and last "unwritten story," "In the Gulf of Desolation," which takes the extraordinary life of Francisco Miranda, the largely expatriate eighteenth- and nineteenth-century Venezuelan nationalist, as its central concentration. Thus the story of a Venezuelan, Manuel Sorzano, which Naipaul hears on a flight to Venezuela from Trinidad, where the two are seated together, is a prelude to the following chapter, for it allows Naipaul to offer a personal account of the way in which Venezuela figures in Trinidadian history, and how its affairs have dominated the political development of the region, during both the colonial and postcolonial periods. Sorzano's story is immediately emblematic of the kind of fluidity and chameleon-like agility that peoples of the region have developed by passing themselves off as culturally something they are not. He tells Naipaul of his extraordinary fortune in having found gold coins in a building where he was engaged in demolition. The small fortune has helped establish his family, the personal details of which gather interest only as Naipaul refigures them through the filter of his own observation that Sorzano is in fact a Trinidadian Hindu like himself, and not the Venezuelan he passes as. It is Naipaul's "racial eye" that sees through the transformation that his traveling acquaintance assumes. Rather than deception, though, Naipaul attributes the phenomenon to living "intuitively," "with no idea of being lost or in a void" (*A Way in the World*, p. 229).

In addition to his "racial eye," Naipaul also deploys his thesis about the failure of cultural hybridity when it does not allow for a connectedness with that which is productive in the constituent traditions. Sorzano's trip to Trinidad in order to purchase Indian records and foods are as talismanic a gesture as were Ganesh's in *The Mystic Masseur*. The implication is that the amelioration they will offer to the family crisis belongs to superstition rather than faith. Thus, this portrait of a modern

Venezuelan family, made up as it is of so many cultural features of the region, including Sorzano's son's enlistment in the Guardia Nacional, serves as a prelude to the Miranda chapter by illustrating the consequences of the nationalist machinations of the nineteenth century whose agendas, according to Naipaul, could not help but contribute to the kind of confusion he has just depicted. The personage who best embodies the originary conditions for this kind of confusion in Naipaul's mind is Francisco Miranda, whom he calls Simon Bolívar's precursor.

Claiming there is no historical myth attached to Miranda, as there is to Columbus and Raleigh, Naipaul's resurrection of him is curious. On the one hand he cites Miranda's career with being every bit "as fabulous and original" as Columbus' and Raleigh's, and he recognizes Miranda as having been a necessary symbol of his era because he lent his compatriots a metropolitan myth that was strategically deployed when convenient. On the other hand, if Miranda's reputation as a romantic figure espousing revolution failed to evolve its own historical myth, the presumption that follows is that his failure has already been recorded, in a manner of speaking. His uses for Naipaul, therefore, rest elsewhere, principally as yet another reinvented man, but possibly the first of his kind, who consequently is precursor to a Naipaulian pantheon of colonial and postcolonial "mimic" men rather than Bolívar. When Naipaul recalls his own early impression of Miranda, he states, "I saw him in some of my own early promptings (and the promptings of other people I knew)" (*A Way in the World*, p. 252), he acknowledges the "feeling of incompleteness" of the colonial, from which he himself has escaped, but not, perhaps, a figure such as Lebrun.

The subsequent account of Miranda's life, as "the first South American of Culture (and often the first South American)" (*A Way in the World*, p. 252), is a predictable narrative filled with the unprecedented global wanderings and political swayings of Miranda, his quirky habits and anecdotal experiences. What is missing, however, is a scrutiny akin to Benedict Anderson's thesis, in *Imagined Communities*, about the modal journey of the secular "pilgrimage" created by colonial administrative units and the new mobilities they established (Anderson, pp.53–65). Miranda's Creole status, and his independence from a specific governmental structure, was a unique circumstance for embarking on his remarkable journeys; nevertheless, his career did represent one of the first manifestations of a life created by the colonial encounter rather than simply by himself. Thus, Naipaul's revelations of his counterfeit claims at different Euro-American courts, are less expository than they are meant to be. The chapter, however, concentrates mainly upon Miranda's last sojourn in Trinidad, before being imprisoned in Puerto Rico, and finally Spain.

Drawing much of his information from Miranda's papers, the story of their preservation being one of the threads of the chapter, Naipaul also revisits his extensive researches for his own history, *The Loss of El Dorado*. But, because "The Gulf of Desolation: An Unwritten Story" is Miranda's story, the events central to *The Loss of El Dorado* and its central characters fall into a slightly different relief, much as Raleigh's story in "A Parcel of Papers" did. And, as in the previous "unwritten story," the humanness of the historical personages and social actors is stressed, providing portraits of the register of human responses within the political machinations of the men of empire making their careers in a social structure straining and changing with the times. The narrative ends with back-to-back exerpts from the correspondence between Miranda in the Caribbean and his common-law wife, Sally, in London. The small domesticities of their exchange remain poignant, and serve to underscore the anomalous nature of one of the first copiously documented "South American" lives.

The last chapter, "Home Again," is again autobiographical, recalling Naipaul's sojourn in Uganda during the mid-1960s. And, again, within just a few paragraphs, Naipaul depicts his expatriate compound in such a way as to describe a microcosm of the larger colonial structures from which the country was trying to emerge. The always slightly sinister political ambiance is complemented by Naipaul's own discomfort with his status there, which is complicated by the kinds of historical connections that he finds. The Asian community is being politically besieged, colleagues Naipaul is comfortable with nevertheless discomfort him in their acceptance of the government's new practice of socialism, South African exiles and "revolutionaries" do not fit his expectations, and students at the university astonish him with their political arrogance. The occasion for his recollection, however, is his meeting with Blair, the compatriot from Trinidad who worked in the registrar-general's department with Naipaul. As was the case with an examination of Lebrun's career, Blair's also serves as one of the gauges Naipaul uses to measure the quality and direction of his own. And while a kind of textual meeting between Phyllis, Naipaul, and Lebrun underwrites the last portion of "On the Run," Blair's and Naipaul's actual meeting in Uganda, so many years after their last, coupled with the last report of Lebrun in Africa, carries with it an odyssean quality, not in its epic dimensions, but in its calculation of the conditions placed upon the three of them by their different understandings of their island "inheritance."

Where Lebrun appears to have slipped dangerously back into a racial indentification, still in the name of revolution, Blair is depicted as having steered a more pragmatic course. Rather than endorsing a politics of "racial redemption," Blair's advisory role in Uganda, it turns out, shows him to have sublimated that aspect of his "inheritance," now allowing him to operate in a political dimension that transcends such narrow concerns. This ability, Naipaul suggests, is also the cause of his brutal murder, by authorities who do not subscribe to Blair's failure to indict Uganda's Asian community as they had hoped. Naipaul also suggests that the untimeliness of Blair's death makes it difficult to assess whether at a later point, with more international success, Blair would have stayed his course. Nevertheless, he redeems Blair by imagining a literary ending to his life. In an imaginary sequence credited to the inflections of a Poe story, Naipaul rewrites Conrad's Kurtz as he lies dying: "And I feel that if, as in some Edgar Allen Poe story, at the moment of death, while the brain still sparked, a question could have been lodged in that brain – 'Does this betrayal

mock your life?' – the answer immediately after death would
have been 'No! No! No!'" (*A Way in the World*, p. 379).

Blair's truth, offered by his death, allows Naipaul to close *A
Way in the World* in the same conditional tense that he has used
in his two previous African-set fictions, "In a Free State" and *A
Bend in the River*. "In a Free State" envisions the ancient artist
insular in his fiction of a complete world, but the narrator
denies the present tense by looking forward to the defeat of
Egyptian soldiers, seventeen months after his visit, "trying to
walk back home, casting long shadows in the sand" (*In a Free
State*, p. 246). Similarly, *A Bend in the River* concludes in an
apocalyptic moment, and then describes a scene that either
was not seen, or has not yet happened: "The steamer started up
again and moved without lights down the river away from the
area of battle. The air would have been full of moths and flying
insects. The search light, while it was on, had shown thousands, white in the white light" (*A Bend in the River*, p. 278). In
A Way in the World, the passage from Africa to Trinidad for
Blair's burial is also reconstructed in the same frame of probability: Naipaul finds out that "the box would have been taken
away in an ambulance to Port of Spain, and then the shell of
the man would have been laid out in Parry's chapel of rest" (*A
Way in the World*, p. 380). A similar frame of probability has
characterized all the narratives in this volume, reiterating once
again Naipaul's fascination with what he feels he, Naipaul,
could have been against what he feels he is. In the light of
Naipaul's latest conclusion, it is probable that he has now
embarked on an extensive program of rewriting, for the more
he writes, it seems, the more there is for him to return to.

CHAPTER 8

Conclusion

> The book before always turned out to have been written
> by a man with incomplete knowledge.
> (V.S. Naipaul, *Finding the Centre*)

The critical industry that Naipaul's works have generated has taken on an aspect similar to his own agenda of rewriting. In March 1994 the University of Tulsa inaugurated and opened its Naipaul archive, which houses all his existing manuscripts through 1984, as well as his professional correspondence. Thus, it is only a matter of time before another generation of scholars produces a body of critical writings that document, in even more detail than Naipaul has himself, the process whereby a Writer emerges from the recesses of Europe's old imperial world. Nevertheless, the query that can always be reiterated is the one that looks into the relationship that has developed between Naipaul *the writer* and the Naipaulian world view. Whether one is discomforted or illuminated by Naipaul's investigations into the failures of modernity, the fact persists that his language, his style, his attention to form, and his expressive dimensions have maintained a brilliance and mastery that have become landmarks in contemporary writing in English. Naipaul the writer, who I understand to be distinct from the romantic young colonial aspiring to become a Writer, embodies one of the possible paradoxes of postcolonial literature – namely, the disjunction between the materiality of language and the materiality of history. For example, when Fanon opens his study, *Black Skin, White Masks*, with the statement that, "To speak means to be in a position to use a certain syntax, to grasp the morphology of this or that language, but it means above all to assume a culture, to support the weight of a civilization,"[1] he distills the complex formulations of psychoanalytical discoveries about language acquisition and the formation of consciousness to point out the psychopolitical ramifications of colonial socialization. The ambivalence bred of functioning in a subordinated relation to the "language of the oppressor" has been to a large extent the central crisis informing much postcolonial and Caribbean writing. The figure of Caliban is of course the literary archetype evoked to exemplify this phenomenon, but, as Roberto Fernández Retamar has noted, at least one writer thought the figure of Ariel best represented the Creole relationship to the Old World.[2] Naipaul's writing positions him as an Ariel figure, whose latent capability has been animated by the power represented in Europe's books. Naipaul's symbolic order, then, most clearly spelled out in his novels, hinges upon a literary tradition and sensibility that are deeply invested in locating, and then articulating, the power of an aesthetic force that transcends the limitations of particular concerns even while it houses them within the parameters of an idea of a larger order.

To say as much is only to join the consensus of opinion that even Naipaul's most divergent critics endorse. Nevertheless, it is his subscription to this function of "the novel," and narrative, that also accounts for his achievement, and his achievement is that he has indeed found a place within the "tradition" he once stated was not his. What the young Naipaul failed to acknowledge, however, were the historical processes of a transforming culture and social order that constituted the conditions of the modern novel's development. The destabilization of old orders in seventeenth- and eighteenth-century Britain, after all, created social upheavals commensurate in magnitude to the upheavals associated with colonization. Thus, Naipaul's early anxieties about his lack of a tradition can now be seen to have been, in part, his response to his colonial status, which, rather than eliciting resistance from him, resulted in his urgent need for acceptance by the governing metropole. This need, in turn, is the origin of his idealization of England, and its literary tradition, which he finally begins to review in *The Enigma of Arrival*.

The idea of "civility," proposed as England's development of empire and universalized through its conflation with "modernity," is, of course, less the work of empire than it is of the narrativization of historical processes engendered by empire. The literary tradition of the novel so central to Naipaul's writing pulse, it must be remembered, evolved its realist mode not only, to oversimplify a complex process, as a "reflection" of rapidly changing social milieux, but also as a response to them. As response, the careful calibration between social propriety, moral concerns, and human relations could not have emerged as it did without the work of empire informing its possibilities.[3] In the same way that colonial discourses constructed "difference" in order to subordinate colonial subjects, so nineteenth-century European national consciousness sublimated the work of empire to help contain the profound social stresses at home. Thus the realist novel's expanded registers of consciousness, sensitive to the urgencies of changing social orders, arrived at an articulation of "civility" (or its absence) achieved through "The principle of organization, and the principle of development,"[4] mediated by intense moral proccupations, which F.R. Leavis in particular understood as one of the aesthetic triumphs of the novelists of the "Great Tradition."

Naipaul's major novels, including *A House for Mr. Biswas*, *The Mimic Men*, *Guerrillas*, *A Bend in the River*, and *The Enigma of Arrival*, all employ a structure that conforms to the realist tradition of composing representations with, in Lukacs' term, "a totality" of being, of life, or of its world.[5] Lukacs' location of the novel's formal relation to "reality" fits Naipaul's treatments since the worlds he evokes all depend on a definition of partial or absent "totality," to the extent, indeed, that their "incompleteness" is what dictates their principles of organization and development. Rather than simply a "thematic" preoccupation, the "incompleteness" I am referring to, Naipaul's "half-made societies" and postcolonial situations, require the quality of consciousness of Naipaul's first- and third-person narrative voices as the novels' philosophical registers that allow for the narrative articulation of those worlds.

The domestic dramas and the life-span of Mohun Biswas in *A House for Mr. Biswas*, for instance, are the necessary temporal and spatial loci for that novel's wonderfully rendered, but displaced, consciousness of its protagonist. Towards the end of his story, for example, when he negotiates the purchase of the house on Sikkim Street, Naipaul presents Biswas as forced to equate his position with that of the protagonist of a Maupassant short story:

Once Mr. Biswas had read a story by a French writer about a woman who worked for twenty years to pay off a debt on an imitation necklace. He had never been able to understand why it was considered a comic story. Debt was a fearful thing; and with all its ifs and might-have-beens the story came too near the truth: hope followed by blight, the passing of the years, the passing of life itself, and then the revelation of waste: Oh, my poor Matilda! But they were false! (*A House for Mr. Biswas*, p. 564)

Encapsulated in this reference is a complex lesson in Biswas' election to a bourgeois social order. Rather than defining Biswas in relation to Europe, however, Naipaul displays an extraordinary economy in taking a short story and formalizing its relation to the novel: "the passing of life itself, and then the revelation of waste" is shown as knowledge or an awareness that needs to be immediately repressed in order for Biswas to buy the house. Employing the conditional tense that Naipaul later uses to close his African-set narratives, the third-person narrative voice intervenes with the following observations:

If it had not been raining he might have walked around the small yard and seen the absurd shape of the house. He would have seen where the celotex panels on the eaves had fallen away, providing unrestricted entry to the bats of the neighbourhood . . . He would not have been deceived into cosiness by the thick curtain over the back doorway on the lower floor. He would have seen that the house had no back door at all . . . He had only a picture of a house cosy in the rain, with a polished floor, and an old lady who baked cakes in the kitchen. (*A House for Mr. Biswas*, pp. 565–566)

What Biswas could not see, but which nevertheless informs the substance of his transaction, is then removed even further away from the "world" of the Maupassant short story. The *reasoning* that seals the closure of his purchase can only take place after Biswas unexpectedly receives $400 for the materials of the failed house at Shorthills:

Between eight hundred dollars and one thousand two hundred dollars there is a great difference. Eight hundred dollars are petty savings. One thousand two hundred dollars stand for real money. The difference between eight hundred and five thousand is immense. The difference between one thousand two hundred and five thousand is negotiable. (*A House for Mr. Biswas*, p. 567)

Biswas' good fortune is presented to us with an economy that intensifies rather than diffuses the traumatic nature of this transaction. A poignancy bordering on the banal is suggested in the synopsis of the Maupassant story, but the very process whereby Biswas then enters a similar narrative as he, too, is about to be locked into a financially compromised position suggests instead his arrival at a consciousness that releases him from all the constraints that hitherto defined his dependencies. The ironic inflection in the principles of organization and development here lies between the narrative voice and Biswas' third-person position, where the overview of how he brings real change into his life is also presented as his entry into *false consciousness*. Not only does this pivotal moment in the novel develop the resolution of the plot – a house for Mr. Biswas – but as resolution, it also reveals the necessarily idealized nature of desire. Naipaul's tableau, "a picture of a house cosy in the rain, with a polished floor, and an old lady who baked cakes in the kitchen," could not be more emblematic of a commodified desire, even though the novel never really seems aware of its own implicit socialist critique.

Both the economy and expressiveness of Naipaul's style have long been celebrated. Whether fiction or non-fiction,[6] the careful precision of his language has always been able to maintain a largely ideological and rhetorical response to his writing. Thus, it is the categories of analysis or knowledge he employs that elicit disagreement, his interpretation of situations and ideas that generates dissent, and the license of his own, personal authorization that is questioned. In particular, it is the alliance of Naipaul's command of English and his repeatedly demonstrated skill as a craftsman that lends his views of the world credence and acceptance among his advocates. The late Irving Howe echoed the tensions surrounding Naipaul's status *as a writer* and the timbre of his views. In the Epilogue appended to *Politics and the Novel* (1992),[7] he opens his section on Naipaul with the acknowledgment that he is among Naipaul's "uneasy admirers": "Uneasy because of his surplus of disgust and paucity of tenderness, but an admirer because he writes with a strict refusal of romantic moonshine about the moral charms of primitives or the virtues of bloodstained dictators" (Howe, p. 265). Commenting primarily on the novels up until and including *A Bend in the River*, Howe is concerned with Naipaul's "control of his feelings, control of his language" in the interests of "novelistic tact," and detects in *A Bend in the River* "signs of a new patience." Nevertheless, he suspects that Naipaul "seems right now to be a writer beleaguered by his own truths, unable to get past them," and that "we ought simply to be content that in his austere and brilliant style he holds fast to the bitterness before his eyes (Howe, pp. 267–268). While Howe is uneasy rather than ambivalent, his difficulties with Naipaul's vision stem ultimately from the demands of a literary technician.

Perhaps it is worth stating once more that while postcolonial history continues to amass an astonishing number of political, social, and cultural casualties, in the form of tryannical leaders, "fundamentalisms," deeply corrupt elites, civil strife accompanied by unbelievable carnage, the escalation of refugee populations, and many other modern horrors, none of these situations can adequately be understood as self-generated, and self-perpetuated phenomena, whose origin may lie in inherent, essentialized attributes or shortcomings of any given peoples or societies. And yet, broadly speaking, much of Naipaul's work, despite its intense scrutiny, has suggested as much. The new note of sympathy that Howe felt he detected in *A Bend in the River*, however, and the increasingly auto-biographical transparency of Naipaul's work since *The Enigma of Arrival*, hint at a more nuanced view of the world in the work of the last decade.

The Enigma of Arrival's acknowledgment of the narrator's imaginary England, in particular, is rendered in terms that are fascinatingly evocative of a postcoloniality more rounded, complex, and realized than in the development of any of his earlier characters, including Salim in *A Bend in the River*, and the essay, "Prologue to an Autobiography." "Naipaul's goodwill, however, is a somewhat dangerous thing," Sara Suleri reminds us (Suleri, "Naipaul's Arrival," p. 171). Thus, *A Turn in the South* reinscribes many of his customary attitudes even though the setting is not customary. Similarly, the new bouyancy of tone in *India: A Million Mutinies Now* is both unexpected and at the same time attaches to an unsatisfactory mode of inquiry to match its spirit of reassessment. Nevertheless, it is also written with an attention to the detail of its settings that even a familiarity with Naipaul's descriptive talents does not completely anticipate. Finally, his ability to sustain a setting and depict landscape becomes pivotal to the development of *A Way in the World*, and in this latest work the emergence of yet another archeological stratum settles into place. Perhaps the development of his treatment of Amerindians can serve as a measure of Naipaul's current attitude towards the world he has spent his life discovering.

It begins in *The Middle Passage*, where Naipaul confesses that:

I had tried hard to feel interest in the Amerindians as a whole, but had failed. I couldn't read their faces; I couldn't understand their language, and could never gauge at what level communication was possible. Among more complex peoples there are certain individuals who have the power to transmit to you their sense of defeat and purposelessness: emotional parasites who flourish by draining you of the vitality you preserve with difficulty. The Amerindians had this effect on me. (*The Middle Passage*, p. 102)

In time, through his researches for *The Loss of El Dorado*, Naipaul becomes more acquainted with the region's Amerindian past, particularly as it receded in the wake of European enterprises. Thus, by the time of *Guerrillas*, he is able to write them into the historical landscape of his island, to open a chapter, midway through the narrative, that attempts to trace the history of destabilization experienced on the island to foreshadow the novel's impending events. Finally, with *A Way in the World*, as we have already seen in the previous chapter, Naipaul invests his Amerindian characters with a voice, and attempts to recuperate his first encounters with them by refiguring the experience of his initial visit to the hinterlands of British Guiana and Surinam into a fictional sketch, "New Clothes: An Unwritten Story."

While this indicates an expanded development of Naipaul's purview of the region, I am not certain that it also constitutes more than a modification of his terms – of classifications, human potentialities, and communal possibilities. What is almost certain, though, is that Naipaul will continue to write with the same vigor, precision, and conviction whatever direction his reflections take him.

Notes

I INTRODUCTION

1 V.S. Naipaul, "Conrad's Darkness," in *The Return of Eva Peron with The Killings in Trinidad* (New York: Vintage, 1981), p. 233.

2 Sara Suleri, "Naipaul's Arrival," in *The Rhetoric of English India* (University of Chicago Press, 1992), p. 152. An earlier version of this chapter appeared in *The Yale Journal of Criticism* 2, 1 (1988): 25–50. Future page references will be taken from *Rhetoric*.

3 V.S. Naipaul, "Trinidad," in *The Middle Passage: Impressions of Five Societies – British, French and Dutch – in the West Indies and South America* (New York: Vintage, 1981), p. 68.

4 Homi K. Bhabha, "Signs Taken for Wonders: Questions of Ambivalence and Authority under a Tree Outside Delhi, May 1817," in Henry Louis Gates Jr. (ed.) *"Race," Writing, and Difference* (University of Chicago Press, 1985), pp. 165, 166, 168.

5 V.S. Naipaul, *The Loss of El Dorado: A History* (London: André Deutsch, 1969; repr. New York: Vintage, 1980); *A Turn in the South* (New York: Knopf, 1989). The characterization of these three publications as a "slave society trilogy" is Rob Nixon's in his essay, "V.S. Naipaul: Postcolonial Mandarin," *Transition* 52 (1991): 107, and his subsequent full-length study, *London Calling: V.S. Naipaul Postcolonial Mandarin* (London and New York: Oxford University Press, 1992).

6 Frantz Fanon, *Black Skin, White Masks*, trans. Charles Lam Markmann (1952; New York: Grove Press, 1967). Fanon of course is not alone. Among Naipaul's contemporaries, Sam Sevlon, Derek Walcott, Edward Kamau Brathwaite, George Lamming, and Wilson Harris all try to come to terms with or capitalize rather than shun or avoid the hybridity of their origins. See Simon Gikandi, *Writing in Limbo: Modernism and Caribbean Literature* (Ithaca: Cornell University Press, 1993), and Edouard Glissant, *Caribbean Discourse*, trans. Michael Dash (Charlottesville: University of Virginia Press, 1989).

7 George Lamming, *The Pleasures of Exile* (1960; repr. London: Allison and Busby, 1984).

8 V.S. Naipaul, "Jasmine," *The Times Literary Supplement*, June 4, 1964; repr. in *The Overcrowded Barracoon* (New York: Vintage, 1984), p. 23.

9 Homi K. Bhabha, "Representation and the Colonial Text: A Critical Exploration of Some Forms of Mimeticism," in Frank Gloversmith (ed.) *The Theory of Reading* (New Jersey: Barnes and Noble, 1984), p. 94. The quotation from "Jasmine" is also cited in the same essay.

10 See Gikandi's *Writing in Limbo*, a detailed and complex rendering of these "anxieties" among the first generations of Caribbean writers.

11 Charles Michener, "The Dark Visions of V.S. Naipaul," *Newsweek*, November 16, 1981: 108.

12 Peter Webb *et al.* "The Master of the Novel," *Newsweek*, August 18, 1980: 34.

13 For more extended analyses on the issue of Caribbean "exile" see Jan Carew's "The Caribbean Writer and Exile," in *Fulcrums of Change: Origins of Racism in the Americas and Other Essays* (Trenton, N.J.: Africa World Press, 1988), pp. 91–114; Rob Nixon's *London Calling*, and Gikandi's *Writing in Limbo*.

14 See for example, Kenneth Ramchand, *The West Indian Novel and its Background* (London: Faber and Faber, 1970); Gareth Griffiths, *A Double Exile* (London: Marion Boyars, 1978); M.M. Mahood, *The Colonial Encounter: A Reading of Six Novels* (London: Rex Collins, 1977); Jeffrey Meyers, *Fiction and the Colonial Experience* (Ipswich: The Boydell Press, 1972); William Walsh, *A Manifold Voice* (London: Chatto and Windus, 1970), *Commonwealth Literature* (London: Oxford University Press, 1973), and *Readings in Commonwealth Literature* (London: Oxford University Press, 1973); George Lamming, *The Pleasures of Exile* (London: Michael Joseph, 1960); Wilson Harris, *Tradition, the Writer, and Society* (London: New Beacon, 1967); Amon Saba Saakana, *The Colonial Legacy in Caribbean Literature* (Trenton, N.J.: Africa World Press, 1987); and collections such as Hena Maes-Jelinek (ed.) *Commonwealth Literature and the Modern World* (Brussels: Didier, 1975); Alastair Niven (ed.) *The Commonwealth Writer Overseas: Themes of Exile and Expatriation* (Brussels: Didier, 1976), and Edward Baugh (ed.) *Critics on Caribbean Literature* (London: George Allen and Unwin, 1978).

15 For a particularly astute reading of postcolonial dialogism see Christopher L. Miller's study, *Theories of Africans: Francophone*

Literature and Anthropology in Africa (University of Chicago Press, 1990). Also see M.M. Bakhtin, *The Dialogic Imagination*, ed. Michael Holquist, trans. Caryl Emerson and Michael Holquist (Austin: University of Texas Press, 1981).

16 Hughes' "Manifesto" appears in his 1926 essay, "The Negro Artist and the Racial Mountain," repr. in Nathan Higgins (ed.) *Voices from the Harlem Renaissance* (New York: Oxford University Press, 1976). Among the most useful analyses of the negritude movement are Abiola Irele, *The African Experience in Literature and Ideology* (London: Heinemann, 1981) and Miller's *Theories of Africans*. See also Ellen Conroy Kennedy (ed.) *The Negritude Poets* (New York: Thunder's Mouth Press, 1989); "Introduction" to *Aimé Césaire: The Collected Poetry*, trans. Clayton Eshelman and Annette Smith (Berkeley: University of California Press, 1983); A. James Arnold, *Modernism and Negritude: The Poetry and Poetics of Aimé Césaire* (Cambridge, Mass.: Harvard University Press, 1981). It should also be noted that the development of "magic realism" within the tradition of Caribbean and Latin American hispanic literature parallels in interesting ways the issues of representation that the negritude poets confronted. Alejo Carpentier's formulation of *the marvellous real* in the Prologue (trans. Heather Martin) to his novel *The Kingdom of this World*, trans. Harriet de Onis (1949; repr. New York: Farrar, Straus and Giroux, 1989) outlines the difference of this form of representation from those of the surrealist movements.

17 Sara Suleri, "Naipaul's Arrival," p. 149.

18 *Ibid.*, p. 169.

19 Thomas Babington Macaulay, "Minute on Indian Education," in *Selected Writings*, ed. John Clive (University of Chicago Press, 1972). For a comprehensive study of the anglicist program of colonial literary education see Gauri Viswanathan's *Masks of Conquest: Literary Study and British Rule in India* (New York: Columbia University Press, 1989). Also see Suleri, *The Rhetoric of English India*, and Homi K. Bhabha, "Of Mimicry and Man: The Ambivalence of Colonial Discourse," *October*, 28 (Spring 1984): 125–133, repr. in *The Location of Culture*, pp. 85–92. Of particular interest is the very readable essay by Edward Kamau Brathwaite, "English in the Caribbean," in *Opening up the Canon* (Baltimore: Johns Hopkins University Press, 1980), and C.L.R. James' "Discovering Literature in Trinidad: the 1930s," in *Spheres of Existence: Selected Writings* (London: Allison and Busby, 1980).

20 It should be noted that in his 1989 publication *A Turn in the South*, Naipaul is reminded of his early introduction to Booker T.

Washington's *Up from Slavery* (1900) and his teacher's subtle valorization of a nascent Pan-Africanism.

21 It is important to note that "mobility" in the colonial context is tantamount to "migrancy." This is of particular significance to the postcolonial era, where migrancy has become the major trope of much of its contemporary fiction. The most famous example of course is Salman Rushdie, *The Satanic Verses* (New York: Viking, 1989).

22 V.S. Naipaul, "Prologue to an Autobiography," in *Finding the Centre: Two Narratives* (New York: Knopf, 1984), pp. 18–20.

23 See Reinhard W. Sanders, "The Impact of Literary Periodicals on the Development of West Indian Literature and Cultural Independence," in Maes-Jelinek (ed.), *Commonwealth Literature and the Modern World*, p. 25. For a cogent and useful review of the uses of "Commonwealth Literature" as a designation, see Salman Rushdie's "'Commonwealth Literature' Does Not Exist," in *Imaginary Homelands: Essays and Criticism 1981–1991* (New York: Viking, 1991), pp. 61–70. The editorial commentaries of the first years of *The Journal of Commonwealth Literature* are also instructive about the debates and disagreements that have attended the phrase since its inception.

24 This is the opening statement of Naipaul's novel, *A Bend in the River* (London: Deutsch, 1979). The much-quoted full sentence reads, "The world is what it is; men who are nothing, who allow themselves to become nothing, have no place in it." Further page references will be used from the 1980, Vintage edition.

25 William Walsh, *V.S. Naipaul* (London: Oliver Boyd, 1973), p. 21.

26 George Sampson, *The Concise Cambridge History of English Literature*, 3rd edn. rev. by R.C. Churchill (Cambridge University Press, 1972), pp. 933–934.

27 Alfred Kazin, "V.S. Naipaul: Novelist as Thinker," *New York Times Book Review*, May 1, 1977: 7, 20, 22.

28 Selwyn R. Cudjoe, *V.S. Naipaul: A Materialist Reading* (Amherst, Mass.: University of Massachusetts Press, 1988), p. 4.

29 Anthony Appiah, "Strictures on Structures: The Prospects for a Structuralist Poetics of African Fiction," in Henry Louis Gates Jr. (ed.) *Black Literature and Literary Theory*, (New York: Methuen, 1984) p. 146.

30 Chris Searle, "Naipaulicity: A Form of Cultural Imperialism," *Race and Class* 26, 2 (Autumn 1984): 45–62.

31 Rob Nixon, *London Calling: V.S. Naipaul Postcolonial Mandarin* (New York and London: Oxford University Press, 1992). Joan Dayan, "Gothic Naipaul," *Transition* 59 (1993): 158–170.

32 Hayden White, "The Forms of Wildness: Archaeology of an Idea," in *Tropics of Discourse: Essays in Cultural Criticism* (Baltimore: Johns Hopkins University Press, 1978), pp. 151–152.

33 C.L.R. James, *The Black Jacobins: Toussaint L'Ouverture and the San Domingo Revolution* (1938: repr. New York: Vintage, 1989). Edward Said, *Orientalism* (New York: Vintage, 1978) and *Culture and Imperialism* (New York: Knopf, 1993). Aijaz Ahmad, *In Theory: Classes, Nations, Literatures* (London: Verso, 1992). Gayatri C. Spivak, *In Other Worlds: Essays in Cultural Politics* (New York and London: Methuen, 1987) and *Outside in the Teaching Machine* (New York and London: Routledge, 1993). See also Dorothy Hammond and Alta Jablow, *The Africa That Never Was: Four Centuries of British Writing About Africa* (New York: Twayne, 1970); and Patrick Brantlinger, *Rule of Darkness: British Literature and Imperialism, 1830–1914* (Ithaca: Cornell University Press, 1988).

34 David Walker's *Appeal* (1829; repr. New York: Hill and Wang, 1965) is a series of four articles which Walker, a free black, distributed to the slave states with ingenious subterfuge. His indictments against American slavery were considered to be the most incendiary materials of his times, and severe punishments were meted out to those found in possession of his works. Also see Houston A. Baker's Introduction to *The Narrative of the Life of Frederick Douglass* (1845; London: Penguin, 1982), for an account of the "white" endorsements required for the publication of "slave narratives." J.J. Thomas' *Froudacity: West Indian Fables by James Anthony Froude Explained* (1889; repr. London: New Beacon, 1969) is also the model Searle uses in his essay, "Naipaulicity." See in particular C.L.R. James' Introduction to Thomas' *Froudacity*, "The West Indian Intellectual," pp. 23–48. The quotation is from p. 23.

35 For a notorious example see Miller's account of Joseph de Gorbineau's *Essai sur l'inégalité des races humaines* (1853–1855) in *Blank Darkness*, pp. 16–18; and Joan Dayan's account of Moreau de Saint-Mery's *Description topographique physique, civile, politique et historique de la partie française de l'Isle Saint Domingue* in "Gothic Naipaul," pp. 167–168. Also see Robert Knox, *The Races of Men* (1850) and Brantlinger's description in *Rule of Darkness*, pp. 21–24. Also helpful is Reginald Horsman, *Race and Manifest Destiny* (Cambridge, Mass.: Harvard University Press, 1989).

36 James Mill, *The History of British India*, ed. John Clive (University of Chicago Press, 1975), p. 13.

37 Also included in the scholarship initiated by Said's *Orientalism* are works that critique it such as Ahmad's *In Theory*.

2 BEARINGS

1 For introductory and nicely balanced background surveys of the region's history, politics, and cultural developments, see the collection of essays, Sidney W. Mintz and Sally Price (eds.), *Caribbean Contours* (Baltimore: Johns Hopkins University Press, 1985), Franklin W. Knight and Colin A. Palmer (eds.), *The Modern Caribbean* (Chapel Hill and London: University of North Carolina Press, 1989), and David Lowensthal's *West Indian Societies* (London: Oxford University Press, 1972). Also instructive is Alfred W. Crosby, *Ecological Imperialism* (Cambridge and New York: Cambridge University Press, 1993).

2 See Philip D. Curtin, *The Atlantic Slave Trade: A Census* (Madison: University of Wisconsin Press, 1969); and Gordon K. Lewis, "The Contemporary Caribbean: An Overview," in Mintz and Price (eds.), *Caribbean Contours*, p. 223.

3 Again see Lowenthal's *listing* of the different significations given over time to the term "Creole" in *West Indian Societies*, p. 32. Within a contemporary "official" discourse furthermore both H. Hoetink and Gordon K. Lewis caution against reading the Caribbean with "a single language focus" that divides the region between its European-language areas and which results in the subordination of local Caribbean issues to the management-seeking needs of First World economic, political, and ideological priorities. H. Hoetink, "'Race' and Color in the Caribbean," in Mintz and Price (eds.), *Caribbean Contours*, p. 56; Lewis, "The Contemporary Caribbean," p. 228. Another related example of problematic taxonomy is in the Slave Codes enacted and variously followed by the European powers. They became further complicated when territories changed hands, when a lag transpired between the metropoles and local Caribbean application, and when one European code conflicted with another. See Lowensthal, *West Indian Societies*, p. 40. Also see Joan Dayan's "Gothic Naipaul," *Transition* 59 (1993): 167–168, where she brilliantly pits the "legal illogic" of white classifications of "mixed blood" against Naipaul's denigrations of negro/slave "fantasy" life in *The Loss of El Dorado*.

4 Another, minor, taxonomic problem of nomenclature arises with the use of "East Indian." While it has long been the preferred term in the Caribbean to minimize confusion with "West Indian," peoples originating from the Indian subcontinent are known as "Asian" or "Indian" in Africa, "South Asian" in the United States, and by nation of origin – Indian, Pakistani, Bangla

Deshi – in Britain. At the time of independence and partition in India in 1947, Indian subcontinentals in the British empire were automatically labeled "Indian" if Hindu, and "Pakistani" if Muslim, regardless of the region of their origin.

5 Bruce King's recent study for the Macmillan Modern Novelists series, *V.S. Naipaul* (London and Hong Kong: Macmillan, 1993), contains an appendix outlining the role Naipaul's relatives and close family associates played in the early political life of modern Trinidad. In addition to Naipaul's father supplying the basic material for *A House for Mr. Biswas*, which is a well-documented event, several other protagonists and characters in the early fiction are apparently composite portraits drawn from Naipaul's actual family. His source material therefore is as much if not more familial than it is sociological. The implicit measures of "civility" he employs, consequently, stem from a community learning to participate in a colonial-administered political enterprise, understood as a manifestation or result of the "civilizing mission" itself.

6 See George Lamming's *The Emigrants* (1954; repr. London: Allison and Busby, 1980), *The Pleasures of Exile* (1960; repr. London: Allison and Busby, 1984); and Wilson Harris, *Tradition, the Writer and Society* (London and Port of Spain: New Beacon, 1967).

7 See Mervyn C. Alleyne, "A Linguistic Perspective on the Caribbean," in Mintz and Price (eds.), *Caribbean Contours*, p. 169, for a more detailed explanation of code-switching in the Caribbean context.

8 The most common comparisons used to describe Naipaul's early stories were with Dickensian categories of satire and social commentary. In *London Calling*, Rob Nixon convincingly argues that Naipaul's narrative model in his travelogues remains primarily that of British Victorian travel writing, complete with its imperialist prejudices, even though Naipaul distances himself from both Georgian travel writing and more contemporary forms of "tourist" adventures.

9 See Benedict Anderson's enormously influential study, *Imagined Communities: Reflections on the Spread of Nationalism* (1983; repr. London: Verso, 1991). Subsequent page references are from the 1991 edn.

10 The expression, "the way information comes," is borrowed from Sara Suleri's *Meatless Days* (University of Chicago Press, 1989). It is employed in relation to the Pakistani press and its often hapless role in defining an emerging nation.

11 Ramchand, *The West Indian Novel and its Background*, p. 6.

12 See Suleri, *The Rhetoric of English India*. In particular, see chapter 5, "The Adolescence of *Kim*," and chapter 6, "Forster's Imperial Erotic."

13 Fredric Jameson, "Third–World Literature in the Era of Multinational Capitalism," *Social Text* 15 (Fall 1986): 69.

14 In particular see Aijaz Ahmad, "Jameson's Rhetoric of Otherness and the 'National Allegory'" *Social Text* 17 (Fall 1987): 3–25. This essay has since been included in *In Theory*, pp. 95–122.

15 Two other Caribbean novels that are exemplary of this "need" are Jacques Roumain's *Gouverneurs de la Rosée*, trans. Langston Hughes and Mercer Cook as *Masters of the Dew* (1944; London: Heinemann, 1977), and Edouard Glissant's *La Lézarde*, trans. Michael Dash as *The Ripening* (1958; London: Heinemann, 1985).

16 Homi K. Bhabha (ed.) *Nation and Narration* (London and New York: Routledge, 1990), p. 1.

17 Gordon Rohlehr, "The Ironic Approach: The Novels of V.S. Naipaul," in Louis James (ed.), *The Islands in Between: Essays in West Indian Literature* (London: Oxford University Press, 1968), p. 122. Lamming, *The Pleasures of Exile*, pp. 224–225.

18 It should be noted that Trinidad's first election under universal adult suffrage took place in 1946, one year before the partition of India, and the subcontinent's independence from Britain. Trinidad and Tobago were granted self-government in 1956, and became fully independent in 1962.

19 In *India: A Million Mutinies Now* (1990) Naipaul never really questions the logic of contemporary Hindu nationalists' sectarian demands within a secular–democratic polity; instead, he is heartened by their appearance of political organization which, he feels, signals India's graduation into modernity.

20 The reference is to Homi K. Bhabha's allusion in "Of Mimicry and Man: The Ambivalence of Colonial Discourse," *October* 28 (Spring 1984): 125–133, to Anderson's portrait of Chandra Pal in *Imagined Communities*, pp. 92–93. "Of Mimicry and Man" is also collected in Bhabha's *The Location of Culture* (London and New York: Routledge, 1994), pp. 85–92.

21 Lamming, *The Pleasures of Exile*, p. 225.

3 HOME

1 Selwyn R. Cudjoe, *V.S. Naipaul: A Materialist Reading* (Amherst, Mass.: University of Massachusetts Press, 1988), p. 54.

2 See Naipaul's "Foreword" to Seepersad Naipaul, *The Adventures of Gurudeva and Other Stories* (London: André Deutsch, 1976).

3 Rob Nixon, *London Calling: V.S. Naipaul Postcolonial Mandarin* (London and New York: Oxford University Press, 1992), p. 3.

4 "My Aunt Gold Teeth" and "The Mourners," two other stories collected in *A Flag on the Island*, are also set within the narrative voice's familial setting, but each is an isolated episode that does not rely upon the narrator's participation, even though he is the principal audience in "The Mourners." "My Aunt Gold Teeth" introduces the theme of slippage, more developed in *The Mystic Masseur*, that happens as a result of cultural encounters, in this case religion. The aunt's recourse to rituals and icons of Christianity mixed to suit her version of Hinduism during her personal ceremonies of appeasement is a favorite of Naipaul's, and permeates all his early work. "The Mourners" is far less culturally specific, and is an exercise, almost, of rendering an incident between the borders of realism and naturalism. The monotony and repetition of the doctor and his wife's intonation over the death of their child, and the narrator's reluctant acquiescence to their grief are more a study of the inevitable inadequacies of expressing loss than an examination of a ritual peculiar to a time and a place.

5 The passage goes on to name the author of the column as Dr. Samuel S. Pitkin, a name too similar to Nathaneal West's Lemuel Pitkin in *A Cool Million* (1935) to be ignored. West's unfortunate Pitkin, it must be remembered, suffers dreadful bodily harm.

6 In chapters 4 and 5, "Passenger: A Figure from the Thirties," and "On the Run," of *A Way in the World* (1994), Naipaul outlines the sequence of his growing awareness of James and his work. James is referred to as Lebrun, for reasons that are not entirely clear, unless we assume that a character *based* on an actual person allows for a kind of artistic license. Nevertheless, it would appear that at the time of *The Middle Passage*, Naipaul was not familiar with *The Black Jacobins*.

7 James' *The Black Jacobins* also offers a refreshing critique of the political origins of the abolitionist movement in Britain. Rather than attribute the movement to primarily humanitarian and rational motives, he outlines Pitt's recruitment of Wilberforce as a strategic move to undermine France's wealthiest colony, San Domingo (*The Black Jacobins*, pp. 50–57). Alejo Carpentier, *El Reino de Este Mundo*, (EDIAPSA, Mexico, D.F., 1949) trans. Harriet de Onis as *The Kingdom of this World* (1957; repr. New York: Farrar, Straus and Giroux, 1989). Carpentier's "Prologue" to the novel is where he outlines "the marvellous in the real,"

while the novel is his attempt to realize it. See also Fredric Jameson, "On Magic Realism in Film," *Critical Inquiry* 12 (Winter 1988): 301–325.

8 A recent essay, entitled "A Handful of Dust: Return to Guiana," *New York Review of Books* 38, 7, April 11, 1991: 15–20, revisits his hosts, Cheddi and Janet Jagan. The essay is discussed below, in chapter 7.

9 Mary Louise Pratt, *Imperial Eyes: Travel Writing and Transculturation* (London and New York: Routledge, 1992), pp. 90–107. Pratt's analysis can also be coupled with James' (above) for a fuller understanding of the political investments surrounding European representations of the Caribbean in the late eighteenth and early nineteenth centuries.

4 ABROAD

1 Reprinted in *The Overcrowded Barracoon*, pp. 23–29.

2 For examples of interpretations that examine Naipaul's ability to capture an "English" essence, see Timothy Weiss, *On the Margins: The Art of Exile in V.S. Naipaul* (Amherst: University of Massachusetts Press, 1992), pp. 87–90; Peggy Nightingale, *Journey through Darkness: The Writing of V.S. Naipaul* (St. Lucia and London: University of Queensland Press, 1987), pp. 71–83; and John Thieme, *The Web of Tradition: Uses of Allusion in V.S. Naipaul's Fiction* (London: Hansib, 1987), pp. 93–109.

3 See Naipaul's essay, "Conrad's Darkness," where he states: "And I found that Conrad – sixty years before, in a time of great peace – had been everywhere before me" (*Return of Eva Peron*, p. 233).

4 See Peter Hughes, *V.S. Naipaul* (London: Routledge, 1988), pp. 11–13 for an interesting observation about the ellipses in Naipaul's biographical blurbs.

5 Also see John Thieme's "A Hindu Castaway: Ralph Singh's Journey in *The Mimic Men*," *Modern Fiction Studies* 30 (Autumn 1984): 505–518, for a detailed examination of the "shipwreck" metaphor and its linkage with the originary myth of *Robinson Crusoe* which Naipaul deals with in *The Loss of El Dorado*.

6 See Karl Miller, "V.S. Naipaul and the New Order: A View of 'The Mimic Men,'" in Edward Baugh (ed.), *Critics on Caribbean Literature* (New York: St. Martin's Press, 1978), pp. 75–83.

7 See John Hearne, "The Snow Virgin: An Inquiry into V.S. Naipaul's *The Mimic Men*," *Caribbean Quarterly* 23, 2–3 (June–September 1977): 31–37.

8 Naipaul's treatment of charismatic leadership and the rituals associated with cult followings is a sharp contrast to Carpentier's in *The Kingdom of this World*. Rather than dismiss the "Voodoo" associated with the historical figures of Mackandal and Boukman, Carpentier instead accords it a political viability that is not measured against the norms of rationality that characterized the revolutionary excitement of the late eighteenth century.

9 James R. Lindroth's "The Figure of Performance in Naipaul's *The Mimic Men*," *Modern Fiction Studies* 30 (Autumn 1984): 519–529, for example, charts Ralph Singh's evolution as a series of self-conscious enactments whose various audiences complete the dialectic of his mimicry.

10 Homi K. Bhabha, "Of Mimicry and Man: The Ambivalence of Colonial Discourse," in *The Location of Culture*, p. 86. Emphasis in the original.

11 Nixon's *London Calling* has an excellent section on Naipaul's arbitrary selectivity, and reductionist tendencies while characterizing Trinidadian and colonial societies as "simple." See pp. 121–129. It is also now evident that Naipaul's latest publication, *A Way in the World* (1994), attempts to reinvest in his original historical paradigm for Trinidad by re-examining both Raleigh's enterprise and the affects of Luisa Calderon's trial from a novelistic rather than historiographical perspective. See chapter 7, below.

12 Cudjoe's study, *V.S. Naipaul*, makes the following important observation: "In another context and with a different emphasis, the historical facts [of *El Dorado*] could have yielded quite different conclusions" (p. 119).

13 Again, see Nixon's *London Calling* for its comparison of *El Dorado* with Eric Williams' almost contemporaneous *History of the People of Trinidad and Tobago* (London: André Deutch, 1962), and James' *The Black Jacobins*.

14 Suggesting that Naipaul's project is "historically skewed" is not meant to be directly synonymous with the current phrase, "politically incorrect." Nevertheless, it is worth referring to Rob Nixon's explanation of why *The Loss of El Dorado* was greeted as a reactionary document by a generation who had successfully negotiated independence from Britain. See *London Calling*, pp. 121–129.

15 See Angus Calder, "Darkest Naipaulia," *New Statesman* 82 (October 8, 1971): 482–483; and Francis Wyndham, "V.S. Naipaul," *The Listener* 86 (October 7, 1971): 461–462, for early reviews. Also see Nan Doerksen, "'In a Free State' and

'Nausea,'" *World Literature Written in English* 20 (Spring 1981): 105–113, and Andrew Gurr, "The Freedom of Exile in Naipaul and Doris Lessing," *Ariel* 13 (October 1982): 7–18.

16 It is also worth noting that Santosh's "self-awareness" arises out of his acknowledgment of an Indian form of racial discrimination where to be "black," a *hubshi*, is tantamount to being subhuman. The grafting that Naipaul practices between different kinds of racism and prejudicial attitudes obscures rather than reveals their disparate origins.

17 For a chilling exercise in exploring the relationship between the views about Africans projected through the narrative voice, the principal characters, and those of Naipaul in the era of "In a Free State," Paul Theroux's tribute to Naipaul, "V.S. Naipaul," *Modern Fiction Studies*, 30 (Autumn 1984): 445–455 should be consulted.

5 THE WORLD

1 Alastair Niven, "V.S. Naipaul's Free Statement," in Maes-Jelinek (ed.) *Commonwealth Literature and the Modern World*, p. 69.

2 Naipaul's success in presenting the "Third World" to the First as a more or less undifferentiated historical phenomenon, is ironically captured in the error in the back-cover blurb of the 1984 Vintage edition of *The Overcrowded Barracoon*: "In this wide-ranging collection of essays, V.S. Naipaul considers his own background – what it means to be an Indian who was born and raised in Trinidad; his reactions to India on visiting it for the first time; figures and movements in the West; and, finally, the situation in the Caribbean: in Anguilla, St. Kitts, Trinidad, British Honduras and Mauritius."

3 Frantz Fanon in *Black Skin, White Masks* first signaled this phenomenon which he attributes to the systematic self-denigration of subject peoples achieved by colonial education. See chapter 1, "The Fact of Blackness." Also see Albert Memmi, *The Colonizer and the Colonized*, trans. Howard Greenfield (Boston: Beacon Press, 1967).

4 See Michael Neill's excellent essay, "Guerrillas and Gangs: Frantz Fanon and V.S. Naipaul," *Ariel: A Review of International English Literature* 4 (October 13, 1982): 21–62.

5 See, for example, Nightingale, *Journey through Darkness*, pp. 171–190. Also see Nixon's *London Calling*, pp. 127–128, for an account of Naipaul's reaction to the 1970 Black Power agitation in Trinidad after having already established his intractable thesis in *The Loss of El Dorado*.

6 See in particular Nissim Ezekiel, "Naipaul's India and Mine," in Adil Jussawalla (ed.) *New Writing in India* (London: Penguin, 1974), pp. 77–90.

7 Ashis Nandy, *The Intimate Enemy: Loss and Recovery of Self under Colonialism* (Delhi: Oxford University Press, 1983).

8 The volume Nandy refers to is Nirad C. Chaudhuri, *The Continent of Circe* (London: Chatto and Windus, 1965).

9 Reprinted in *The Overcrowded Barracoon*, pp. 76–97.

10 V.S. Naipaul, "Argentina: Living with Cruelty," *New York Review of Books* 39, 3 (January 30, 1992): 13–18 and "The End of Peronism?" *New York Review of Books* 39, 4 (February 13, 1992): 47–53.

11 V.S. Naipaul, "The End of Peronism?", p. 48; Joseph Conrad, *Heart of Darkness*, ed. Robert Kimbrough (New York: Norton, 1988), pp. 31–33.

12 See Nixon's *London Calling*, p. 101, for some sober figures about the former Belgian Congo's situation at the time of independence.

13 Placide Tempels, *Bantu Philosophy*, trans. Colin King (Paris: Présence Africaine, 1959). Incorporated within this category of religion, or systems of belief, is the history of Europe's anthropological and commercial usage of its discovery of African art. Principal among the texts associated with these "explanations" of African culture are those of Leo Frobenius, (see in particular Miller's *Theories of Africans*), and the works of the Mission Dakar–Djibouti before the Second World War. James Clifford's *The Predicament of Culture: Twentieth-Century Ethnography, Literature and Art* (Cambridge, Mass.: Harvard University Press, 1988) offers a very useful insight about the Mission in chapters 2 and 6, "Power and Dialogue in Ethnography: Marcel Griaule's Initiation," and "Tell about Your Trip: Michel Leiris."

14 G.W.F. Hegel, "Introduction," in *The Philosophy of History*, trans. J. Sibree (1833–1836; repr. New York: Dover, 1956), p. 91.

15 This aspect of the novel can be compared to Nadine Gordimer's novel, *A Guest of Honour* (London: Penguin, 1970). The theme of outside experts' "interference" in African politics is explored again in Naipaul's *A Way in the World*, where the character of Lebrun is credited with recommending an ultimately vicious socialist program in a West African nation.

16 See Fatima Mernissi, *The Veil and the Male Elite: A Feminist Interpretation of Women's Rights in Islam* (1987; New York: Addison Wesley, 1991) and *Beyond the Veil* (Bloomington: Indiana University Press, 1987); Asma Jahanghir and Hina Jilani, *The Hudood Ordinances: A Divine Sanction?* (Lahore, 1990); and Sara Suleri,

"Woman Skin Deep: Feminism and the Postcolonial Condition," *Critical Inquiry* 18 (Summer 1992): 756–769.

17 It should be pointed out that Zulfikar Ali Bhutto's outlawing of the Ahmadi community in the 1970s, when they were declared "non-Muslim," was not only a capitulation to the religious right in Pakistan, but also to pressure from Saudi Arabia.

18 Naipaul's 1991 essay, "Our Universal Civilization," *New York Review of Books* 39 (January 31, 1991): 22–25, does return to the topic of Islam. He claims the religion's contemporary practice is the antithesis of modernity and progress because it denies history. The essay is discussed at greater length in chapter 7, below.

6 RIGHT OF ABODE

1 Salman Rushdie, *Shame* (London: Picador, 1983) p. 29.

2 Joseph Conrad, *Heart of Darkness*, ed. Robert Kimbrough (New York: Norton, 1988), p. 148; pp. 11–12.

3 Edward Said, "Intellectuals in the Post-Colonial World," *Salmagundi* 70–71 (Spring–Summer 1986): 44–64; and Conor Cruise O'Brien, Edward Said and John Lucas, "The Intellectual in the Post-Colonial World: A Discussion," *Salmagundi* 70–71 (Spring–Summer 1986): 65–81.

4 Said, "Intellectuals in the Post-Colonial World," p. 53.

5 I do not mean to suggest that analyses about social or political disadvantage which identify problems solely within the groups targeted are open to argument. The tendency to dehistoricize readings happens in both liberal and conservative camps. For a cogent review of "blaming the victim" arguments, see Stephen Steinberg, *The Ethnic Myth* (Boston: Beacon Press, 1987).

6 The books referred to are *Miguel Street, A House for Mr. Biswas, The Middle Passage, An Area of Darkness, The Loss of El Dorado, The Overcrowded Barracoon, The Return of Eva Peron with The Killings in Trinidad, In a Free State*, and *Among the Believers*. The list of course is not comprehensive. Why, for example, are the concerns explored in *Guerrillas* and *A Bend in the River* subordinated to those voiced in *The Middle Passage, The Loss of El Dorado*, and *In a Free State*? "The Journey" does suggest that the initial failure of *The Loss of El Dorado* was a turning point for the writer and that out of that disappointment arose the alternative site of "Africa."

7 Arnold Rampersad, "V.S. Naipaul: Turning in the South," *Raritan* 10, 1 (Summer 1990): 27.

8 Rampersad's review carefully charts the ways in which Naipaul tends to dismiss the accomplishments of African Americans while he tends to valorize those of his white interviewees.

9 Rob Nixon proposes an amusing and instructive transposition: *The South: A Wounded Civilization*, but also points out that Naipaul's sympathies for the frontier/pioneer mythology propagated by southern apologists overrides his Indian narrative's impatience with mythologized "pasts." See Nixon, *London Calling*, p. 168.

10 Rob Nixon is quite correct in disputing Naipaul's choice of "mutiny" to characterize the expression of manifold group "particularities" in contemporary India. See *London Calling*, p. 170.

11 Akeel Bilgrami, "Cry, the Beloved Subcontinent," *The New Republic* (June 10, 1991): 30–34. Bilgrami himself offers a valuable overview of the historical antecedents informing current Indian and Hindu politics. The review itself places in sharp relief the absence of the same in Naipaul's book.

12 I refer only to the "ignorance" suggested by Edward Said when he points out that Naipaul ignores a huge body of scholarship that has been written during his life time about the historical and political composition of the areas he habitually travels to. Obviously, Naipaul chooses to focus his attention on alternative sources that are congenial to him.

13 Akeel Bilgrami's review cited above is particularly useful in explaining how any search for a Hindu essentialism, especially through caste prohibitions, is nothing other than an endorsement of the hegemonic tendencies of the brahminical elite.

14 It is worth noting that Naipaul continues to use the term "Mohammadan," most pointedly in *A Way in the World*. As a gesture towards what he perceives to be a deification of Islam's prophet – which no Muslim would claim – it remains a deeply "orientalist" usage.

7 ONE WAY

1 Naipaul's specific formulation occurs in his critique of an Iranian novel, Nahid Rachlin's *Foreigner*,: "the other world where it was necessary to be an individual and responsible; where people developed vocations, and were stirred by ambition and achievement, and believed in *perfectability*," ("Our Universal Civilization," p. 25, emphasis added).

2 Spivak, "Reading *The Satanic Verses*," in *Outside in the Teaching Machine*, p. 236. Emphasis in original.

3 "Work of the imagination" is Naipaul's description, spoken during an interview with Charlie Rose, *The Charlie Rose Show*, PBS, June 1, 1994.

4 Stephen Schiff, "The Ultimate Exile," *New Yorker*, May 23, 1994: 60–71.

5 It is worth comparing Antonio Benítez-Rojo's treatment of Caribbean asymmetry to Naipaul's. Benítez-Rojo finds a productive force in the islands' turbulent histories. See Antonio Benítez-Rojo, *The Repeating Island: The Caribbean and the Postmodern Perspective*, trans. James E. Maraniss (Durham, N.C., and London: Duke University Press, 1992).
6 See Stephen Schiff, "The Ultimate Exile," p. 62.

8 CONCLUSION

1 Frantz Fanon, *Black Skin, White Masks*, trans. Charles Lam Markmann (New York: Grove Press, 1967), pp. 17–18.
2 Roberto Fernández Retamar refers to José Enrique Rodó, *Ariel*, (Madrid: Espasa–Calpe S.A., 1948) in his *Caliban and Other Essays*, trans. Edward Baker (Minneapolis: University of Minnesota Press, 1989), pp. 11–16. Rob Nixon offers a useful review of the use of the Caliban theme in black writing in his "African and Caribbean Appropriations of *The Tempest*," *Critical Inquiry*, 14 (1987): 557–578.
3 Said's *Culture and Imperialism* is largely concerned with this relationship between the development of the novel and the work of empire. Gayatri C. Spivak offers an excellent reading of Charlotte Bronte's "repression" of empire in *Jane Eyre*. See her "Three Women's Texts," in Henry Louis Gates Jr. (ed.) *"Race," Writing and Difference*, pp. 262–280.
4 F.R. Leavis, *The Great Tradition*, (New York: George W. Stewart, 1947), p. 7.
5 Georg Lukacs, *The Theory of the Novel*, trans. Anna Bostock (1920; repr. Cambridge, Mass.: MIT Press, 1971). I am only referring to Lukacs' employment of the term as the capability lost to modernity.
6 Naipaul's move away from the traditional novel, and the increased blurring in his recent work between fiction and non-fiction, does not affect interpretations of his work. As Rob Nixon points out, "he has remained by and large a formally unadventurous novelist while pursuing complementary effects through non-fiction" (*London Calling*, p. 5).
7 Irving Howe, *Politics and the Novel*, (1957; repr. New York: Columbia University Press, 1992).

Bibliography

WORKS BY NAIPAUL

The publication dates of both the Penguin (UK) and Vintage (USA) editions are included.

The Mystic Masseur. London: André Deutsch, 1957. Repr. Harmondsworth: Penguin, 1964 and New York: Vintage, 1984.

The Suffrage of Elvira. London: André Deutsch, 1958. Repr. Harmondsworth: Penguin, 1969 and New York: Vintage, 1985.

Miguel Street. London: Andre Deutsch, 1959. Repr. Harmondsworth: Penguin, 1971 and New York: Vintage, 1984.

A House for Mr. Biswas. London: Andre Deutsch, 1961. Repr. Harmondsworth: Penguin, 1969 and New York: Vintage, 1984.

The Middle Passage: Impressions of Five Societies – British, French and Dutch – in the West Indies and South America. London: Andre Deutsch, 1962. Repr. Harmondsworth: Penguin, 1969 and New York: Vintage, 1981.

Mr. Stone and the Knights Companion. London: Andre Deutsch, 1963. Repr. Harmondsworth: Penguin, 1969 and New York: Vintage, 1985.

An Area of Darkness. London: Andre Deutsch, 1964. Repr. Harmondsworth: Penguin, 1968 and New York: Vintage, 1981.

The Mimic Men. London: Andre Deutsch, 1967. Repr. Harmondsworth: Penguin, 1969 and New York: Vintage, 1985.

A Flag on the Island. London: Andre Deutsch, 1967. Repr. Harmondsworth: Penguin, 1969.

The Loss of El Dorado: A History. London: Andre Deutsch, 1969. Repr. New York: Knopf, 1970. Harmondsworth: Penguin, 1973 and New York: Vintage, 1984.

In a Free State. London: Andre Deutsch, 1971. Repr. Harmondsworth: Penguin, 1973 and New York: Vintage, 1984.

The Overcrowded Barracoon and Other Articles. London: André Deutsch, 1972. Repr. New York: Knopf, 1973, Harmondsworth: Penguin, 1976, and New York: Vintage, 1984.

Guerrillas. London: André Deutsch, 1975, New York: Knopf, 1975. Repr. Harmondsworth: Penguin, 1976 and New York: Vintage, 1980.

India: A Wounded Civilization. New York: Knopf, 1977. Repr. Harmondsworth: Penguin, 1979 and New York: Vintage, 1977.

A Bend in the River. New York: Knopf, 1979. Repr. Harmondsworth: Penguin, 1980 and New York: Vintage, 1980.

The Return of Eva Peron with The Killings in Trinidad. New York: Knopf, 1980. Repr. Harmondsworth: Penguin, 1981 and New York: Vintage, 1981.

A Congo Diary. Los Angeles: Sylvester and Orphanpos, 1980.

Among the Believers. New York: Knopf, 1981. Repr. Harmondsworth: Penguin, 1982 and New York: Vintage, 1982.

Finding the Centre: Two Narratives. New York: Knopf, 1984. Repr. Harmondsworth: Penguin, 1985 and New York: Vintage, 1986.

The Enigma of Arrival. New York: Knopf, 1987. Repr. Harmondsworth: Penguin, 1988 and New York: Vintage, 1988.

A Turn in the South. New York: Knopf, 1989.

India: A Million Mutinies Now. London: Heinemann, 1990.

A Way in the World. New York: Knopf, 1994.

OTHER SELECTED WRITINGS AND INTERVIEWS

"Among the Republicans," *New York Review of Books*, October 25, 1984, pp. 5, 8, 10, 12, 14–17.

"Argentina: Living With Cruelty," *New York Review of Books* 39, 3 (January 30, 1992), pp. 13–18.

"A Conversation with V.S. Naipaul," Interview by Bharati Mukherjee and Robert Boyers, *Salmagundi* 54 (1981), pp. 4–22.

"Critics and Criticism," *Bim* 10, 38 (January–June): 74–77.

"The End of Peronism?" *New York Review of Books*, 39, 4 (February 13, 1992), pp. 47–53.

"India's Cast-Off Revolution," *Sunday Times* (London), August 25, 1963, p. 17.

"An Island Betrayed," *Harper's* 268, 1606 (March 1984): 62–72.

"Life, Literature and Politics: An Interview with V.S. Naipaul," Cathleen Medwick, *Vogue*, August 1981, pp. 129–130.

"Meeting V.S. Naipaul." Interview by Elizabeth Harwick, *New York Times Book Review* (May 13, 1979), pp. 1, 36.

"Our Universal Civilization," *New York Review of Books* 39, (January 31, 1991), pp. 22–25.

"A Plea for Rationality," in I.J. Bahadur Singh (ed.)*Indians in the Caribbean*. New Delhi: Sterling, 1987, pp. 17–30.

"Trollope in the West Indies," *The Listener*, March 15, 1962, p. 461.

"The Ultimate Exile," Interview by Stephen Schiff, *New Yorker*, May 23, 1994, pp. 62–71.

"V.S. Naipaul: It's Out of This Violence I've Always Written," *New York Review of Books*, September 16, 1984, pp. 45–46.

"V.S. Naipaul: Novelist as Thinker," Interview by Alfred Kazin, *New York Times Book Review*, May 1, 1977, pp. 7, 20–21.

"V.S. Naipaul Tells How Writing Changes a Writer," *Tapia*, December 2, 1973, pp. 11–12.

"V.S. Naipaul: A Transition Interview by Adrian Rowe-Evens," *Transition* 40 (1971): 56–62.

SELECTED WORKS ABOUT V.S. NAIPAUL

Applewhite, James. "A Trip with V.S. Naipaul," *Raritan* 10. 1 (Summer 1990): 48–54.

Bilgrami, Akeel. "Cry the Beloved Subcontinent," *The New Republic*, June 10, 1991, pp. 30–34.

Bordewich, Fergus. "Anti-Political Man: V.S. Naipaul Reconsidered," *Working Papers* 9, 5 (September/October 1982), pp. 36–41.

Boxhill, Anthony. *V.S. Naipaul's Fiction: In Quest of the Enemy*, Frederickton, N.B.: York Press, 1983.

Cudjoe, Selwyn. *V.S. Naipaul: A Materialist Reading*, Amherst: University of Massachusetts Press, 1988.

Dayan, Joan. "Gothic Naipaul," *Transition* 59 (1993): 158–170.

Elliot, Michael. "Naipaulia," *New Republic*, November 16, 1987, pp. 13–14.

Eyre, M. Banning. "Naipaul at Wesleyan," *South Carolina Review* 14, 2 (Spring 1982): 34–47.

Ezekiel, Nissim. "Naipaul's India and Mine," *Literary Criterion*, (Summer 1965) repr. in Adil Jussawalla (ed.), *New Writing in India*, London: Penguin, 1974, pp. 77–90.

Goodheart, Eugene. "V.S. Naipaul's Mandarin Sensibility," *Partisan Review*, 50 (1983): 244–256.

Gorra, Michael. "Naipaul or Rushdie," *Southwest Review* (Summer 1991): 374–389.

Gurr, Andrew. *Writers in Exile: The Creative Use of Home in Modern Literature*, Atlantic Highlands, N.J.: Humanities Press, 1981.

Hamner, Robert. *V.S. Naipaul*, New York: Barnes and Noble, 1973.

(ed.) *Critical Perspectives on V.S. Naipaul*, Washington, D.C.: Three Continents Press, 1977.

Hassan, Dolly Zulakha. *V.S. Naipaul and the West Indies*, New York: Peter Lang, 1989.

Howe, Irving. *Politics and the Novel*, New York: Columbia University Press, 1992. Orig. pub. 1947.

Hughes, Peter. *V.S. Naipaul*, London: Routledge, 1988.

Jarvis, Kelvin. *V.S. Naipaul: A Selective Bibliography with Annotations*, Metuchen, N.J.: Scarecrow Press, 1989.

Kelly, Richard. *V.S. Naipaul*, New York: Continuum, 1989.

Kermode, Frank. "In the Garden of the Oppressor," *New York Times Book Review*, March 22, 1987.

King, Bruce. *V.S. Naipaul*, London and Hong Kong: Macmillan, 1993.

McSweeney, Kerry. *Four Contemporary Novelists: Angus Wilson, Brian Moore, John Fowles, V.S. Naipaul*, Kingston: McGill– Queen's University Press, 1983.

McWatt, Mark (ed). *West Indian Literature and its Social Context: Proceedings of the Fourth Annual Conference on West Indian Literature*, Cave Hill: University of the West Indies, 1985.

Modern Fiction Studies, 30, 3 (Autumn 1984).

Morris, Robert, K. *Paradoxes of Order: Some Perspectives on the Fiction of V.S. Naipaul*, Columbia: University of Missouri Press, 1975.

Neill, Michael. "Guerrillas and Gangs: Frantz Fanon and V.S. Naipaul," *Ariel* 13, 4 (October 1982): 22–62.

Nightingale, Peggy. *Journey through Darkness: The Writing of V.S. Naipaul*, St. Lucia and London: University of Queensland Press, 1987.

Nixon, Rob. *London Calling: V.S. Naipaul: Postcolonial Mandarin*, New York and London: Oxford University Press, 1992.

O'Brien, Conor Cruise, Edward Said, and John Lucas. "The Intellectual in the Post-Colonial World: A Discussion with Conor Cruise O'Brien, Edward Said and John Lucas," *Salmagundi* 70–71 (Spring–Summer 1986): 65–81.

Rai, Sudha, *V.S. Naipaul: A Study in Expatriate Sensibility*, New Delhi: Arnold Heinemann, 1982.

Ramchand, Kenneth. *The West Indian Novel and its Background*, London: Faber and Faber, 1970.

Rampersad, Arnold. "V.S. Naipaul: Turning in the South," *Raritan* 10, 1 (Summer 1990): 24–39.

Richmond, Angus. "Naipaul: The Mimic Man," *Race and Class*, 24, 2 (1982): 125–136.

Robbins, Bruce. "Homelessness and Worldliness," *Diacritics*, 13 (Fall 1983): 69–77.

Rohlehr, Gordon. "The Ironic Approach: The Novels of V.S.

Naipaul," in Louis James (ed.), *The Islands in Between: Essays in West Indian Literature*, London: Oxford University Press, 1968.

Searle, Chris. "Naipaulicity: A Form of Cultural Imperialism," *Race and Class* 26, 2 (Autumn 1984): 45–62.

Sheshadri, Vijay. "Naipaul from the Other Side," *Threepenny Review* 22 (Summer 1985): 5–6.

Suleri, Sara. "Naipaul's Arrival," *Yale Journal of Criticism* 2, 1 (Fall 1988): 25–50.

Swinden, Patrick. *The English Novel of History and Society, 1940 1980: Richard Hughes, Henry Green, Anthony Powell, Angus Wilson, Kingsley Amis, V.S. Naipaul*, New York: St. Martin's Press, 1984.

Theroux, Paul. *V.S. Naipaul: An Introduction to his Work*, New York: Africana, 1972.

Thieme, John. *The Web of Tradition: Uses of Allusion in V.S. Naipaul's Fiction*, Hertford, U.K.: Hansib, 1987.

Walcott, Derek. "The Garden Path," *New Republic*, April 13, 1987, pp. 27–31.

Walsh William. *V.S. Naipaul*, London: Oliver Boyd, 1973.

Weiss, Timothy. *On the Margins: The Art of Exile in V.S. Naipaul*, Amherst: University of Massachusetts Press, 1992.

White, Landeg. *A Critical Introduction*, London: Macmillan, 1975.

SELECTION OF OTHER RELATED WORKS

Ahmad, Aijaz. *In Theory: Classes, Nations, Literatures*, London: Verso, 1992.

Anderson, Benedict. *Imagined Communities: Reflections on the Spread of Nationalism*, London: Verso, 1983. Rev. edn. 1991.

Asad, Talal. *Anthropology and the Colonial Encounter*, London: Ithaca Press, 1973.

Ashcroft, Bill, Gareth Griffiths, and Helen Tiffen (eds.). *The Empire Writes Back*, London and New York: Routledge, 1989.

Bakhtin, M.M. *The Dialogic Imagination*, ed. Michael Holquist, trans. Caryl Emerson and Michael Holquist, Austin: University of Texas Press, 1986.

Baugh, Edward (ed.). *Critics on Caribbean Literature*, London: Allen and Unwin, 1978.

Benítez-Rojo, Antonio. *The Repeating Island: The Caribbean and the Postmodern Perspective*, trans. James Maraniss, Durham and London: Duke University Press, 1992.

Bhabha, Homi K. *The Location of Culture*, New York and London: Routledge, 1994.

"The Other Question: The Stereotype and Colonial Discourse," *Screen* 24, 6 (1983): 18–36.

"Representation and the Colonial Text: A Critical Exploration of Some Forms of Mimeticism," in Frank Gloversmith, (ed.) *The Theory of Reading*. Totowa, N.J.: Barnes and Noble, 1984.

"Signs Taken for Wonders: Questions of Ambivalence and Authority under a Tree Outside Delhi, May 1817," in Henry Louis Gates Jr. (ed). *"Race," Writing, and Difference*, Chicago: University of Chicago Press, 1985.

(ed.) *Nation and Narration*, London and New York: Routledge, 1990.

Bongie, Chris. *Exotic Memories: Literature, Colonialism and the Fin de Siècle*, Stanford: Stanford University Press, 1991.

Brantlinger, Patrick. *Rule of Darkness: British Literature and Imperialism, 1830–1914*, Ithaca: Cornell University Press, 1988.

Césaire, Aimé. *Discourse on Colonialism*, 1955; trans. Joan Pinkham. New York: Monthly Review Press, 1972.

Chamberlin, Edward J. *Come Back to Me My Language: Poetry and the West Indies*, Urbana and Chicago: University of Illinois Press, 1993.

Chatterjee, Partha. *The Nation and its Fragments: Colonial and Postcolonial Histories*. Princeton: Princeton University Press, 1993.

Nationalist Thought and the Colonial World, Minneapolis: University of Minnesota Press, 1993. Orig. pub. 1986.

Clifford, James. *The Predicament of Culture: Twentieth-Century Ethnography, Literature and Art*, Cambridge, Mass.: Harvard University Press, 1988.

Crosby, Alfred. *Ecological Imperialism*, Cambridge University Press, 1993.

Dirks, Nicholas (ed.) *Colonialism and Culture*, Ann Arbor: University of Michigan Press, 1992.

Fabian, Johannes. *Language and Colonial Power*, Berkeley: University of California Press, 1986.

Fanon, Frantz. *Black Skin, White Masks*, trans. Charles Lam Markmann, New York: Grove Press, 1967. Orig. pub. 1952.

Gates, Henry Louis Jr. (ed.). *Black Literature and Literary Theory*, New York: Methuen, 1984.

"Race" Writing and Difference, University of Chicago Press, 1986.

Gikandi, Simon. *Writing in Limbo: Modernism and Caribbean Literature*, Ithaca and London: Cornell University Press, 1992.

Hammond, Dorothy and Alta Jablow. *The Africa that Never Was: Four Centuries of British Writing about Africa*, New York: Twayne, 1970.

Haraway, Donna. *Primate Visions: Gender, Race, and Nature in the World of Modern Science*, London and New York: Routledge, 1989.

Simians, Cyborgs and Women: The Reinvention of Nature, New York: Routledge, 1991.

Hitchcock, Peter. *Dialogics of the Oppressed*, Minneapolis and London: University of Minnesota Press, 1993.

Hulme, Peter. *Colonial Encounters: Europe and the Native Caribbean 1492–1797*, London and New York: Routledge, 1986.

Irele, Abiola. *The African Experience in Literature and Ideology*, London: Heinemann, 1981.

Jahangir, Asma and Hina Jilani. *The Hudood Ordinances: A Divine Sanction?* Lahore, 1990.

James, C.L.R. *The Black Jacobins: Toussaint L'Ouverture and the San Domingo Revolution*, New York: Vintage, 1989. Orig. pub. 1938.

Jameson, Fredric. "Third World Literature in the Age of Multi-national Capitalism," *Social Text* 15 (Fall 1986).

JanMohammad, Abdul. *Manichean Aesthetics: The Politics of Literature in Colonial Africa*, Amherst: University of Massachusetts Press, 1983.

Knight, Franklin W. and Colin A. Palmer (eds.). *The Modern Caribbean*, Chapel Hill and London: University of North Carolina Press, 1989.

Lawrence, Karen R. (ed.). *Decolonizing Traditions: New Views of Twentieth-Century "British" Literary Canons*, Urbana and Chicago: University of Illinois Press, 1992.

Lowenthal, David. *West Indian Societies*, London: Oxford University Press, 1972.

Maes-Jelinek, Hena (ed.). *Commonwealth Literature and the Modern World*, Brussels: Didier, 1975.

McGee, Patrick. *Telling the Other: The Question of Value in Modern and Postcolonial Writing*, Ithaca: Cornell University Press, 1992.

Memmi, Albert. *The Colonizer and the Colonized*, trans. Howard Green-field, Boston: Beacon Press, 1967.

Mernissi, Fatima. *Beyond the Veil*, Bloomington: Indiana University Press, 1987.

The Veil and the Male Elite: A Feminist Interpretation of Women's Rights in Islam, New York: Addison-Wesley, 1991.

Miller, Christopher L. *Blank Darkness: Africanist Discourse in French*, University of Chicago Press, 1985.

Theories of Africans: Francophone Literature and Anthropology in Africa, University of Chicago Press, 1990.

Mintz, Sydney W. and Sally Price (eds.) *Caribbean Contours*, Balti-more: Johns Hopkins University Press, 1989.

Mudimbe, V.Y. *The Invention of Africa: Gnosis, Philosophy and the Order of Knowledge*, Bloomington: Indiana University Press, 1988.

Nandy, Ashis. *The Intimate Enemy: Loss and Recovery of Self under Colonialism*, Delhi: Oxford University Press, 1983.

Niven, Alastair (ed.). *The Commonwealth Writer Overseas: Themes of Exile and Expatriation*, Brussels: Didier, 1976.

Nixon, Rob. "African and Caribbean Appropriations of *The Tempest*," *Critical Inquiry* 14 (1987): 557–578.

Parry, Benita. "Problems in Current Theories of Colonial Discourse," *Oxford Literary Review* 9, 1–2 (1987): 27–58.

Pratt, Mary Louise. *Imperial Eyes: Travel Writing and Transculturation*, London and New York: Routledge, 1992.

Retamar, Roberto Fernández. *Caliban and Other Essays*, trans. Edward Baker, Minneapolis: University of Minnesota Press, 1989.

Rushdie, Salman. *Imaginary Homelands: Essays and Criticism 1982–1991*, New York: Viking, 1991.

Said, Edward. *Culture and Imperialism*, New York: Knopf, 1993.
Orientalism, New York: Vintage, 1978.
"Orientalism Reconsidered," *Europe and its Others, Proceedings of the Essex Conference on the Sociology of Literature, July 1984*. Vol. 1, Colchester: University of Essex, 1985.

Spivak, Gayatri, C. *In Other Worlds: Essays in Cultural Criticism*, New York and London: Methuen, 1987.
Outside in the Teaching Machine. New York and London: Routledge, 1993.
The Post-Colonial Critic: Interviews, Strategies, Dialogues, ed. Sarah Harasym. London: Routledge, 1990.

Spurr, David. *The Rhetoric of Empire: Colonial Discourse in Journalism, Travel Writing and Imperial Administration*, Durham and London: Duke University Press, 1993.

Suleri, Sara. *The Rhetoric of English India*, University of Chicago Press, 1992.

Tiffin, Chris and Alan Lawson (eds.). *De-Scribing Empire: Post-colonialism and Textuality*, London and New York: Routledge, 1994.

Viswanathan, Gauri. *Masks of Conquest: Literary Study and British Rule in India*, New York: Columbia University Press, 1989.

White, Hayden. *Tropics of Discourse: Essays in Cultural Criticism*, Baltimore: Johns Hopkins University Press, 1978.

White, Jonathan. *Recasting the World: Writing after Colonialism*, Baltimore and London: Johns Hopkins University Press, 1993.

Index

Aeneid (Virgil), 146
Affective memory, 140
Afghanistan, 153
Africa, 5, 26, 113–114, 117, 118,
    163–164, 178
  and black consciousness, 11
  postcolonial, 142–152
  revised scrutiny of, 194
  see also specific locales
African Americans, *see* Blacks
Ahmadis, 156–157
Algeria, 12
Alienation, 114, 116
Amerindians, 225–226
Among the Believers (Naipaul), 16, 125,
    152–58, 165, 178, 184, 197
Anderson, Benedict, 39, 41, 215
Anguilla, 124
Antigua, 86
Apollinaire, 171
Appeal (Walker), 25, 231 n. 34
Appiah, Anthony, 22–23, 25
Applewhite, John, 181, 185, 186
Area of Darkness, An (Naipaul), 16, 79,
    90, 92–100, 122, 132–133, 134, 136,
    168, 187, 194
Argentina, 138, 139–140, 199, 200
Ariel figure, 220
Atlanta (Ga.), 180

Baldwin, James, 182
Banana Bottom (McKay), 11
Banjo (McKay), 11
Bantu Philosophy (Tempels), 146
Bend in the River, A (Naipaul), 16, 17, 42,
    79, 118, 124, 137, 138, 140,
    141–152, 206, 218, 221, 224, 225
Berrio, Antonio de, 110
Bhabha, Homi K., 4, 6, 24, 28, 49, 106

Bhave, Vinoba, 135
Bilgrami, Akeel, 187, 241 nn. 11, 13
Black Jacobins, The (James), 24, 82, 210,
    235 nn. 6, 7
Black power, 125, 130–131, 132
Blacks, 10–11
  in America, 179–183
  in Trinidad, 81, 111, 204
  see also Black power; Slavery
Black Skin, White Masks (Fanon), 6, 12,
    24, 219
"Bogart" (*Miguel Street*), 36, 37, 80
Bombay (India), 188
Brazil, 180
Breton, André, 12
British Guiana, 84, 226
British Honduras, 124
"B. Wordsworth" (*Miguel Street*), 38,
    64

Calcutta (India), 188
Calderon, Luisa, 109, 112
Caliban (literary figure), 220
Calypso, 83
Camoens (poet), 191
Caribbean area
  and colonial control, 25, 30
  culture, 5, 9
  history, 4, 30–31
  revised scrutiny of, 194
  slavery in, 181
  writers, 9–10, 13
  see also specific locales
Carpentier, Alejo, 82
Carter, Martin, 200
"Caution" (*Miguel Street*), 39
"Ceremony of Farewell, The" (*The
    Enigma of Arrival*), 175, 176
Césaire, Aimé, 10, 11, 12, 24, 82

Charleston (S.C.), 180–181
Chaudhuri, Nirad C., 136
Chirico, Giorgio de, 171
Churchill, R.C., 21
Civility, 221, 233 n. 5
Class, 56, 102
Colonialism, 83, 111
  allegory of, 44
  Caribbean, 25, 30
  colonialists' version of, 24–26
  scholarship on, 24–25
  in Trinidad, 13–14, 63
Colonialist reflexivity, 24
Columbus, Christopher, 207–208, 215
"Columbus and Crusoe" (*The
  Overcrowded Barracoon*), 123
Commonwealth literature, 15
Congo, 140
Conrad, Joseph, 3–4, 73, 92, 139, 146,
  149, 163, 164, 209
"Conrad's Darkness" (essay), 3, 4, 141,
  168, 209
Country music, 184–185
"Crocodiles of Yamoussoukro, The"
  (*Finding the Centre*), 161–163, 174,
  178, 211
Cudjoe, Selwyn R., 22, 25, 52, 61
Cullen, Countee, 11
Cultural authenticity, 6, 83
Culture, 5–6, 83

Damas, Léon, 10
Dayan, Joan, 23, 25
Decolonizing the mind, 6–7
Deracination, 115
Determinism, 103
Domestic situations, 41–42
Du Bois, W.E.B., 11, 183

East Indian communities, 31–32, 52,
  232 n. 4
El Dorado, 109
Eliot, T.S., 90
"Enemy, The" (*Miguel Street*), 65–67,
  72
English literature, 4, 19
English tradition, 89, 220–21
English in the West Indies, The (Froude),
  25, 78
Enigma of Arrival, The (Naipaul), 18, 79,
  114, 159, 168–177, 185, 187, 194,
  220, 221, 224–225
Ethics, 165, 196

Ethiopia, 83, 130
Existentialism, 9, 10, 91
Expatriate mentality, 117

False consciousness, 223
Family histories, 187, 189
Fanon, Frantz, 6, 12, 24, 81, 86, 219
Fantasy, 111, 163–164, 182
Fictive technique, 37–38
  see also Narrative technique
Finding the Centre (Naipaul), 18,
  161–168, 202
Flag on the Island, A (Naipaul), 16, 32,
  45, 65, 107–108, 114
Forster, E.M., 99, 124, 195
France, 12, 86
Freedom, 114–115
Froudacity (Thomas), 25
Froude, James Anthony, 25, 79
Fundamentalism, 194, 197

Gandhi, Indira, 80, 124
Gandhi, Mahatma, 52, 97, 110, 135,
  193
  "South African eye," 134, 136, 145
Garvey, Marcus, 11
"George and the Pink House" (*Miguel
  Street*), 43
Georgetown (British Guiana), 84
Greene, Graham, 81, 209
Guerrillas (Naipaul), 16, 17, 42, 86, 124,
  125–132, 137, 141, 149, 221, 225
Guyana, 199, 200

Handful of Dust, A (Waugh), 199
Harlem Renaissance, 10–11
Harris, Wilson, 33
Heart of Darkness (Conrad), 3, 4, 73, 92,
  139, 140, 146, 149, 163, 173
Hegel, G.W.F., 26, 148, 149
Helms, Jesse, 185
Hinduism, 45–47, 51, 52–53, 82, 134,
  135, 177, 188–189, 241 n. 13
History of British India, The (Mills),
  26–27
Hoetink, H., 28
Homosexuality, 117, 127
House for Mr. Biswas, A (Naipaul), 15,
  32, 33, 34, 35, 45, 48, 58–77, 81, 82,
  91, 100, 168, 211, 221, 222
Howe, Irving, 224
Hughes, Langston, 10
Humanism, 19, 22

Idea of Order, 4
Imagined Communities (Anderson), 215
"Imagined community," 39
"In a Free State" (*In a Free State*),
    116–118, 125, 202, 206, 218
In a Free State (Naipaul), 16, 79, 90,
    113–121, 127
India, 13, 110, 122, 180
    in *An Area of Darkness*, 92–100, 194
    British perspectives on, 99, 192
    British power in, 27, 193
    independence movements, 52
    under Indira Gandhi, 124, 132
    see also India: A Million Mutinies Now;
        India: A Wounded Civilization
India: A Million Mutinies Now (Naipaul),
    18, 140, 186–195, 197, 199, 225
India: A Wounded Civilization (Naipaul),
    16, 124, 132–137, 145, 168, 182,
    194
Indonesia, 153, 157
Interview technique, 187–188,
    190–191
Intimate Enemy, The (Nandy), 135, 187
Iran, 153, 154, 155
Islam, 153–158, 184, 194, 197–198
Ivory Coast, 96, 161, 162, 163, 164, 174,
    211
"Ivy" (*The Enigma of Arrival*), 172

"Jack's Garden" (*The Enigma of Arrival*),
    169–170
Jagan, Cheddi, 199, 200
Jamaica, 83, 86, 130
James, C.L.R., 24, 25, 82, 210,
    235 nn. 6, 7
Jameson, Fredric, 48, 49, 51, 52, 54
"Jasmine" (essay), 88
Java, 197
Jones, Sir William, 192, 193
"Journey, The" (*The Enigma of Arrival*),
    171–172
Justice, 166, 167, 182

Kazin, Alfred, 21–22
Kenya, 118
Knowledge, 164, 165
    see also Self-knowledge

Lamming, George, 6, 33, 50, 54,
    56–57
Laye, Camara, 81
Leavis, F.R., 20, 221

Literacy, 14, 34–35, 38, 200
Literature, 88–89
London Calling (Nixon), 23, 207,
    233 n. 8, 237 n. 11
Loss of El Dorado, The (Naipaul), 5, 16,
    18, 90, 109–113, 123, 131, 139, 178,
    181, 182, 202, 203, 212, 216, 225,
    237 n. 14
"Love Song of J. Alfred Prufrock, The"
    (Eliot), 90
Lukács, Georg, 221

Macaulay, Thomas, 137
Magic, 163
Magic realism, 82, 229 n. 16
Malaysia, 153, 156
Manhattan Institute, 196
Martinique, 11, 86
Mauritius, 124
McKay, Claude, 11
Middle Passage, The (Naipaul), 5, 16, 32,
    50, 52, 77–87, 93, 110, 123, 142,
    164, 168, 178, 181, 199, 202, 206,
    225
Migrancy, 230 n. 21
Miguel Street (Naipaul), 15, 32, 33–44,
    45, 57, 58, 64, 80
Mills, James, 26–27, 28
"Mimic man," 53–54, 106
Mimic Men, The (Naipaul), 16, 17, 54,
    90, 100–106, 121, 125, 127, 143,
    150, 221
Miranda, Francisco, 214, 215–216
Mississippi, 181, 183–184
Mobility, 14, 230 n. 21
Modernity, 168–169, 185, 188, 193, 196,
    197, 219, 221
Morris, Foster, 207–9
"Mourners, The" (*A Flag on the Island*),
    235 n. 4
Mr. Stone and Knights Companion
    (Naipaul), 16, 90–92
Muslims, *see* Islam
Mutability, 159
"My Aunt Gold Teeth" (*A Flag on the
    Island*), 235 n. 4
My Diary in India in the Year 1858–9
    (Russell), 192
Mystic Masseur, The (Naipaul), 15, 32,
    33–34, 39, 44–48, 51–54, 55, 57, 58,
    83, 100, 150, 177, 214

Naipaul, Seepersad, 63

Naipaul, Shiva, 177
Naipaul, V.S.
  affinity for English tradition, 10
  autobiographical writings, 13,
    159–160, 168, 177, 203, 216, 224,
    233 n. 5
  background, 13
  career, 7–8, 14–19
  and colonialism, 27–28
  Conrad's influence, 3–4, 73, 139
  early work, 32–58
  idiom, 17–18, 122
  Kazin on, 21–22
  language use, 37, 223–224
  postcolonial thesis, 125, 126
  recent phase, 161–195, 201–218
  schooling, 14
  second decade of writing, 90–120
  as spokesperson for postcolonial
    world, 20
  travel and travel writing, 3, 17–18,
    23, 77–87, 92–100, 167, 178–195,
    207–208
  world view, 125, 219
  as writer, 219–220, 224
  see also specific works
Nandy, Ashis, 135–136, 187
Narrative technique, 34, 190, 191, 202,
  212, 214
Nation, concept of, 49
Nation and Narration (Bhabha), 49
National allegories, 50
Negritude, 11, 12
New Criticism, 90
Newspapers, 39–40, 48
New Yorker, 201
Nightingale, Peggy, 155
Nihilism, 103
Niven, Alastair, 121
Nixon, Rob, 5, 23, 25, 63, 95, 162,
  178–179, 207, 233 n. 8, 237 nn. 11,
  14, 242 n. 6

O'Brien, Conor Cruise, 166
"On the Run" (*A Way in the World*),
  209–213, 217
"One Out of Many" (*In a Free State*),
  114, 115–116
Orientalism (Said), 24, 27
"Our Universal Civilization" (lecture),
  196, 197
Overcrowded Barracoon (Naipaul), 16,
  122–124, 130, 132–133, 164

Pakistan, 153, 156–157, 160
"Parcel of Papers, A" (*A Way in the
  World*), 212–213, 216
Passage to India, A (Forster), 124
Philosophy of History, The (Hegel), 26
Picaroon society, 83
Picton, Governor, 109, 112
Pleasures of Exile, The (Lamming), 6
Port of Spain (Trinidad), 113, 203–204
Postcolonial condition, 100–103, 119
Postcolonial history, 5
Postcolonial intellectuals, 165
Postcolonial self-reflexivity, 24
Postcolonial "stability," 105
"Power" (*The Overcrowded Barracoon*),
  130
Pratt, Mary Louise, 85, 236 n. 9
Présence Africaine (journal), 10
Presley, Elvis, 184
"Prologue to an Autobiography"
  (*Finding the Centre*), 18, 36, 38,
  161–162, 166–167, 168, 225

Race, 82, 84, 102, 179, 204, 205
  see also Blacks
Raleigh, Sir Walter, 109, 110, 112, 203,
  212–213, 215, 216
Ramchand, Kenneth, 44
Rampersad, Arnold, 178
Ras Tafarians, 83, 129
Rednecks, 181, 183–184
Reincarnation, 177
Retamar, Roberto Fernndez, 220
*Return of Eva Peron with The Killings in
  Trinidad, The* (Naipaul), 16, 125,
  137–141, 164
Rhetoric of English India, The (Suleri),
  26–27
Rohlehr, Gordon, 50, 54, 57
Roman verité, 78
"Rooks" (*The Enigma of Arrival*), 175
Rosenthal, David, 28
Rushdie, Salman, 160, 198
Russell, William Howard, 191–193

Said, Edward, 24, 27, 165–166,
  241 n. 12
Sartre, Jean-Paul, 12
Satanic Verses, The (Rushdie), 198
Satire, 32, 35, 46, 48, 49, 50, 51, 55,
  56–57, 81
Schiff, Stephen, 201
Searle, Chris, 23, 25

Self-absorption, 135
Self-discovery, 160
Self-knowledge, 15, 106
Senegal, 11
Senghor, Léopold Sédar, 10, 11–12
Shadowed Livery, The (Morris), 208
Shame (Rushdie), 160
Shia Islam, 154, 184
Slavery, 80, 85, 109, 110, 111, 131, 181, 182, 186, 231 n. 34
Social comment, 91
Souls of Black Folks, The (Du Bois), 183
Soustelle, Jacques, 122–123
South (U.S.), 179–186
South Africa, 85, 97, 117, 125, 129, 145
South Carolina, 180–181
Spain, 139–140
Spivak, Gayatri, 24
St. Kitts, 124
Stedman, John, 85
Suffrage of Elvira, The (Naipaul), 15, 32, 33, 34, 35, 45, 48, 54–56, 58, 83, 100
Suleri, Sara, 3, 12, 25, 26, 95, 173, 174, 225
Surinam, 5, 83, 85–86, 226
Surrealism, 12

Tanzania, 118
"Tell Me Who to Kill" (*In a Free State*), 116
Tempest, The (Shakespeare), 146
Tennessee, 184–185
Third World, 2, 19, 121, 137–41, 161, 165, 178, 238 n. 2
Thomas, J.J., 25, 26
Tobacco culture, 185
Torture, 112
Tradition(s), 6, 83, 185, 197
   see also English tradition
Trinidad, 178
   black power movement in, 132
   blacks in, 81, 111, 204
   colonial, 13–14, 63

and concept of "nation," 49
ethnic and class divisions, 56, 232 n. 3
history of, 109–113, 181, 207–208
Indian communities, 31–32, 45–47, 51, 52, 62, 82
political aspects, 52, 204–205
slave population in, 131
travel writing about, 79–82, 207
in *Way in the World*, 201–218
   see also Miguel Street
Truth, 166, 167, 182, 188, 201
Turn in the South, A (Naipaul), 5, 18, 178–186, 187, 188, 225
Tuskegee Institute, 183

Uganda, 118, 216–217
United States, 178–186
Universalism, 22, 23, 33, 81–82, 196, 197, 200
University of Tulsa, 219
Up From Slavery (Washington), 183, 229 n. 20

Venezuela, 110, 214–215
Virgil, 143, 146

Walker, David, 25, 231 n. 34
Walsh, William, 20, 22
Washington, Booker T., 182–183, 229–230 n. 20
Waugh, Evelyn, 199
Way in the World, A (Naipaul), 18, 112, 197, 201–218, 225, 226
West Indian culture, 5
West Indian literature, 15, 21
White, Hayden, 23
Williams, Eric, 77
Williams, Hosea, 180
Women, 41–42, 58, 62, 156
Writing process, 161, 164

Zaire, 140
Zanzibar, 118, 147
Zia-ul-Haq, 153